screamfree MARRIAGE

Also by Hal Runkel

ScreamFree Parenting:
The Revolutionary Approach to
Raising Your Kids by Keeping Your Cool

screamfree MARRIAGE

Calming Down,
Growing Up,
and Getting Closer

Hal Edward Runkel, LMFT
with Jenny Runkel

Crown Archetype
New York

Library of Congress Cataloging-in-Publication Data
Runkel, Hal Edward.
Screamfree marriage : calming down, growing up, and getting closer / Hal Edward
Runkel, with Jenny Runkel. — 1st ed.
p. cm.
1. Marital conflict. 2. Marriage—Psychological aspects. 3. Married people—
Psychology. 4. Marital quality. I. Runkel, Jenny. II. Title. III. Title:
Scream free marriage.

HQ734.R798 2010
646.7'8—dc22

2010020100

ISBN 978-0-7679-3277-6
eISBN 978-0-7679-3279-0

PRINTED IN THE UNITED STATES OF AMERICA

Book design by Donna Sinisgalli
Jacket design by Fritz Miller Studios

1   3   5   7   9   10   8   6   4   2

First Edition

Dedicated to

Jon Kaplan

*You're more than just a business partner and dear friend;
you're a brother who, in so many ways,
makes my life, and this ScreamFree mission, possible.*

Contents

ScreamFree™: \ˈskrēmˈfrē\: learning to relate with others in a calm, cool, and *con*nected way, taking hold of your own emotional responses no matter how anyone else chooses to behave; learning to focus on yourself and take care of yourself for the world's benefit.

Hold On—
This May Not Be the Marriage Book for You

I used to believe that marriage would diminish me,
reduce my options—that you had to be someone less
to live with someone else when, of course,
you have to be someone more.

—CANDICE BERGEN

Why did you pick up this book?

There may be a number of reasons. You may be engaged or newly married, and you've just started reading every marriage book on the planet. Perhaps you've got a great marriage and want to keep it that way. Maybe you enjoyed reading my first book, *ScreamFree Parenting,* and you're hoping to apply those same calming principles to your marriage. Or perhaps, and perhaps most importantly, you may really be hurting. You may believe you're in the worst marriage ever, or at least believe that yours is worse than ever. And you may be desperately searching for some guidance and some hope.

Whatever your motivation for reading these pages, I have one request at this point: Hold on. This may not be the book for you. That's because this is not your ordinary marriage book. This is probably the first marriage book you've seen that says much of what you have been taught about marriage—how it works and how to make it better—is not only wrong, but actually harmful. And this is definitely the first marriage book you've ever seen that says the best thing you can do for your marriage is to become *more* self-centered, learning to focus less on your spouse and more on yourself . . . for the benefit of you both.

I know that sounds at best bold, and at worst arrogantly insensitive. Your pain and desire for real improvement are probably speaking louder than any words I may say here. In fact, you may think there's no way I can understand all that you've been through, or all you're going through, just to make your marriage work day by day.

And you'd be right.

I do not know you personally, and I cannot ever fully know your plight. No one can. But my highest recommendation to you still remains the same—hold on.

Hold on to your present marital state as it is right now. If you're happily or unhappily married . . . or just beginning to wonder which. If you're single and searching . . . or single again and searching again. If you're in the process of separation, and headed toward divorce court. Stop whatever you're doing, and just hold on. I believe that the vision for marriage I'm presenting here is so potentially life-changing for you that I'm asking you to cease doing anything further about your situation, at least until you hear me out.

What I'm offering here is an invitation to let go of the damaging lies about marriage, and then behold some fundamental truths. Truths such as:

- **If You're Not Under Control, You Cannot Be In Connection,** because the greatest barriers to true connection with your spouse are not busy schedules or incompatible interests. The greatest barrier to real connection is your own "screaming," your own emotional reactivity. Thus, learning to pause and think clearly is the absolute first, and best, step toward true intimacy. And . . .

- **It's Not What You Have in Common, It's What You Have Inside,** because reliance on common interests and compatibility is the foundation for a superficial friendship, whereas reliance on personal integrity in the midst of constant change is the foundation for a deep, lasting marriage. And . . .

- **The Only Communication Skill You Need to Learn Is Authentic Self-Representation (ASR),** because connection is not about using some artificial active listening technique. True connection is about fully representing your *self* (your thoughts, your preferences, your positions, your intentions) in word and action so that, at the very least, your partner has a chance to *know* you. And . . .

- **It's Better to Get "Rubbed the Wrong Way" than Never to Get Rubbed at All,** because in-your-face conflict is always a better path to true intimacy than cold avoidance, especially if you want to experience truly heartfelt connection (and possibly even mind-blowing, scream-*filled* sex). And . . .

- **If You Want a Warm Marriage, You Have to Walk through Fire,** because every couple in every culture throughout history has had to negotiate several natural fires of commitment, and those partners who can keep their cool and walk through each fire with cool integrity have the best chance of creating a truly warm, close relationship. And . . .

- **Intimacy Always Begins with an "I,"** because taking the risk of boldly pursuing your partner with your truest self, your deepest feelings and desires—in short, your "I"—is the only way to the close, naked, and even spiritual intimacy we all crave.

Now, these "truths" may fly too much in the face of notions about marriage that you truly hold dear. If so, then again, this may not be the marriage book for you.

Moreover, you may not even be looking for any new "truths" about marriage; you may be honestly searching for the latest and greatest techniques to manage your spouse, "train your husband," improve your communication, etc. If so, then again, you may need to look elsewhere.

I believe all people function best when given clarity about their situation—the truths about their situation—and then given clarity about their specific choices within that situation. Which choice you make is up to you and can never be determined by another, even a so-called expert like me. But I do believe that all you are looking for, and all you really need in order to radically transform your marriage into the connection of your dreams, can be found within these pages. Here you will discover timeless, life-changing principles and countless stories and illustrations that show these principles in clear practice. These stories are real-life examples of real-life partners who have bravely chosen to end bad patterns and create new ones, all by simply Calming Down, Growing Up, and Getting Closer. As you might guess, the names and details of these stories have been changed to protect confidentiality, but all the stories are true. And you can definitely find yourself in them. And yet, I will not tell you exactly what to do. Except for this:

Hold on.

Hold on to your belief, however small, that you are *not* crazy and *not* alone—your marriage is difficult, very difficult, and that makes you just like most married people.

Hold on to the hope that you are more capable of introducing lasting change into your marriage, and into your whole life, than you may know. Like the weary traveler caught in the thickest part of the jungle, the open meadow of calm joy may be closer than you realize.

Most of all, hold on to your *integrity,* that truest and most principled part of yourself.

Your integrity is the part of you that speaks loudest when you're quiet, informing you of your most deeply held principles and the most passionate dreams for your life. This is the part of you that said, "I do," and it's the part that wants you to keep saying it (or at least *wants to want* you to keep saying it). Your integrity is that part of you that carries the greatest potential for profound, love-affirming, and life-changing decisions, and because of that, it is to your integrity that I am trying to speak most clearly. I am writing this book directly to your integrity, because your integrity knows that life and marriage are difficult, and that no growth in life or marriage can happen without clarity, challenge, and truth.

Your integrity also knows what you want *most,* and the very fact that you're reading this book testifies to your deepest dream: You want to experience a great marriage, one that offers warmth, maturity, peace, connection, and intimacy unlike anything you've ever experienced or enjoyed.

To have this type of marriage, you're most likely going to have to do a lot of unlearning. Again, hold on, because if you dare to keep turning these pages, you're in for a bumpy ride—a ride that may turn all that you've been taught about marriage upside down. You're about to stop dreaming of, and start moving toward, the warm, close marriage you've always wanted.

Just hold on.

Hal Edward Runkel, LMFT
Duluth, Georgia
August 2010

A Word about Structure and Authorship

As you've undoubtedly noticed, mine is not the only name and face on this book. My wife of seventeen years, Jenny, is listed as an assistant writer on this project. In truth, she is both more and less than that. She is more than cowriter, in that she is truly the co*creator* of the whole ScreamFree message, copractitioner of the ScreamFree principles in our home and work life, and Director of Content for everything The ScreamFree Institute, our not-for-profit organization, produces.

Jenny is less than cowriter, however, in that she does not share ultimate responsibility for the content of this book. That belongs to me alone. I alone should be held accountable for the ideas, the tone, and certainly the errors and missteps contained within these pages. You will therefore not see the pronoun *we* here, as if we, as a couple, are ganging up to promote ourselves as the ideal couple, and thus telling you how to really be married. No, we both frowned on that idea from the very beginning.

What we thought would be far more helpful, and this is the reason her name is on the book, is for Jenny to serve as a very hands-on editor throughout this writing. Here's why:

1. While my expertise as a licensed marriage therapist gives me credibility, it can also preclude me from seeing things from a non-therapeutic, non-expert point of view. While I always court feedback from my fellow

family professionals, I am not writing this book to experts; I want to take the best therapeutic expertise and translate it into the working dialogue of regular couples. Jenny is well educated and well informed, that's for sure, but she has a very keen sense of how my words can come across to non-experts.

2. Obviously, Jenny is a woman and a wife. Incorporating her distinctive thoughts can help mitigate some of the effects of my inescapable bias as a man and a husband. Yes, I work very hard to account for as much of my bias as possible, but I know that without Jenny's helpful (and sometimes painful) correction, it would be far more prevalent.

screamfree
MARRIAGE

partone

Calming Down,

Growing Up,

Getting Closer

If I get married, I want to be very married.
—AUDREY HEPBURN

Almost everyone wants to get married. Little girls dream about big weddings, and sooner than they admit, boys fantasize about the girl of their dreams. Young women take this desire for matrimony several steps further, attending bridal shows and showers with fervor, and savoring every romantic comedy at the movies. Young men, despite their feigned fears of commitment, still fervently continue that search for a dream-girl worthy of marrying for life. And yes, they also watch those romantic comedies.

That's right. Even most guys see rom-coms, and not just because they're on a date. It's also because every romantic comedy has, as its goal, the couple ending up hitched. The characters want to experience it, the characters' friends encourage it, and the audience is dying to see it happen. Romantic movies don't get made if the characters don't get married. Just look at all the classics, as well as the success of *When Harry Met Sally* in the '80s, *Sleepless in Seattle* in the '90s, and, of course, *The 40-Year-Old Virgin* in the last decade. We all love these movies because, in addition to being incredibly entertaining, they capitalize on one truth: Almost everyone wants to get married.

Even the current gay marriage controversy offers more evidence of this fact. What gets lost in the whole debate is what it says about marriage itself: Even such "nontraditional" relationship partners want desperately to experience the official status, the spoken commitment, the tradition of marriage.

Yep, almost everyone wants to *get* married. Very few of us, however, want to really *be* married.

Being married, being *really* married, asks more of us than any movie could ever show onscreen. In truth, not even premarital counseling, or watching our own parents have a fantastic relationship, could adequately prepare us. Being married—being truly married for life—requires us to develop a level of maturity that few other experiences in life can match—a maturity character-ized by intense vulnerability, generous amounts of forgiveness, and undying patience. And that's all just in the first year! (And, of course, every year thereafter.)

As the years add up, marriage quickly stops feeling like a rom-com and starts feeling like a sitcom. "Marriage is like a never-ending, unfunny episode of *Everybody Loves Raymond*," says a character in *Knocked Up*. Sometimes, it's even worse, like an episode of *Roseanne*. One of my favorite sitcom scenes from the past twenty years was watching a yawning, stretching John Goodman, Roseanne's TV husband, walking out the front door, claiming a newfound freedom, "Ahhh . . . you know, this wife and kids thing has been nice and all . . . but I gotta go."

Now, because of your particular situation, you may not find that very funny—you may be married to someone who feels just like that. And that may make you want to scream. Or you may be the one who's just ready to run (another form of "screaming"). Either way, that's okay. Part of this maturity process, this grow-ing up, means growing honest with yourself and all your feelings and experiences. And when we're honest about our marriages, we have to admit that most of us have a lot in common. As we get and stay married, we all begin to realize the following:

- Whoa, my spouse and I really are two different people;
- This is harder than I thought it would be;
- No matter how hard I try, conflict is unavoidable, and, perhaps:
- If I want to see a change here, I'm probably going to have to initiate it myself.

The problem is not coming to those realizations about your-self. As you'll see in the first chapter, calmly focusing on yourself and your true feelings is the first step toward creating the relationship you really want. The problem comes when those of us who eventually recognize these truths do so with a great amount of confusion and resentment. We recognize these truths, but we do not want to accept them, because, darn it all, it's not supposed to be like this! We're supposed to be compatible! We're supposed to get along! We're supposed to see problems from the same standpoint, and handle them the same way, and no one person should ever feel more responsible for making it better! Right?

That's where *ScreamFree Marriage* comes in. This is a message that frees all of us confused and resentful spouses to openly feel just that, confused and resentful. We *should* all feel that way—not because of our marriages, but because of all the marital advice and expertise that has led us astray. People are not divorcing at higher rates than ever *just* because they are acting or relating badly (they are). Marriages are also breaking up because spouses are trying to squeeze their marriage into paradigms that, in the name of relationship expertise, are actually making things worse.

ScreamFree Marriage is among the first marriage books to expose all those lies and thus free you (and possibly your partner) to fully experience, recognize, and confront the counterproductive patterns that are keeping you stuck and making your marriage so difficult. By leading you through this process, I hope to help you transform your marriage into the one you dreamed of. It all begins with one uniquely ScreamFree principle:

If you want a warm, lasting marriage, you have to learn to keep your cool.

In *ScreamFree Marriage*, "keeping your cool" does not refer to simple anger-management techniques or artificial rules of engagement (fighting fair). No, becoming ScreamFree in your marriage refers to something far more optimistic. Here, *keeping your cool* means discovering and holding on to your truest self—and having the courage to openly pursue your truest desires—even in the midst of your greatest conflicts. It means willingly and calmly facing the natural fires of marital commitment, and actually growing up—and getting closer—through them.

Entering into such conflicts with integrity is not an easy task; it's not supposed to be. Developing a marriage built on passion, commitment, and deep connection means committing yourself to a new way of relating. It means keeping your cool as you face conflicts with your spouse that may have previously set you off in some form of "screaming." Being ScreamFree means holding on to your deepest desires for connection and boldly making yourself vulnerable . . . *without knowing how your spouse will respond.* It means viewing old marital patterns through new lenses, no longer seeing those patterns as indications of irreconcilable differences, but rather as opportunities to grow your personal integrity and transform your relationship. It's not a journey for timid spirits, but the rewards are certainly worth the struggle.

The ScreamFree Revolution

In my first book, *ScreamFree Parenting,* I introduced the power of keeping our cool—staying both calm *and* connected as we lead our kids into adulthood. By focusing less on our kids' behavior, and focusing much more on our own, we learned to stop taking responsibility *for* our children and start fulfilling our responsibilities *to* them. This groundbreaking approach doesn't aim to eliminate the natural difficulties of parenting, but instead embraces those challenges as precisely the growth opportunities needed to reclaim leadership in our families and bring peace to our homes.

Well, that's the approach of *ScreamFree Marriage* as well. This book is going to ask you to focus on yourself and calm yourself down, so that you can learn to embrace the natural conflicts of marriage and actually grow up and grow closer through them. And in Part One of this book, you are going to learn about a revolutionary new approach to addressing even the most hardened of marital problems.

This approach is so revolutionary that it may not make much sense right away. It may even come across as so jarring, or so pointless, that you'll be tempted to dismiss it out of hand. I say *jarring* because this approach is so different from almost everything you've heard before that you'll think it cannot possibly be valid. I say *pointless* because this approach is so simple you'll be tempted to think that it cannot possibly be transformative.

Obviously, I believe it is both incredibly valid and powerfully transformative. I see this approach work every week in couples with histories and problems and patterns all across the spectrum. When one partner chooses to follow this approach, as challenging as it may be, those histories gain new futures, those problems find solutions, and those patterns, well, they change forever.

The truth is this: You do not have to say all the right things at all the right times in order to have a great marriage. You do not have to know your spouse inside and out and sacrifice your life in order to meet his/her needs.

As you will see, all you have to do in order to build and enjoy the close marriage you've always craved is Calm Down, Grow Up, and Get Closer.

And I know you can do it. Ready? Let's get started.

Chapter 1

If You're Not Under Control,
You Cannot Be In Connection

Sometimes when people are under stress, they hate to think,
and it's the time when they most need to think.

—BILL CLINTON

According to Facebook (aka Timesuck), I am now "connected" to "friends" on four continents. With a few simple clicks and keystrokes, I am instantaneously in touch with interesting people from all walks of life. I am now reacquainted with a college buddy, reminiscing about the time we poured instant mashed potato flakes all over our roommate in the shower. (It was awesome.) I am now newly acquainted with some South Korean fans of the movie *Magnolia* (my favorite film). I am even now able to join a growing movement of Informed Baseball Fans Against the Designated Hitter. I'm part of a movement!

Apparently, Facebook and all the other exploding social-networking sites know me pretty well. The same goes for my cell provider. What they all seem to know about me is that I have an intense craving. I have a deep longing for something, something that I'm not always fully aware of. But all these companies know what I want. They call it by one name.

Connection.

We human beings crave this thing called connection. We want it so badly that we'll gladly part with almost any amount of monthly fee or hours spent just to taste it. And this quest for connection is so powerful and so universal, we'll take it however we can get it. Especially in this digital age. We connect to the Internet so that we can reconnect with our high school friends. We stay connected through our wireless network so that we can connect to our circle via voice or data. We'll even venture onto ChatRoulette and fleetingly "connect" with random strangers (and their body parts) from all over the world.

Connection.

In so many ways, we as people and as a society are experiencing more "connection" than ever. So why is it that, despite all this connection, we still crave even more? I believe that our growing ability to connect through technology has not lessened our anxiety about being *dis*connected; it's *magnified* it exponentially. Think about travel, for instance. This week I went from my home in Atlanta to work with military families in Colorado. Now, a hundred years ago, this trip would've taken a week or so by train and buggy. After my eventual arrival, it would've taken roughly another week for me to get a postcard back to my own family telling them that I had arrived safely. So think about how much time they would have had to wait, wondering about my safety! For weeks on end, they would have had to find a way to stop worrying, calm their anxieties, and go on with life.

Contrast that with how things are now. As soon as the airplane lands, after a mere three-hour flight, we'll all be whipping out our smartphones to let our loved ones know that we made it to our destination safely. This doesn't sound like the calming, strengthening freedom promised by increased connection; this sounds like a weakening dependence on superficial lifelines, all in 140 characters or less. This doesn't sound like true connection; it sounds like anxious addiction.

So what's the problem here? More important, what's the solution?

Well, the first problem is that these superficial pseudo-connections via technology have no chance of fulfilling our deepest desires. Not by a long shot. See, these electronic relationship providers are getting better at giving us the illusion of true, intimate connections, capable of transcending life's anxieties and increasing our human capabilities. But what the digital age calls "connecting" is really just *acquainting*. We're acquainting ourselves with each other as never before. But we all want something more than mere acquaintance. We want something deeper. Something private. Something exclusive.

And we always have.

The Answer Is . . . Marriage?

For seemingly ever, couples have been pairing up and trying to forge a special connection called marriage. On every continent, in every culture throughout history, people have been hitching their families and futures together, for better or for worse. Since our earliest history, humans have been longing for, and sacrificing for, the chance to connect with that one special other. Cavemen scratched out pictures about it. Every language has crafted poetry about it. We have always had a longing to experience an intimate, exclusive connection with someone. And of course, we still do. We want to choose someone, and have that someone choose us back. We want to share secrets with that special someone, and have him or her confide in us right back. We long to experience a unique bond with that one person above all others, and share a union that can transcend any crisis, reprioritize any other commitments, and leave us feeling stronger than when we were by ourselves.

Connection.

Now, I know what you might be thinking. You might be thinking that not everyone craves this kind of connection. For instance, you may not be certain that your spouse still wants a connection with you. Or maybe you're not sure that you still want a connection with your spouse. You may be wondering if you've ever *had* such a true connection in your current relationship, or if you *ever will*. What I want you to know is that I hear you. Throughout this book I will try my best to speak directly to that hurt and those concerns. But also know this. If you're having these concerns, and any of these concerns bother you, then you can be sure of one thing: You *do* still want connection. And I believe your spouse still wants it, too. We *all* want it.

How do we know this?

First of all, look at the latest research, which coincides with my clinical experience as a marriage and family therapist. The vast majority of both men and women report an equally strong desire for a close, emotional connection. That's right: *Men report a strong, emotional connection as their main desire.* You may find that hard to believe, thinking that all men want is a prostitute and a maid rolled into one, but the evidence is clear. Why else would all these men still be getting *re*married, even after horrible divorces, even after finding out that second and third marriages fail at a rate of 60–70%? Why else would all the research say that married men are happier, have greater financial success, and live longer?

Likewise, women still report that a close, emotional connection is their main relationship desire. Despite all the feminist advances of the last forty years, enlightened women have not abandoned the quest for intimate connection. Why else would so many still clamor for the white wedding and the white picket fence, even though the research says that married women are *un*healthier, *un*happier, and die *sooner* than their single counterparts?

The second way we can tell that all of us still crave connection is by just watching TV. Producers and advertisers know exactly what we all desire most, and it is all about intense, romantic connection. Think about it. Why buy a particular deodorant? Why else watch a ridiculous reality show about contrived mate selections? Why take a blue pill and risk a four-hour erection?

Connection.

We want to make our bodies ready for it, we like to fantasize about it by watching others, and we are willing to risk life and er, limb, to get a chance at it.

That's where marriage is supposed to come in. Marriage is society's way of answering the question, "What am I supposed to do with this lifelong, seemingly insatiable desire for true, chosen, mutual connection?"

Why, you get married, of course. And then you live happily connected ever after.

Right?

Yet here I am, writing a marriage book for folks supposedly already "connected." Here I am, obviously assuming that scores of already-married people, or soon-to-be-married people, are still battling to create and maintain this lifelong connection. Here I am, the supposed marital expert, still struggling every week to do the same in my own marriage.

And here you are, presumably one of those already-connected and yet still struggling people, reading this marriage book. Here you are, consciously thinking about your current connection—and looking for a hopeful, helpful message of transformation and joy.

So, if you and I are both married, then why are we still searching for help? Family, history, and culture have told us that marriage is the ultimate answer to our longing. Is there something wrong? Is there something wrong with the nature of our particular marriages, or is there something wrong with marriage itself? Is there something that is still preventing us from experiencing and enjoying the kind of connection we all crave most?

Well, if I may be so bold, yes. There is something wrong. And that's what this whole book is about.

The answer is this: We all scream too much.

We're either screaming at our spouses on the outside, or screaming at ourselves on the inside. We scream because we react to the anxiety of the relationship and the anxiety of the moment. We scream in marriage because we don't know how else to handle the inherent differences between us. We want to be close to someone, so we get married. We then want to get closer to that person because we think that by doing so we'll eliminate the anxiety brought on by our differences. The irony is, however, that when we get anxious about being distant, we scream, and screaming doesn't make us closer; it makes us even more distant. Of course, the opposite is true as well. Demanding our space in reaction to a sense of too much closeness doesn't work in marriage, either. In fact, it usually backfires, creating an anxious closeness that actually feels suffocating.

Now, I hear what some of you are thinking. "But I don't ever scream at my spouse." And that's what I used to think as well. But what I mean by "screaming" is not just yelling with a raised voice. *Screaming* is the term I use to describe the greatest enemy we all face in our marriage: emotional reactivity. That's a big, clinical expression to describe the process of letting our anxious emotions override our clear thinking. Getting emotionally reactive means allowing our worst fears or worries to drive our choices, instead of our highest principles. And whenever we allow ourselves to be driven by our anxiety, we usually create the very outcome we were hoping to avoid in the first place.

I don't just know this on a clinical level. I, the so-called marriage and ScreamFree expert, know this truth on the most personal level possible. Allow me to take you back seventeen years or so, to a time when Bill Clinton was a new president, *The X-Files* was a new TV phenomenon, and I was almost a new divorcé after only three days of marriage.

Trouble in Paradise

See, back in 1993, it took me three days to realize I was actually married. I know this sounds ridiculous, but it's true. There I was, with my beautiful bride, Jenny, eating a fabulous lobster dinner in an open-air restaurant in Hawaii. The food was delicious, the place, and Jenny, were gorgeous, and, of course, the weather was perfect. But once I realized I was really married, none of that mattered. All that mattered to me at that point was getting the heck outta there.

But let's back up. First of all, you need to know that Jenny and I were relative babies at the time of our nuptials. I was twenty-one and she was twenty. We were the first among all our friends to get hitched, which for a narcissist like me was sheer bliss. I loved all the attention and anticipation building up to that fateful day, and I could not understand how anyone could ever get "cold feet." I dove into everything about the wedding process, from the menu planning to the apartment hunting to the honeymoon details.

So with all this anticipation and preparation, I just couldn't stop thinking about, dreaming about, and planning on being together forever. All I wanted was to be *together,* all the time.

Jenny, however, was in a different place. She wasn't apprehensive, mind you (she was getting to marry me, after all!), but she was definitely concerned about things like finances, things like the transition from single, college kids to a new family unit, and things like whether her husband was taking all of this seriously enough. She knew that she loved me, but she wasn't sure that she could be a good spouse, capable of loving me, gulp . . . forever.

And this gave her a need for some space. She needed to take some time alone so that she could really ask herself, "Am I at all ready to become a lifelong partner?"

Well, of course she wasn't. In the astute words of Dr. David Schnarch in *Passionate Marriage,* no one can be ready for marriage *before* marriage because nothing prepares us for marriage *except* márriage. But at least Jenny was asking some good questions. My questions, on the other hand, were only about the event itself, and my focus was only on making public, and official, our *togetherness.* I was only concerned about getting joined as one, and getting on with our happily ever after. So I didn't take any space for any real, individual questions. Questions like whether I was up for the challenge of being a husband, or whether I could really see myself married to one woman for the rest of my days. These would have been good personal reflections, ones that could have helped me find my pause button, calm my genuine anxieties, and avoid the unpleasant situation I was about to create.

Fast-forward to the honeymoon. We were finally together, and I was wonderfully happy. For three days. Then there we were, enjoying a fine lobster, and something hit me. A feeling of dread and panic like nothing I'd experienced before. And it couldn't have come over me at a worse time. Out of the blue, all of a sudden, I lost it. I am telling you with all the seriousness I can muster. I. Freaked. Out.

I looked across the table and saw Jenny—really *saw* her, as if for the first time. She was not just my girlfriend anymore, she was my wife, my one and only, till death do us part. My pulse rate skyrocketed, I broke into a cold sweat, and things got blurry. It was as if she were stretching farther and farther away, like the door in that scene from *Poltergeist.* Questions started swirling in my head. *Could I really stay with this one woman, as wonderful and beautiful as she is, for the rest of my life? What was I thinking? I am only twenty-one years old! Oh, God, did I really just get . . . married????* All those questions that I should have been asking myself for months before the ceremony were now suddenly flooding my brain. It was at that time that I abruptly stood up, turned to my lovely young maiden, and asked her the worst question you can ask on a honeymoon . . .

"WHAT HAVE I DONE???"

Jenny stared at me midbite, with her little lobster bib rustling in the wind. She cocked her head to one side and lifted her eyebrows in disbelief. She was trying to make sense of what she'd just heard. Next thing I knew my fork dropped from my fingers, clanging on the plate and drawing the attention of everyone around us. I didn't care; I just wanted out. And as A Flock of Seagulls sang in the '80s, "I ran, I ran so far away." I left my new bride with the unfinished lobster, the unpaid check, and a very uncertain future.

Three days. Welcome to marriage.

Now, obviously, that's not the end of the story. Once on the streets of Honolulu, I stopped to catch my breath. I tried to calm my panic with self-talk. "It's okay, Hal, you just need some space. You just need some time apart. It's gonna be okay." Of course, space and time apart was not what I got that day. Jenny chased after her new husband, and she eventually caught up with me. In her own breathless, confused panic, she screamed to get my attention. I turned around and started screaming myself.

"I don't know if I can handle this!" I confessed. "I don't know if I can handle being together, all the time, forever! I feel like I'm about to lose my mind!" I was really losing it, right there on Oahu. "I mean, geez, I try to get away just now, and here you are, right behind me!"

It was at that point I became aware that in my hasty exit, and all during my grand speech, I was still wearing the silly plastic lobster bib from the restaurant.

It was actually perfectly appropriate that I was wearing a bib, because I was definitely acting like a baby. I was doing what so many of us do in our relationships: I was allowing myself to become immaturely, emotionally *reactive*. And emotional reactivity is our greatest enemy when it comes to creating great relationships. Let me say that again. Emotional reactivity is our greatest enemy when it comes to creating great relationships.

See, emotional reactivity, what I call "screaming," doesn't just make things worse; it actually creates the very outcomes we were hoping to avoid. Take this lobster bib incident. What was I, in my panic, trying to accomplish? I was trying to give myself the space that, truth be told, all relationships require—even couples on their honeymoon. But because I had been so anxiously *attached* up to and through the wedding, I reactively bounced to the other extreme as soon as I felt the least bit claustrophobic. So I freaked out and ran away. But did this give me the space I so desperately needed? Of course not! How could it have? How could I expect that such an immature action as running away was going to do anything but backfire? That's why Jenny ran after me; my extreme reactivity practically invited her to.

That's the power of emotional reactivity; that's the power of screaming. It just leads to more reactivity from our spouse, which creates the very outcome we were hoping to avoid in the first place.

The Power of Screaming

The truth is, we all "scream" in our marriages, because we all get anxiously reactive. And this reactivity can take several aggressive forms, like yelling, raging, or even hitting. It can also manifest itself through passive-aggressive behavior, like shutting yourself down and shutting your partner out. All are different, yet equally powerful, examples of getting reactive. There are, in fact, many ways to scream.*

Your husband criticizes you in public, and you lash out right back with something even crueler. Or maybe you shut down and shut him out for the next week.

Your wife complains that you don't do enough around the house, and you launch into a defensive, name-calling tirade about all you do at work *to pay* for that house. Or maybe you do the opposite. Maybe you weakly acquiesce with some sort of "Yes, dear" promise that you have no intention of keeping.

These are all emotional reactions of one kind or another, knee-jerk moves that feel natural at the time. But these reactions have no chance of creating the kind of response, or relationship, that you really want. And that's why I talk so much about them. I refer to all these reactions as "screaming" because: (1) literal screaming is the most common form of emotional reactivity; and (2) *Emotional-Reactivity-Free Marriage* as a book title doesn't really flow off the tongue very well.

But understanding what to call it is not nearly as important as understanding what it does to our relationships. First of all, allowing ourselves to become flooded with relationship anxiety actually prevents us from any kind of productive interaction. Ever heard it said, "I was so angry, I couldn't see straight?" Well there's some physiological truth to that statement. In his book *People Skills,* Dr. Robert Bolton points out that

> emotional arousal actually makes us different people than who we are in moments of greater calmness. When

---

*For a full, descriptive list of the five main ways we get reactive, the five ways we "scream" in our marriages, please see Appendix A at the end of the book. But be sure to mark this page and come right back.

we are angry or fearful, our adrenaline flows faster and our strength increases by about 20 percent. The blood supply to the problem-solving part of the brain is severely decreased because, under stress, a greater portion of blood is diverted to the body's extremities.

[Also, an increase in] adrenaline suppresses activity in areas at the front of the brain concerned with short-term memory, concentration, inhibition, and rational thought. This sequence of mental events allows a person to react quickly to [conflict], either to fight or to flee from it. But it also hinders the ability to handle rational problem solving.

Whenever we give in to the natural anxieties of marriage ("Is it always going to be like this?"; "Does she even care about me anymore?"; "Is he cheating?"), we make it harder for our brains to function clearly. And when our brains stop working, we start to scream in one way or another. And you know what? In a cruel, but poetic twist, our screaming actually makes it easier for those original anxieties to become reality.

For instance, ever nag your spouse about coming home on time, only to find that the more you nag, the more she comes home late . . . and resentful? Your emotional reactivity actually makes the worst outcome more likely, because no one wants to rush home to a nagging, needy spouse.

The same holds true for the "Is he cheating?" scenario. Say your husband mentions a new female coworker he really gets along well with. They complement each other's skills, and they've just been made partners on a big project. This will require a lot of hours and close contact with each other, and you start to get concerned. Now, a ScreamFree, principled, responsive move might be to calmly address your concerns with your husband directly, as soon as you start to feel those concerns. (And this book will help you figure out how to do this.)

Contrast that with what your anxiety tells you to do. You lash out openly, accusing him of cheating and/or no longer loving you. Or you passive-aggressively start to spend more time away from him, especially when he pursues you, hoping to hurt him just as he's hurting you. Or—and I've seen this happen too many times to count—you could terrorize this other woman by calling her names or making accusations and threats.

What's the logical conclusion of the story? Why, of course, your husband is less attracted to you, he's angry at you, and he's now much more likely to seek out time at work, time with the new coworker. In your reactivity, you've just shown your husband the worst side of yourself, in hopes that doing so would somehow bring him back, closer to you. And that, of course, just backfires. He now doesn't want to be closer to you, except maybe out of pity or resentment-filled obligation. Now, ironically, he wants to be closer to *her*. Your screaming made the outcome you feared that much more likely to occur.

That's the incredible power of emotional reactivity; that's the incredible power of screaming. And that's why calming yourself down is the most important step you can take to introduce positive change in your marriage.

Whatever you take from this book, take this: Learning to stay calm, when everything in and around you compels you to scream, is the first and best step you can take to revolutionize your relationship. Staying calm will always end a reactive pattern and start something positive. Always. That's why this book is called *ScreamFree Marriage*. And that's why Calming Down is the first step in the revolutionary formula you're about to encounter in chapter 3.

But it's not just about calming down. It's about learning to stay calm *and connected* at the same time. Some of us can easily stay calm by simply running away from the situation, avoiding any possible conflict that might arise. But that's not being Scream-Free; such running away is just another form of screaming. Staying calm *and* connected means remaining in the conflict and authentically representing your position. Staying calm and connected means saying no to the screaming inside you and saying yes to calmly pursuing the honesty and intimacy you want most. And, most important, staying calm and connected requires you to stop focusing on your spouse and start focusing on yourself.

It's Not You, It's Me

The greatest thing you can do for your marriage is to learn to focus more on yourself. Yes, I believe you actually need to become more *self*-centered. Now, before you call this crazy talk, hear me out. Every great marriage is a self-centered marriage because every great marriage requires two *centered selves*. Every great marriage is a bond between two whole, centered people. These two strong individuals actively work on improving themselves for the other's benefit, without necessarily depending on the other to do the same. These two are afraid of neither separation nor togetherness, and work to seek a balance of both. These two pay more attention to their own behavior, which they can control, than their spouse's, which they, thankfully, cannot.

Only with such an approach can anyone experience what we all crave—true intimacy with another separate and mysterious soul, one who consciously chooses to share with us his/her life, choices, hopes, and dreams.

Now, I understand that you may not be familiar with this model for marriage. You may have been inundated your whole life with teachings on self-sacrifice, compromise, meeting one another's needs, and the constant quest for compatibility. In chapter

2, we will directly combat those lies. All such marriage expertise advises focusing more on your spouse, as opposed to yourself, and is thus inherently misguided, misleading, and actually harmful to your marriage.

What I'm proposing is a new model for marriage. It's actually not new, because it's the model I believe we were meant to follow from the beginning. This model is just new to most of us, particularly as laid out in a marriage book.

But I'm definitely not the first person to say it. In fact, there is a legacy of relationship expertise that has been articulating this "two centered selves" model for centuries. Almost every religious and philosophical tradition has a strong emphasis on growing in self-awareness and self-control. The Greeks taught us that, above all else, we should know ourselves. The Hebrew Bible cites self-control as more valuable than riches, and has a rich legacy of God holding everyone responsible for their own individual choices (regardless of the choices of the people around them, even their spouses). Islamic tradition preaches that the "real jihad," the most important battle of all, takes place within the self. Jesus taught us to take out the plank in our own eye instead of worrying about the speck in our neighbor's, a prescription to focus more on our own behavior than anyone else's. Christianity also teaches that one of the fruits of the Holy Spirit, one of the ways you can tell that someone is led by God, is self-control. And Gandhi, perhaps summing up all these traditions, exhorts us all to "first, be [yourself] the change you want to see in the world."

Now, most of us have at least heard of these ideas, but we rarely implement them in our relationships. We commonly think of them as ethereal tenets to be used in general rather than practices to be put into action, and this is most unfortunate.

But applying this model of relating with others is definitely possible. And it all begins with one shift. As I said at the beginning, you have to learn to focus on yourself. Obviously, not in a

"I only care about myself" kind of way. That type of self-absorbed approach is not at all what we're talking about. Truth be told, being self-absorbed is not focusing on yourself, it's *getting others* to focus on you. Whenever we need others to think, feel, or act a certain way to suit our own needs, we are focusing on others *for our own benefit,* and that's the height of self-absorption. See, being self-absorbed is not being self-focused, it is actually being *other*-focused. It's focusing on others so that you can either get them to focus on you or get *them* into a mood—or get *them* to behave in a way—that makes *you* feel better.

Now, you may not see yourself in this light, but that's just the problem. We often don't see ourselves at all. So here's a little test.

1. Do you ever get angry that your spouse doesn't meet your emotional needs? Think of the wife who constantly complains to her girlfriends about her husband's lack of romance, but never openly addresses it with him. Think of the husband who justifies his affair because at least *she* appreciates him. That's other-focused thinking.

2. Do you ever try to "make" your spouse happy (as if that's really possible), because it just makes your life easier? Think of the wife who compromisingly accepts her husband's strip club habit because it relieves her of the anxiety of dealing with her own sexuality. Think of the husband who "yes-dear"s his wife's every plea just to get her off his back. That's all other-focused as well.

And why is other-focused thinking so wrong? Because whatever we human beings focus on, we inevitably try to manage, improve, or control. We cannot help it—it's simply in us to want to increase our influence upon whatever we set our gaze. If you don't believe me, then I want you to try something. Take the biggest picture or painting in your home and turn it until it is visibly crooked. Then, see how long you can look at it without wanting to straighten it. Go ahead, see if you can last ten minutes.

Now, this desire to straighten the picture doesn't mean you're suffering from obsessive-compulsive disorder; it just means you're human. And thankfully so. Where would we be without this desire to improve what we see? We'd still be living in caves, that's where we'd be (and all our cave drawings would be crooked).

But there's a problem when this innate desire gets applied to relationships, particularly marriage. Ever had much success controlling or changing your spouse? See, as natural as it is to want to change another person, or even improve that person's situation, it's also our human nature to *resist being changed by another*. That's why trying to get your spouse to eat better and lose weight rarely works. That's why you resent and resist your spouse's efforts to do the same thing with you, or to give you any unsolicited advice.

As perplexing as this may be, when you think about it, you wouldn't want it any other way. This is because any change you "get" your spouse to make, whether it's talking more about your relationship or doing more at bedtime with the kids, is not the genuine change you wanted in the first place. You don't want to change your spouse, you want your spouse *to want to* change. You want it to be his decision. You want him to *want* to change his housecleaning habits. You want her to *want* to give you more compliments. You want him to *want* to grow up whenever Mom comes to town. That way you can still respect him as an equal, independent partner, choosing to act differently on his own—not just because you asked him to.

And, believe it or not, that's the real power of focusing on ourselves, of becoming more "self-centered." See, when you are actively centered on yourself, you are more conscious of your own behavior than your spouse's. You're more concerned about knowing and representing your real feelings and desires than you are with getting your spouse to do the same. And most important, you are most concerned with staying calm and connected, making sure that, at the very least, you are not reactively contributing to the very patterns you want to avoid.

When focusing on yourself and staying calm is your number one priority, you learn how to push your own pause button. You learn to create a space for yourself between stimulus—your spouse pushing your buttons—and your response. That way you can then *choose* what you do next, out of your highest principles and desires, rather than simply react without thinking. And the best part? Creating such a pause for yourself, in turn, creates a new space for your partner to do the same. By simply creating a small pause, a calm, centered spouse can transform any marriage into a deeper, lifelong connection. I honestly and absolutely believe that, and that's why I'm writing this book.

And that's why this entire book is about the power of calm in your marriage. The most powerful force you can introduce into your marriage is the simple power of calm. By staying both calm and connected, you have the power to stop any argument in its tracks, identify and change any dysfunctional pattern, and transform any relationship into one you've always dreamed about. By just staying calm and connected, you can remain focused on adhering to your principles instead of clinging to your anxieties. By staying calm and present, you can become a calming presence for your marriage and your whole family.

I want you to imagine yourself as such a calming presence. Your wife attacks you verbally, for instance, accusing you of a slew of wrongs—some accurate, most not. With a careful pause, you calmly reply, "Honey, thank you for telling me; believe it or not I really do want to know how you feel. Please *tell me more* about how you really feel about all of this." Your spouse is dumbstruck, not knowing who you are, or what she's supposed to do next.

Or let's say you catch your spouse in a lie about an expense on the credit card bill. With absolute calm, you bring it to his attention and exclaim, "I'm assuming you were just mistaken about this, but I just wanted to make sure I don't need to call the bank." He secretly rejoices at the chance you've given him to save face, and agrees with your assessment. "Yeah, that was me. I think I got it wrong the first time we talked about it. Sorry about that."

Or how about this: You go out of your way to create a special evening with just you and your wife. You arrange the babysitting, make the reservations, the whole bit. You really go all out, hoping for a special, intimate night. But your wife, for whatever reason, just never gets into it. She frets about the kids, checks her watch throughout the evening, and cannot wait to go to sleep as soon as you get home. While everything in you wants to scream out with anger or shut down with resentment, you remain calm, choosing to sleep on all your thoughts and feelings. The next day, with absolute clarity, you tell her that you were hurt by her actions, that you had hoped for something special. You don't ask her to respond, you just inform her how you feel. And then you calmly leave the room. She is now forced to sit with her own thoughts and feelings, contemplating her actions and reflecting on what she wants most. The strength you feel in your own self-respect is empowering, to say the least. It's almost better than the sex you hoped for last night. (Almost.)

"Let's Be Careful Right Now"

Now, you may be reading those scenarios above with a skeptical, or even a cynical eye. *Yeah, right, Hal. First of all, I can't imagine myself doing and saying those things. Second, even if I did, even with all this calm you're talking about, there's no way my spouse would respond anything like the spouses in those examples. No way.*

Or, maybe you're saying to yourself that you've tried those things, and it's never worked. It's always made things worse.

You may be right. I don't know you, I don't know your spouse, and I don't know your history. But I'm asking you now to just hold on. Keep reading. I am going to try my very best to give you clear, actionable principles to put into practice. And I am going to give you clear, inspiring stories of what this all can look like, and how it has worked for real-life couples.

And along those lines, I want to close this chapter with one such story.

In her brilliant reflection on marriage, *Committed,* Elizabeth Gilbert gives us a true and powerful example of successfully introducing calm and, as a result, a deepened connection. As I retell her story, including a few excerpts, look for the critical moments of choice, those moments where anxious reactivity would have been far easier—and quickly destructive. Look also for the courageous choices to calm down in the midst of torrential chaos, and how those choices saved, and strengthened, a committed relationship.*

Let's first set the scene. For a variety of detailed reasons that you'll have to pick up the book to fully understand (and I highly

---

*Before we start, a warning. Some of you may be a little put off that this story involves a couple not yet officially married. Yes, they had made a personal, and even spiritual, commitment to one another, but not in an official ceremony. They had both been through horrible divorce experiences, and thus were each turned off to the whole idea of an official, state-sanctioned marriage. Their journey toward such an arrangement, however, is in fact the whole story and subject of Gilbert's book. My hope is that any opinions and feelings you may have about their arrangement will not cloud your appreciation for their dilemma or their courageous choices, and that you will still be able to profit from seeing their growth as individuals and as a couple.

recommend that you do), Gilbert and her fiancé found themselves trapped in quite a hellish limbo. Wanting to stay together for life in America, Gilbert and Felipe, as he's called, have to go through a year of bureaucratic waiting and processing. He was deported by the United States, and in order for him to reenter the country, he and Gilbert, an American citizen, had to get married. So they had to wait for his native Brazil to process his records. They had to wait for the U.S. Consulate in his current home of Australia to process his visa interview. They had to wait for, well, almost everything.

So, in the meantime, they traveled. And then they traveled some more. Gilbert and Felipe decided to find the cheapest, and yet still interesting, place they could think of—Southeast Asia. In a few humidity-ridden countries like Vietnam, Cambodia, Laos, and Malaysia, this waiting, wandering couple set out on a journey of coping . . . and hoping.

For this couple, trying to start a life together, these were some fairly excruciating circumstances. It was hot. It was humid. They were tired. They were in what seemed like perpetual limbo, not knowing when, or even if, they could legally live together in America. And in the midst of all this, they were each facing their greatest fear—the fear of getting attached in marriage again. Both of them had survived very messy and painful divorces, and neither wanted any part of that experience again. They did, however, want each other. They did crave the experience of a deeper, life-long connection.

So they each decided, on their own, to endure. Of course, that led to an increased knowledge of each other. And that, even in the best of circumstances, leads to friction. On a twelve-hour, un-air-conditioned bus ride through the jungle, it can lead to war.

In an effort to pass the time and make the best of their predicament, Gilbert kept scheduling mini-excursions for the both of them to see various sites. While this was moderately successful for a while, it was losing its effect. Like so many solutions we come up with, these excursions were beginning to cause more problems than the issues they were meant to resolve.

Such was the case with this twelve-hour expedition into the mountains of Laos. Four hours in, while losing the battles against sweat and nausea and claustrophobia, Felipe began to lose it. Now, according to Gilbert, seeing Felipe "lose it" was nothing new. Here's how she described it:

> Even under the best of circumstances, Felipe has the bad habit of sometimes snapping impatiently at people he feels are either behaving poorly or interfering somehow with the quality of his life. This happens rarely, but I wish it would happen never. All over the world and in many languages I have watched this man bark his disapproval at bungling flight attendants, inept taxi drivers, unscrupulous merchants, apathetic waiters, and the parents of ill-behaved children. Arm-waving and raised voices are sometimes involved in such cases.
>
> I deplore this.

What was new on the bus ride was how reactive Gilbert herself became in this battle. She surprised herself with her own volatility, and volume. The two of them became engaged in a full-fledged fight. Felipe was sick and tired of Gilbert's anxious attempts to "make the best" of the situation. Gilbert, on the other hand, was sick and tired of Felipe being so sick and tired. "I'm just trying to make the best out of this situation, okay? If you have any better ideas or any better plans—please, by all means, offer some!"

The heat, the sweat, the weariness, the waiting, the worry. Above all, the unknown. It was all getting to both of them. And after the back-and-forth explosions came what Gilbert described

as a "heated silence." They each retreated to their separate corners, each mentally rerunning their own arguments. As we can
all testify, these are make-or-break moments for a relationship.
Think about the tensest moments you've gone through in your
relationship. Think about the painful fright of walking on such
tenuous turf, wondering whether you or your relationship could
make it through that moment.

It was exactly in such a moment, that moment, that Felipe
then did something remarkable. Nothing huge, mind you, but remarkable. He obviously wanted this relationship to work. After a
calming pause, with both great restraint and great pursuit, Felipe
gently reached for his fiancée's hand. Then he spoke. Softly, but
surely.

"Let's be careful right now."

That's all he said. In reality, that's all he needed to say. This
is because Gilbert immediately knew what her fiancé was doing.
She knew exactly what he meant.

See, a couple of years before that, the two of them had been
in a similar situation, leading to a similar argument. But just as
the tone in that encounter was turning nasty, and they were beginning to question the relationship's very survival, Felipe paused
and said, "Let's be careful."

"Of what?" Gilbert had asked at that time.

"Let's just be careful of what we say to each other for the next
few hours," Felipe explained. "These are the times, when people
get tired like this, when fights can happen. Let's just choose our
words *very carefully* . . ."

Since that initial episode, both Gilbert and Felipe had
occasionally used this calming interjection to stop a reactive
pattern—and pursue something more response-able.

"Let's be careful right now."

Care-full, indeed. Now back on that bus in Laos. As it had
before, Felipe's calm interjection this time managed to stop their

negative, reactive pattern in its tracks—and created the possibility for something new. Gilbert no longer wanted to fight, because it is just too exhausting to fight with someone who refuses to get reactive. Felipe's calm became *calming*.

And what happened next, I believe, was revolutionary for Gilbert and Felipe's relationship. Felipe put his arm around his mate, and Gilbert began to relax into his chest. Struck again by her supposedly hotheaded Latin fiancé's sudden calm, Gilbert herself took a pause. And then she began to see this man in a wonderful new light, to know this man as a separate being. She began to see that her efforts to make Felipe happy were merely ways to soothe *her* anxiety. Her subsequent reactivity was simply furthering the outcome she was hoping to avoid, namely, his *un*happiness. Seeing him afresh, she was able to see how she was contributing to the pattern, and that she could do something about it.

Making It Personal

Here's what this story makes clear. Huge change doesn't have to begin with a move so radical that you cannot imagine yourself doing it. And it certainly doesn't begin with any effort to change someone else's behavior. It simply begins with one partner staying calm, and inviting the other to follow suit.

And this is where you come in. It is your responsibility to do something different in your marriage. It is your responsibility to make a break with your current patterns of reactivity, finding your own pause button and inviting your spouse to do the same.

Right now, it is up to you. Why, you ask? For two reasons. One, you're the one reading this book, so you're the only one I'm talking to. Obviously, if your spouse were reading this, if I were talking to your spouse, then I'd be saying the same thing to him/her. But the fact that you're reading this right now means that

you're at least curious about having a better marriage. You're at least interested in creating a deeper, lifelong connection. That interest belongs to you, so it is your job to do something about that interest.

Two, you're the only one responsible for your behavior, your choices, your attitudes, your moods, and so on. You cannot, with any measure of integrity, claim that any screaming on your part—in whatever form it takes—is your spouse's fault. "If only my spouse would [start appreciating me, do more around the house, spend less, etc.], then I wouldn't have to [yell, get so upset, shut down, withhold sex, spend more time at work, etc.]." All such "if only" thoughts are inherently weak and weakening, because they place our own remote control in the hands of someone else. And then we complain that they push our buttons! We've all done this in a variety of ways throughout our lives, especially in our marriages.

But we don't have to. Not anymore.

When we begin to willingly focus on ourselves, when we see and feel the self-destructive power of such emotional reactivity, we begin to see and feel everything differently. We recognize that each of us has had a strong hand in creating the very outcomes we were hoping to avoid. Each of us has played a major role in perpetuating the negative patterns we complain about. We also recognize that without one partner having the calm clarity of mind to stop this kind of destructive cycle, there's usually no end to it in sight. Like tribes and countries forever at war, couples can go on screaming indefinitely.

Now, those truths are painful to face and admit. But that doesn't make them any less true. When you claim your innermost desires for true connection, however, these truths become a message of good news. See, it's good news to know that you're a powerful, creative actor in your own life, even if you're learning how your own knee-jerk reactions have created powerfully negative patterns. This is good news because it means, quite simply, that you also have the power to stop those patterns and create new, positive interactions instead. It's also good news to learn about the power of screaming, because that means, quite simply, that all you have to do is stay calm.

Perhaps this means, for you, confronting your own insecure jealousies, evaluating your suspicions with a neutral third party, and calmly representing, directly to your husband, your concerns about his new female coworker . . . *without asking him to give a defense.*

Perhaps this means setting aside your resentments about your wife's lack of expressed appreciation, and instead making an honest list of all the things you appreciate about her, and sending that list to her . . . *without needing her to reciprocate in any way.*

Perhaps it just means pausing during your next heated moment, stepping toward your spouse, and simply suggesting, "Let's be careful right now."

The beauty of all this is that, regardless of what you do with this new truth and responsibility, regardless of how you choose to begin, your next steps will greatly influence your relationship. This is because your moves will begin to come from a place of calm, a place of clear thinking. Thinking about what you want *most,* and thinking about how you can best represent, and pursue, that desire. And that alone gives you the greatest chance of stopping any pattern of reactive screaming. That alone gives you, and your spouse, the greatest chance of encountering and enjoying that experience we've all been craving all along.

Connection.

Chapter 2

It's Not What You Have in Common,
It's What You Have Inside

*I think that there is some merit to a description I once read of a
married couple as "happily incompatible." Ruth likes to say, "If two
people agree on everything, one of them is unnecessary."*
— BILLY GRAHAM

If everyone is thinking alike, then somebody isn't thinking.
— GEN. GEORGE S. PATTON

Shel Silverstein is one of the most beloved children's writers
of the last century. He was capable of penning the silliest poetry,
like *Where the Sidewalk Ends,* and the most poignant of fables,
like the tearjerker *The Giving Tree.*

But two of my favorite Silverstein works don't seem to fall into
any given literary genre. In fact, these two books are two of the
unlikeliest best sellers you'll ever encounter; with so few words,
or even penstrokes of art, they hardly qualify as books at all. But
you'd be hard-pressed to find two more compelling works of relationship wisdom.

In the first book, *The Missing Piece,* we come upon an incomplete circle, looking like a misshapen Pac-Man, searching
the world for a pie piece that'll fit perfectly into his open gap.

We see him try out several possibilities: a square, a rectangle, a small triangle, a large triangle. None fit. Even when he does find a pie piece that seems to match perfectly, the two can't seem to get along for very long, and they both go their separate ways. The book ends, somewhat sadly, with our Pac-Man bumping along, singing his song, "Oh, I'm looking for my missing piece . . ."

In the sequel, *The Missing Piece Meets the Big O,* the Missing Piece herself is the main character. A small triangular pie piece, she sits alone on the road, longing to meet a Pac-Man-like circle to fit herself into. She meets several, but none seem to have missing gaps that match her exact size. Some even have more than one gap! At one point, however, our Missing Piece heroine encounters a Pac-Man with a gap that she could fill just perfectly. Both she and the Pac-Man are thrilled, and they jump into each other, forming their new, complete whole. And life is good . . . for a while.

Then, something unexpected happens: The Missing Piece starts to grow. And grow some more. She starts to grow so much that she outgrows the gap of her partner, making the once-perfect fit a thing of the past. Not knowing what to do, thinking that they can't possibly stay together, they separate and go away from each other, renewing their search for a new, perfect fit.

Thankfully, that is not the end of the story. The end of the story not only takes us into a new meeting of characters; it brings us to a new understanding of relationship itself. And I'll have to leave it to you to go read the book to find out what that powerful conclusion is. For now, it's important to take what wisdom we can.

See, most of us have been sold a bill of goods, a bunch of lies about what relationships are supposed to be like, particularly the most important relationship of all—marriage. The most basic, and insidious, of these lies is that each of us is an incomplete "part . . ." looking for a *part*-ner. According to this lie, we have each been sent on a quest to find our one perfect match, and we've been trying to fit ourselves into one another ever since. We have even been resisting the very growth in ourselves and our marriages we seek, just to keep the mythical perfect original match in place. As Rocky puts it in the first movie, when describing his relationship with Adriane, "I got gaps. She's got gaps. We fill each other's gaps." And we think this sets us up for the ideal match.

These Silverstein books not only point out the fallacy of trying to match ourselves perfectly with another person (a fallacy we'll fully detail in this chapter), these books point out the mistake of trying to match our marriages into some ideal model. We've been exhausting ourselves attempting to wedge our unique, wonderfully imperfect unions into some idyllic model of oneness, without even a correct understanding of the meaning of oneness. No wonder we're periodically frustrated reading marriage-advice articles, or attending marriage seminars, or visiting matchmaker sites, all of which promote and promise harmonious unions of perfect compatibility. These are usually vestiges of a faulty marriage model, one that cannot produce the active, vibrant, resilient relationship we all crave.

The Lies about the Ties That Bind

What I truly believe is that marriages today are in trouble, but not just in spite of all the great marriage advice out there. No, marriages today are in trouble precisely *because of* some misleading, even damaging advice that's been foisted upon couples for way too long. We've been handed aphorisms about soulmates and finding "the one." We've been admonished to compromise, and find peace before bedtime. We've been taught that everything comes down to meeting one another's needs. And what makes all this information so rooted in our psyche is that we've heard all this misinformation from so many various sources.

First of all, our families hand down these false truths, teaching us that "finding someone" is the key to having a full life, even as Mom divorces Dad so she can "find herself." TV shows and movies then spoon-feed more lies to us, leading us to believe that needing or "completing" someone is the telling signal of true love, that the only exciting part of any relationship is the initial attraction, and that once you've found Mr. or Ms. Right it's happily ever after. If a show does depict a married couple, they're always unhappy because they're obviously mismatched, or they've grown apart over the years (Cliff and Clair Huxtable being the obvious exception). Finally, we're bombarded at our place of worship with confusing messages of oneness and submission, coupled with a seemingly contradictory encouragement to develop an individual, personal relationship with God above all else.

We've heard all this messaging designed to make us happy and healthy in our relationships, yet it hasn't helped. In truth, it's hurt us. Our efforts to squeeze our marriage into these ideals has left us exhausted and exasperated, wondering if there can possibly be a better way to be and stay married. Every week in my office I meet or hear about another couple seeking divorce because they have nothing left "in common." They cannot seem to get on the same page, and they can no longer sacrifice themselves to make this marriage work.

Well, obviously, I believe there is a better way—the Scream-Free way—and that's what this book is all about. Specifically, this book is going to show you a way of being married that focuses not on compatibility, but on personal commitment and integrity. It's going to show you how to be married in a way that doesn't depend on finding agreement with your spouse, but rather on embracing your conflicts as the growth opportunity you and your marriage need. The rest of this book is going to show you that it's not what you have in common that makes a deep, lasting connection; it's what you've got inside. What you've got inside you—integrity, passion, commitment—that's what creates and maintains connection.

To that end, this chapter is going to examine three specific lies that keep us stuck, lies that keep us chasing after that elusive compatibility and agreement and commonality. Then we'll point out the fallacies in those lies by advancing some ScreamFree truths that highlight a better way. First, however, a small warning. Some of these lies may be sayings or philosophies that you've held dear for quite some time. Yet my guess is that you have, at some point, wrestled with whether or not they could apply to your marriage, given how much confusion and difficulty you've experienced in real life. So don't be surprised if you feel a little confused by the following challenges to your previous ways of thinking. And don't be surprised if at least a part of you feels somewhat relieved at the same time. Ready for a strong dose of challenging truth? First, here come the lies.

1. Spouses Are Supposed to Meet Each Other's Emotional Needs.

I know that calling this first one a lie runs counter to some of the most popular marital advice out there, so follow me closely here. My intent is not to denigrate anyone's lifework (there are a number of outstanding relationship professionals who have built their whole models on the needs-meeting premise), but I do need to speak what I believe to be the truth. And the truth is that you and your spouse *do not need each other.* What marriages need most are spouses who do *not* need each other.

Sounds radical and jarring, I know. Let's slow down, therefore, and just examine this logically. See, if marriage is about meeting one another's needs, then I am definitely responsible *for* my spouse and her well-being, and I had better do everything I can to focus all my efforts on her. I had better focus my gaze and my energy on discovering what her strongest needs are, and working hard to meet them. Of course, since, according to this model, I also need *my* needs met, then she needs to do the same for me. She needs to focus her energy on discovering and trying to serve my needs.

All we both need, therefore, is a clear picture of what each other's needs are. I need to know what wives need most, and my wife Jenny needs to know what husbands need most. Again, since this model is so prevalent, there are a lot of marriage experts willing to clue us in. Let's start with figuring out my needs first. Most of these experts tell me that because I'm a man, I have one clear, great need. Can you guess what that need is? Of course you can. Since I'm a man, my greatest need is sex. In this model, sex is a *need*. The same way oxygen is a need. The same way shelter is a need. And clothing. This model believes that men have proven, time and again, that they are geared toward sex above all else. So this means that for all men, including me, sex is not just a desire, or a passion for connection. *It's a need*. And it's my greatest need above all.

Now, let's focus on Jenny. Since she is a woman, she has a different greatest need, according to this model. Given that throughout history women have depended on men to care for and protect them, then it is obvious that for all women, including my wife, the greatest need is a sense of safety and security. This is only logical, right? Women have to feel protected and provided for *by someone else* in order to truly live. Why? Because it's a *need*.

So, continuing with the illogic of this model, here's what now has to happen: Jenny and I have to work very hard to meet each other's clear and primary needs in order for us to have a working, compatible relationship. But here's where we all begin to run into a problem: One person needs to go first. Either Jenny needs to provide me with sex, or I need to provide her some sense of security.

Now, traditionally throughout history, society has posited that the husband needs to prove his worthiness as a provider, and once he does, he and his wife can get married and then consummate the union. So he's got to show he's got the goods to provide the necessary goods, and then she'll let him have *her* goods. In to-day's society, however, this seems to have gotten reversed. Today, the woman needs to give it up a little in order for the man to feel strong and motivated enough to go out and provide a secure, stable life for them both. Either way, the logical conclusion is the same: He gets sex as long as he provides her with security, and the wife gets security as long as she gives the husband sex.

Hmmm. Does that sound like prostitution to anyone be-sides me?

Never mind the woman's *desire* for sex—that just compli-cates things. Let's not even talk about desire. For men, it goes beyond the vulnerabilities of desire. This is a *need*, people! It's a *necessity* that *must* be met for the man to function as a husband and a provider.*

Never mind the business of growing ourselves and our chil-dren beyond our long-held stereotypes about men, women, sexu-ality, and who provides for whom. We cannot raise up women as strong, independent individuals (no doubt what you are raising your daughter to be, as I am striving to do with mine), all the while truly believing in our hearts that really and truly, no woman can feel secure and stable without a man. We also cannot raise up men to be mature, self-controlled individuals who respect women as true equals (no doubt what you are raising your son to be, as I am striving to do with mine), all the while truly believing that all men are truly just horndogs, always at the mercy of their hor-mones, always needing their sex "needs" serviced.

---

*This is why so many societies have "circumcised" their young girls (a horrific procedure also known as genital mutilation). By removing the God-given clito-ris (the only body part in either the male or female anatomy explicitly designed for sexual pleasure), these societies reason that they can keep this whole sex matter as uncomplicated as possible. Remove the woman's desire, they reason, and she can just focus on fulfilling this need for her man, without the messy complications of desire.

Now, other marriage manuals tell me that my greatest need as a husband is respect. I need her to respect me, meaning I cannot operate at my best without it. And apparently, according to these other books, if I don't get such respect, then I won't provide her with her greatest need, supportive love. Well, if I'm not getting mine, then I'm not giving you yours! Never mind that I'm not acting in any sort of respect-full way. You owe me because you're my spouse! Take that!

Are you getting the picture here? If our job is to meet one another's needs, then we automatically set up a quid-pro-quo relationship that is only as strong as the mutual cooperation of each partner. There's no reliance on personal integrity here, the idea that my behavior is driven by my highest principles, not by whether or not I believe my spouse is working hard enough to meet my needs. In this faulty model, there's only reliance on what you've done for me lately.

Once a good friend and fellow author, John Alan Turner, and I were both speaking at a family relationships seminar. After our speaking sessions, we both attended a workshop about husbands and wives working to meet these respective needs of respect and love. We listened to the workshop leaders articulate how, in their experience, men who don't feel the respect they need will withhold the love their wives so desperately "require." Men feel undercut, undersupported, and slighted by this unmet need, so they reciprocate in kind. Of course, the women who don't feel loved feel no compulsion to respect their man, and so it goes. The only way out of this stalemate, according to the workshop leaders, is for both husbands and wives to start getting their needs met by the other.

After listening to this for a good long time, my friend John turns toward me and asks, "But what if I'm a grown-up?"

Exactly. Grown-ups love and respect others based on their principles, not on their spouse's perceived reciprocity. Grown-ups serve others regardless of whether they're getting served in return. The needs-meeting model doesn't call people to greater maturity; it simply accepts, and even encourages, spouses to dwell in *immaturity*.

And that brings up the worst part of this needs-meeting model. The worst part of all is that by concentrating so much on our needs, we end up creating two *very . . . needy . . . people*. We end up with two whiny, immature people needing each other, always with the mind-set that if I don't get mine, then you won't get yours, and on and on. And when's the last time you respected an emotionally needy person? Never, that's when. Right now, try to picture in your mind the most emotionally needy person among your friends. Go on, think about it. Does the image of that person invigorate you? Does thinking about spending time with that person excite you? Of course not; it drains you. It wearies you. So why would anyone want to promote a model for marriage that encourages people to focus on their needs? (Now, if you couldn't think of that emotionally needy person right away, guess what— you're it. But don't worry, just keep reading.)

The truth is that spouses do not need each other, and they're not supposed to. Spouses are supposed to be grown-ups, capable of meeting their own emotional needs through a variety of relationships and pursuits. I'm not saying that we adults do not have emotional needs. We do. We each have needs for security, self-worth, a sense of community and usefulness, as well as a deep need to belong to something bigger than ourselves. What I am saying is that we cannot place all of those emotional needs upon one person. Especially if that person is putting the same expectations and requirements right back on us.

The ScreamFree model of relationships is based on each individual taking full responsibility for his/her own emotional needs. That way spouses can freely *want* each other. For example, you do not *need* your husband to do more around the house; you really *want* him to. And that you can ask for (see chapter 6). You do not need your wife to have sex with you, you *want* her to (and you want her to *want to* as well; see chapter 7).

Most of all, you do not need your spouse to validate you. Read that again. Your validation as a human being, that sense of rightfully having a place in your own life, is up to you. We all continue to search for others to validate us, to make us feel whole, valued, useful, and worthy of respect. We chase after popularity with our peers. We crave our parents' approval long into our own adulthood. We look to our kids to make us feel "proud," living vicariously through them in order to make ourselves feel accomplished. (For instance, we work with our kids on their homework every night so we can put the bumper sticker on the back of our car that says, "I'm the proud parent of an honor roll student . . ." And we say the sticker is to build up our kids' self-esteem, but then why is it on *our* car?)

As ugly as these pursuits may be, we especially look to our spouses to provide us with this sense of validation. We look to our spouses to make us feel special, prized, and wonderfully important. And in the beginning, we get a taste of that. As I'm writing these words right now in a Starbucks, I'm overhearing a conversation between two girlfriends, talking about their marriages. In discussing their moving past the "honeymoon" phase, one confessed, "I never told anyone this, but I literally expected my husband to bring home flowers for me every night." (I assure you, this conversation just happened right next to me.)

Of course, as we're looking to our spouse to continue that magical validating experience, our spouse is looking to us to provide the exact same thing. That's why it's so easy to fall into patterns of complete emotional dependence on one another, especially after the newness of our mutual attraction wears off. But needing to feel needed by another is not authentic validation; it's actually a symbol of our *lack* of authentic validation. That's

because, ultimately, validation is an inside job. Validation is only authentic and lasting when it comes from within.

I love the way Dr. David Schnarch puts it in his remarkable book *Passionate Marriage*. He talks brilliantly about how we can all be divided into two camps—those seeking connection whose validation comes from their spouse, and those seeking connection who are grown-up enough to seek validation from within themselves. He even provides two contrasting statements to highlight the difference:

> Other-validated intimacy "sounds" like this: *"I'll tell you about myself, but only if then you tell me about yourself. If you don't, I won't either. But I want to, so you have to. I'll go first and then you'll be obligated to disclose—it's only fair. And if I go first, you have to make me feel secure. I need to be able to* trust *you!"*
>
> Self-validated intimacy in long-term relationships sounds quite different: *"I don't expect you to agree with me; you weren't put on the face of this earth to validate and reinforce me. But I want you to love me—and you can't really do that if you don't know me. I don't want your rejection—but I must face that possibility if I'm ever to feel accepted or secure with you. It's time to show myself to you and confront my separateness and mortality. One day when we are no longer on this earth, I want to know you knew me."*

It is not your spouse's job to validate you, to make you feel secure enough, sexy enough, respected enough, or loved enough for you to return the favor. It is not your spouse's job to meet these "needs" any more than it's your spouse's job to take care of your physical body. Getting the validation you seek is your responsibility, and true validation is not something you *seek from* another; it

derives from a strength of character within that allows you to *serve* another . . . without needing them to serve you in return.

And fully realizing such truth frees you and your spouse to live up to your vows. After all, you said "I do" to a number of commitments that require a lot of inner strength and self-validation. "I do promise to love and cherish you . . . for better and worse, through rich times and poor, through sickness and health . . . until death do us part."

You said "*I* do," not . . . "*We* do." You said "*I* do," not . . . "as long as *you* do, I do." You said "I do," for *life*. And that "I do" is what gets you through times when you don't feel like it, when your spouse isn't sharing the same spirit, when you're tempted to run because your needs don't feel met. The "I do" spirit is exactly what will lead you to grow as a spouse, and grow closer to your spouse, without waiting for him/her to make a reciprocal move.

Okay. Take a deep breath. We've confronted the lie that says marriage is about meeting one another's emotional needs. That was a big lie to confront. In fact, among the biggest. All the others will make more sense once you grasp that one. Ready for another? Read on.

2. Trust and Safety Are the Most Important Qualities in an Intimate Marriage.

Now I'm really talking crazy, right? *All relationships are built on trust! Trust and safety have to be the highest qualities in every marriage!* No, those are the highest qualities in a bus driver. You want your bus driver to be cautious and safe so that you can get to your destination without incident. More often than not, the ride itself isn't what interests you—it's getting there in one piece that is important. In the case of a bus ride, such predictability is wonderful.

But for marriage, trust and safety are vastly overrated. Not just overrated, but misleading. That's because a marriage is

inherently different from a bus ride. A marriage isn't just a trip you make with the hopes of getting "there" in one piece. A marriage is an adventure. It is a journey that changes you and makes you better in the process. Although trust and safety may feel nice, and certainly have their place as *indications* of a growing relationship, most people put far too much emphasis on these feelings. This emphasis actually leads couples away from marital bliss and straight toward complacency, entitlement, and boredom. And boredom is a marriage killer.

Couples who come to me convinced that they've grown apart are usually surprised to hear me say, "No, you haven't . . . and that's the problem." Their problem is that they haven't grown at all. This is because they are often victims of their own bus-driver, warm-blanket mentality. They have worked so hard at keeping things safe between the two of them that they've forgotten what excitement feels like. They have become "comfortably numb," and they wonder why after a few years they start itching for something different.

In her excellent book *Mating in Captivity*, Esther Perel associates our quest for security with a deadening of passion:

> There's a powerful tendency in long-term relationships to favor the predictable over the unpredictable. Yet eroticism thrives on the unpredictable. Desire butts heads with habit and repetition . . . without an element of uncertainty there is no longing, no anticipation, no frisson.

There's hard science to support this theory. In a recent study at the University of Michigan and SUNY–Stony Brook, researchers found a direct link between boredom in marriage and long-term decreased marital satisfaction. Scientists have concluded that the reason for this link lies in a lack of closeness. When couples become bored, or feel as if they are stuck in a rut, their level of closeness decreases significantly, which in turn decreases their overall satisfaction.

So, if trust and safety aren't the cornerstones of a long, healthy, and exciting marriage, what are? Self-respect and self-representation, at the risk of rejection, are the essential qualities that can actually lead to a growing, vibrant marriage.

I can hear you now: Wait a minute . . . do you mean to tell me that feeling *unsafe* in my marriage is the key to happiness? Well, yes—to some extent. Allow me to unpack this a little. We've all heard that trust and safety are the essential qualities and goals of a committed, intimate relationship. When we enter a relationship, we tell ourselves, "I need to be able to trust you. I need to know that you're going to be able to accept me and honor me, and I need that from you before I will entrust myself to you." And some of this is helpful. After all, Jesus was right in his admonition not to cast your pearls before swine.

But here's the problem: How many hoops does your spouse have to go through before he's proven that he's not a pig? And what happens if he does earn that approval, then breaks it once? Then how many more hoops does he have to jump through? It is a myth to think that trust can be earned. It's never earned. It can never be fully earned. At some point, no matter how trustworthy someone appears to be, you still have to *take a risk* in revealing yourself to him/her. You still have to confront your feelings of insecurity, your lack of trust, in order to open yourself up to another.

Think about the first time you said "I love you" to your significant other. Was there no risk in that? Of course not. There was a ton of risk! You had no ironclad way of knowing how he/she would respond—and that was the thrilling part! The same holds true for all couples, no matter how long they've been together. There is always a risk in revealing yourself, taking the courage to represent your position, your feelings, your preferences, your complaints, your requests, anything. There is no escaping the risk—there is only prolonging it (or avoiding it, and any intimacy, altogether).

Every step toward your spouse is a huge risk on your part—whether it's a step expressing some negative feelings toward him ("I find it hard to be attracted to you when you don't take good care of your body") or a step expressing something positive ("Lately, I'm seeing you in a new light, and I'm loving you in a new way, and I just want you to know that").

You can never know just how your spouse will respond—and that's the thrilling beauty of relationship, the thrill that keeps marriages fresh until death do you part. It's also the way that our relationships keep asking us to grow up toward personal maturity. See, upholding the myth of "trust and safety" above all else is actually a pretty immature way of living in relationship. It is basically telling your spouse, "I need to know how you're going to react before I am vulnerable with you." Which is basically a glorified version of the old playground antics of "You show me yours before I show you mine." How do you think your spouse is going to respond? You guessed it: "You show *me* yours before I show *you* mine!"

Again, it creates a quid-pro-quo relationship. *I'll take a little step toward you if you'll take a little step toward me. Oh wait, you didn't take a big enough step. I told you all about my family, which was very hard for me to do, and you didn't respond with enough sympathy and reciprocal vulnerability. You just sat there, not knowing what to say next. Now I'll have to retreat into my shell until you pony up.*

We've all done this in one form or another. We keep score with our spouses to make sure that things are even. To make sure that no one is taking advantage of us. To make sure that we are withholding just enough to keep ourselves . . . you guessed it . . . *safe.*

But safe is dead in a marriage. What keeps a marriage alive

is risk. What keeps a marriage breathing in life is adventure and mystery in the form of risky self-representation—*without know-. ing how your spouse is going to respond*. Digest those words very carefully, because you're about to explore them fully in chapter 3.

Okay: Two lies down, one to go. Still holding on? I know these are tough to wrestle with, and I know these new truths are really forcing you to think. But I promise that your marriage is already beginning to change, just by your beginning to think differently about marriage itself. Here comes lie number three:

3. Oneness Means Having No Boundaries, No Separation, No Individuality.

Perhaps my favorite quote about marriage comes from Rabbi Edwin Friedman: "The reason why most couples separate is because they were unable to separate." Edgy, playful, and right on the money, this quote sums up perfectly what we've been discussing so far. The most successful couples are those who continually see themselves as two separate individuals, continually choosing to commingle, overlap, and join their lives.

But Rabbi Friedman understood quite well the controversy of talking about healthy separation in marriage. As a rabbi, he hailed from a Jewish tradition that, perhaps more than any other religion, touts the idea that "The two shall become one." I also understand that notion, as a former church minister of, and still active follower in, the Judeo-Christian tradition. So I can tell you that neither Friedman nor I take it lightly when we challenge ideas of oneness.

Let me first say that I still tout oneness as the ideal model for marriage. I really do. But as you can tell by now, I teach and try to live a oneness that is carefully defined. This is not a oneness built upon absolute sameness; it's a oneness built upon a balance of separateness and togetherness. This is not a oneness built on two halves coming together to form one whole; it's a oneness built on two wholes coming together to form something larger, some-thing that paradoxically makes both wholes stronger as individu-als. I will, indeed, be talking about and illustrating this model of oneness throughout the rest of this book. I will also lay out for you exactly what this looks like in real relationships, and teach you a step-by-step formula for making it happen in yours.

For now, let's examine the illogic of this lie, which keeps us stuck in old, faulty ideals. This idea of oneness, meaning total unity and total sameness, is the stuff of infatuation fantasy. When two people begin to fall in love and fantasize about their new life together, they each begin to dream about wonderful moments of unity. They dream about doing everything together. They dream about sharing the same living quarters, the same life pursuits, and the same love for opening gifts on Christmas morning (not Christ-mas Eve!). They fantasize about, and secretly expect to share, the same decorating ideas, the same hopes about starting a family, and the same love for the beach. And, of course, they expect to share the same appetites for food, for travel, and, of course, for sex. As one of my college friends put it, after only a year of mar-riage, "I really figured that since we were hungry at the same time, we'd usually be horny at the same time." Ummm, yeah.

As a symbol of this fantasy, a number of couples, Jenny and myself included, performed a very strange ritual during the wed-ding ceremony. Now, thankfully, this practice is not nearly as pop-ular as it once was. But in its heyday, it was all the rage. We call it "lighting the unity candle," and it's designed to symbolize the move from two separate individuals into one new union. You probably know how it works. On a stand, there are three candles—two sin-gle candles on the outside and one larger, ornate wax behemoth in the middle. The two candles on the outside represent the couple as separate individuals. The decorative behemoth represents the new, unified whole. Now, at the beginning of the ceremony, both of the outside candles are lit while the unity centerpiece remains unlit. As soon as the official pronounces the couple "husband and wife," the couple walk over to the candelabra, joined together as one. They each then pick up the lit individual candles, put them together over the wick of the unity candle, and set alight this new symbol of unified oneness. Now, I actually don't have a problem at all with the ritual up to this point.

See, if you're in your right mind, having been educated by wise folks who preach the type of balanced oneness I'm trying to endorse throughout this book, then you probably do the following: You and your spouse light the ornate thing in the middle, and then, leaving your flames of individuality burning brightly, return the single candles to their place. There you have a great representation of a beautiful, functional, balanced marriage. Two individuals, coming together as one, and yet still remaining individuals who neither own, nor need, one another.

Now, if you're like Jenny and me, you are not in your right mind. You bought into the "oneness equals sameness" model, and you, naively, do the following: After bringing your individual selves together to light the beautiful behemoth, showing the world your new status as One and Only One, you then do the unthinkable. You snuff out those two individual candles, leaving two funeral pyres wafting into the open air. Those individuals have died, you see. There is no longer room for uniqueness, individual preferences, or personal development. There is no possibility of experiencing any change, or event, or mood without the other—there is no other! If you're like Jenny and me, you want to show the world that you are determined to live in the la-la land of sameness.

Obviously, though, it doesn't take long after the wedding for these fantasies to bump against the reality of married life. As you read in chapter 1, it took me three days. But despite that fiasco, when we moved into our first house as a married couple, we proudly displayed that unity candle on the mantel. However, not too long after moving in, during a typically scorching Texas summer, we went on a weekend trip. Not knowing anything about caring for a house, I didn't even think about setting the thermostat up to 80 degrees to prevent the house from overheating. Jenny had argued to do just that, but I just turned the thing off, hoping to save on our energy bill. She didn't want the conflict, so off it went. And then off we went. Well, what do you think we found upon returning three days later? The temperature in the house probably soared to 120 degrees, and that did not bode well for our now-deceased houseplants. Nor did it fare well for our magical unity candle. The poor thing had totally collapsed and melted into a gloppy mess. It seems that our newly created "union as one" could not stand the heat of our individual immaturity.

By contrast, after seventeen years together, Jenny and I now have on our mantel at home a very different symbol of our union. It is a wooden statue we found in Siberia, Russia. We had the honor of traveling there in 2009 to present the ScreamFree relationship and leadership philosophy at a retreat bringing together Russians from St. Petersburg in the west to Yakutsk in eastern Siberia. It was a special week, introducing these new ideas of marriage to a country and culture totally foreign to us.

In order to commemorate the occasion, we looked long and hard for a special memento. We found the perfect thing in this hand-carved statue. Viewed from afar, it looks like a tall, singular person with a leather belt around his waist. Upon closer inspection, however, you see that this singular person is actually made up of two individuals, carved to fit together so closely that they appear as one. The leather belt is a tie between them, holding them together at the hands.

But before you think that this oneness is built on two half people who need to complete one another, Jerry Maguire–style, know this: As you pick up the statue, you soon learn that these are two separate statues, two whole people. They are completely capable of standing alone . . . or together.

Jenny and I keep this statue of two statues out in plain sight because it stands in such contrast to our earlier views, and years, of marriage. See, even after our "unity" melted, we were so fused together in pseudo-oneness that we thought any separateness, any disagreement at all, meant trouble. We were supposed to be one, so that meant we were supposed to do everything as one. We were supposed to like all the same things, hate all the same things, and do everything together.

But that is just no way to live. Even though we tried, it couldn't last. Thankfully, we made it through the tough transition from forced sameness to balanced oneness. We learned that Bono from U2 was right, "We're one, but we're not the same." Oneness means two different wholes coming together to form one, all the while retaining the separateness that makes the oneness so profound. If we were truly the same, then there'd be no magic, no mystery behind the life-changing connection that can truly be called "becoming one."

Believe me; you don't want your oneness to mean sameness. Otherwise, you'll be eliminating the very spaces between you and your spouse that make coming together meaningful and genuine. Your lives and choices would overlap out of obligation or fear of conflict; they wouldn't continue to commingle out of the same individual "I do" that connected you initially.

The Love Toilet

Sometimes it takes an absurd example to make us aware of how ridiculous an idea can be once taken to its natural extent. Such is the case with The Love Toilet. Years ago, *Saturday Night Live* created a fake commercial for a dual toilet, one to be enjoyed by those couples who are truly "one."

"You shared vows . . ." the narrator began, showing a starry-eyed couple at the alter. "You share a home . . ." the narrator continued, showing the couple in front of a SOLD real-estate sign. "You share a bed . . ." cue the bedroom scene.

The narrator then leads us into the absurdity. "Why not share the most intimate moment of them all?" he asks, while the camera fades in to a couple sitting cattycorner on a conjoined dual toilet, with each partner placing a loving hand on the common flush button in between them.

The Love Toilet.

Absurd? Absolutely. Satirical? Surely. But brilliantly accurate in spotting the undesirable, but logical, extent of the oneness-means-sameness lie. Leaves you doubting whether anyone could actually believe, much less propagate, such a lie, right?

Well, take note: The Love Toilet actually exists, ruining marriages and bowel movements everywhere. It is a real product, albeit marketed under a different name. It's called the TwoDaLoo, and here's the actual product description:

> The TwoDaLoo is billed as the world's first toilet two people can use . . . at the exact same time. It brings couples closer together and conserves our water supply all with one flush. The TwoDaLoo features two side-by-side toilet seats with a modest privacy wall in between. An upgraded version includes a seven-inch LCD television and iPod docking station.

Finally, the perfect model of oneness. I think I prefer the model standing on our mantel.

Now What?

This was, admittedly, a very theoretical chapter. We started with a Shel Silverstein piece about a lonely Missing Piece. As you can probably tell by now, Silverstein was preaching the ScreamFree, two-centered-selves model for marriage years ago. In his own inimitable way, he was showing us the fallacy of believing in our own incompleteness and our need for another person to make us whole. Where we've taken it further here is to illustrate that, in the same way, you do not need to squeeze your marriage into some perfect fit of compatibility, trust, and oneness.

This was all challenging and informative and, I believe, necessary to understanding why so much of our married lives has been such a struggle. But this chapter has not contained a lot of practical advice to start applying to your marriage tonight.

Well, don't worry, Part Two of this book is going to give you more practical stories and advice than you can handle about the very common conflicts you engage in with your spouse every week. And Part Three is going to tie it all together in a way that will leave you feeling more inspired and ready to act than ever before (I promise).

But first, we have to go through chapter 3. I have to warn you, this may be the toughest chapter you've ever read about your marriage. You may be tempted to throw the rest of the book, and this whole ScreamFree philosophy, out the proverbial (or literal) window. Here's why: We're going to look at all the ways you yourself have created all the problems in your marriage. No, not everything is your fault. Every problem in every marriage is part of a complicated system of patterns created and maintained equally by two partners. But within that system of patterns are choices, choices that you have made all on your own. By examining these choices, you give yourself the best chance of growing into the whole, complete, centered-self your marriage needs.

_____

Chapter 3

If You're Not Part of the Solution,
Then You're Still Part of the Problem

The best years of your life are the ones in which you
decide your problems are your own.
You do not blame them on your mother, the ecology, or the
president. You realize that you control your own destiny.

—ALBERT ELLIS

Okay, let's map out what we've covered thus far. We've established that, above all, we get married because we crave connection. We choose to join, share, and overlap our lives with another because we so love the idea and experience of *connecting* to another individual, one who freely chooses to do the same with us. We want to be chosen, freely and daily, by the very same person we want to choose, freely and daily. (Okay, maybe not daily, but at least weekly.) And that mutual, voluntary choosing creates a connection like no other experience on earth. It is not a forced, obligatory arrangement that leaves us feeling weaker and more immature and more dependent. It is a connection that leaves both parties feeling more prized, more valued, more mature, and more empowered to live as unique, individual, connected selves.

Now, at the same time we've come to these realizations about what we crave most, we've also examined what most gets in our way: the power of emotional reactivity, of "screaming" in all sorts of ways. This reactivity, this screaming, doesn't just make things worse. Whenever we let our anxiety overtake us, we actually help create the very outcomes we were hoping to avoid. Our anxious efforts to force a connection actually prevent us from forging one.

We've learned that in order to truly pursue a deeper, lasting marriage, we must shift our focus. We cannot fix our gaze on our spouse, or even our relationship, if we really want change. In order to bring about real growth, we must focus on the only one we can actually control: ourselves. And control ourselves we must, because emotional reactivity, or "screaming," is our worst enemy.

This became all the more clear in chapter 2, when we announced and examined the various lies that keep feeding our anxiety. These lies have given us false ideals about compatibility, oneness, and meeting one another's needs. They have sent us frantically chasing after these ideals, and left us screaming as we failed to experience them. These lies have led us to pursue ideals of sameness that leave us altogether frustrated and quid pro quo arrangements that leave us nothing but stalemated.

Thankfully, however, such lies are not the last word. Truth always has the last word. You see, there is another way to be married, a model for marriage that doesn't just work, it transforms the very idea of what "works" in marriage. The goal here is not just survival; it's not just avoiding seven-year itches and midlife crises and empty-nest syndromes. No, the goal here is something far more optimistic: turning your common conflicts into a deeper, lifelong connection.

And that's where we're headed in Part Two. There, we'll examine several common conflicts we routinely face as couples. It is an immensely practical section, showing you how the

ScreamFree principles can shape your approach to conflicts surrounding household management, for instance, or issues with in-laws or questions about sexual connection (or disconnection). You will come away with concrete examples of what it means to be ScreamFree in all these areas. And as you read, you will get ready to take action, action that I believe will change the lives of you and your spouse forever.

I know it's tempting to skip ahead to these practical actions, but first, you have to walk through chapter 3 with me. Why? Because this chapter prepares you for all of that practical work. This chapter—as challenging as it is—is the one that teaches you how to make your relationship problems *productive*. That's right. Your relationship problems can actually become the very path to the calmer, warmer, deeper connection you seek. All it takes is a willingness to accept some hard truths, truths about relationships in general and truths about you in particular.

How do you begin to pursue a ScreamFree marriage? What does it look like in stark reality, in clear focus? And how do you get from here (your marriage as it stands right now) to there—your marriage as you've always wanted it to be?

Well, that's what this chapter is all about. We've talked about the "what" of a ScreamFree marriage, and we've talked about the "why"—both why you want what you want and why you've struggled to experience it thus far. Now, we turn to the "how."

And, believe it or not, the "how" is quite simple. It's as simple as following a formula. Notice I didn't say *easy*, because it's definitely not easy. If revolutionizing your relationship were easy, then we'd all be doing it naturally, and you wouldn't be reading a marriage book like this one. No, following this formula is definitely not easy; but the formula itself is quite simple. I've even tried to make it rhythmic and memorable, ready-made for the twenty-first century and all its informational distractions. Ready to ingest this new, simple formula for creating and maintaining the marriage you've always wanted? Here it is:

Calm Down, Grow Up, Get Closer. Repeat.

That's it. All it takes for a marriage to begin, and continue, a lasting transformation is for one partner to voluntarily, and repeatedly, Calm Down, Grow Up, and Get Closer. Then repeat. Taking these three steps, which I will explain and illustrate throughout this chapter, and throughout this book, will give anyone, including you, the best chance to change your marriage into the connection you crave. No, taking these steps will not guarantee getting your partner to respond to you in the ways you've always dreamed. I cannot promise that he or she will suddenly respond to you with newfound respect, admiration, gratitude, or attraction. I cannot even promise that if you follow the formula, your spouse will respond in kind. What I *can* promise is that following this formula will make you a stronger spouse. It will definitely make you a stronger person. And making yourself a stronger spouse and person is exactly what your marriage needs most. It is exactly what gives you and your marriage the best chance to change for the better.

Calm Down, Grow Up, Get Closer. Repeat. Breathe those words in, and get ready to see them again and again throughout this book. This is because I believe in the power of this formula to change lives. This formula is what I lead my clients through as they seek to improve their relationships. I have had the distinct joy of accompanying people as they learn to adopt this formula as their personal relationship mantra, and learn to apply it in even the most anxious and painful situations.

As you can guess by now, this is not a formula designed to change your spouse. It is not even a formula designed to change your relationship. No, the real purpose and hope of this formula is that it changes you. It does this by giving you, and thus your marriage, the chance to experience *the real you*. This formula is an aid to help you confront, discover, and reveal the real you, first to yourself and then to your partner.

I call this process Authentic Self-Representation, or ASR. What every marriage asks of its partners is to authentically give a full representation of their truest selves to one another. This means representing your innermost desires, what you want most out of life and this marriage. It means representing your strongest-held positions, the clear boundaries created by your beliefs about what you will or will not accept, what you will or will not do, and what you will or will not take responsibility for. Authentic Self-Representation means representing your strengths and your weaknesses, your hopes and your fears, your loves and your hates. And in a marriage, it means championing your spouse to do the same. And this formula is the simplest way I've found to effectively get you there.

The Authentic Self-Representation Formula

For the rest of this chapter, I will be leading you step-by-step through the ASR formula by relating a very telling story in the history of my own marriage. As we go, I will be using this story as the ideal illustration of the formula in action. I do not recount this story to highlight my wife, Jenny, as some ideal spouse. I tell it to highlight how anyone stuck in a marital "problem" can change it for the better. All you have to do is follow the formula.

First, let's set the stage for the story. About six years after the lobster incident, Jenny and I were (thankfully) still married and had managed to bring two children into the world. I was finishing grad school, and we were fairly involved in a local church. We found ourselves extremely busy attending services and teaching classes every Sunday morning. And somewhere along the way, we had created a routine that was as dependable as Old Faithful, and just about as eruptive. Every Sunday morning, you see, was the same. Jenny would wake up early and get dressed. Then she would begin the arduous process of rousing the kids and getting them ready for church. I, on the other hand, would wake up late, offer weak promises to help feed and dress the kids, and lollygag my way through the morning. Every Sunday morning. As you'll read on, this friction became more and more heated, usually leading to the two of us blowing up at each other in front of our kids, running late into services, and fuming throughout. Oh, what a wonderful way to go worship God. Now, this problem may seem mild compared to what you're going through, but don't let that fool you. As mild as it may sound, this was not a small problem; it was actually indicative of a pattern that threatened to wreak serious havoc in our marriage.

Calm Down

Now that we've set the scene, we can begin to go through the formula. The first step of the ASR formula is learning to Calm Down. We already talked at length about calming down in chapter 1, so we won't belabor that here. Calming down is the beginning point, and the main gist, of the entire ScreamFree approach. Since emotional reactivity is our prime enemy when it comes to maintaining great relationships, it makes perfect sense that learning to calm such reactivity would be the first, and best, move. Well, of course it is. And in the ASR formula, calming down consists of two steps.

Pause Yourself. The first step in calming down is learning to create a pause for yourself. Now, before you say, "Yeah, right! If I could do that, then I wouldn't need this book!," allow me to offer some help. All of us have "screamed" in our marriages. All of us have "lost" our adulthood one way or another. This is the antithesis of Authentic Self-Representation, because whether we're passive-aggressively stonewalling our spouse or actively yelling our heads off, we're allowing our anxiety to take the reins. This is not authentically representing our self and our true desires; this is letting our fears *mis*represent us, and usually creating the very outcome we most want to avoid.

But just as all of us have "lost it," every one of us has also kept our cool, at least once, in the heat of anxiety. Every one of us, even you, have had a moment of absolute calm and clarity when the situation called for anything but. Think about it for a moment. Think about that time you kept your cool when everyone else was freaking out. Maybe it was that time you held it together, conquered your fear, and delivered that touching, poignant memorial at your grandmother's funeral. Perhaps it was that time your son was throwing a fit in the grocery store and, somehow, you responded with a calm assertiveness you didn't know you had. Maybe it was the time your husband accused you of taking, and misplacing, his keys, and you were able to quietly scan your memory, realize that you did no such thing, and let him know he was mistaken. You even then warmly offered to help him conduct the search.

Each of us has at least one moment of calm clarity in tense situations. And most of us have done this repeatedly. Maybe it's hard to remember right now, because the times you've blown up are far stronger residents in your memory. But those moments, those exceptional moments, are there. And it's your job to recall those moments in as much detail as possible. This is because those moments are your best aid in learning to pause yourself.

How did you do it? What kind of mood were you in? Did you use some technique, like counting to ten, snapping a rubber band around your wrist, taking several deep breaths? If so, then use that technique again. Did you feel yourself tense up? Where? In your forehead, between your shoulder blades, in your gut? How did your body clue you in, at that moment, that you needed to exercise all your calming muscles for one single purpose?

Those are the elements of creating a pause for yourself. This is about creating a break between stimulus—your spouse (or your finances or whatever)—pushing your buttons, and your response. This is about learning to feel those buttons getting pushed, and yet refusing to allow your anxiety to then guide your actions. Your body can clue you in. Your memory can remind you of your capabilities. Your technique can lengthen the moment and clear your head. When tension arises, your number one priority is to just stay calm, *no matter what*. When your buttons are getting pushed, you have to learn to push your own button. Your pause button.

Go to the Balcony.* As you create a pause for yourself, you proceed to the next step of Calming Down. You go to the balcony. You "take it upstairs," as Dr. Major Boglin, my old professor, used to say. This is about mentally taking yourself out of and above the moment, seeking to gain a newfound clarity about the situation. Your goal is to gain a little objectivity. The literal process is moving into your neocortex, that uniquely human part of your brain geared for analytic, self-reflective thought. It's what separates us from the rest of the mammals—our ability to think about ourselves in action. A cow, for instance, cannot think about its choices as a cow, choosing to act in new ways. We humans can, however, when we go to the balcony.

---

*Since writing this, I have discovered that I am not the first to use the balcony metaphor to describe the process of rising above the scene, above your emotions, and viewing the conflict with some objectivity. William Ury employs this exact metaphor in largely the same way in his fantastic books on conflict management, *Getting Past No* and *Getting to Yes*. I apologize for any appearance of plagiary on my part; it was unintentional, and perhaps mine and Ury's use of the balcony metaphor testifies to its effectiveness.

I like the balcony imagery because it suggests rising-above-the-fray or getting-a-bird's-eye-view. Call it using-your-head, call it taking-a-step-back, call it whatever you like. As long as you can conjure up a mental picture, then it'll work. That's because this step is about visualization. It's about learning to see things with a fresh lens, attempting to see things with a fresh perspective. For instance, your wife is harping on you about leaving the dishes in the sink, even though you promised you'd do them before going to bed. Your most reactive parts want to either lash back, recounting all the times she's let you down, or internalize her lashes, "yes-dear"-ing her to shut her up, and letting your resentment build silently.

Pausing yourself and going to the balcony allows you to do something different, to listen intently to your beloved wife, honestly wanting to hear her. You love her, so you don't want to be the source of any pain. At the very same time, you don't believe your sidestepping the dishes deserves this much fury. From the balcony, you can better observe both your wife and yourself in this dialogue. What's the problem here? Is this an isolated incident or is this reflective of a pattern? What else may be going on besides the dishes? Is this event and its fallout just a blip or is it a microcosm of the whole marriage right now? Regardless, what part have you legitimately played in this, and what would be a response that is both warranted and representative of your truest self?

Sound like a pipe dream, to have such lucid thoughts in the midst of a fight? I promise you it's not. Not as you grow in your ability to pause yourself and go to the balcony. Going back to our Sunday morning story, you'll see that Jenny demonstrated an incredible, if previously underused, ability to calm herself down. As you read on, you'll see her take a remarkable pause, learning to interrupt herself in the midst of a heated, ongoing conflict. This interruption, this pause, allowed her to gain a new appreciation of the situation, seeing her problem with me as something bigger than that. She was able to see that this friction was actually an opportunity to focus on herself and her own growth—for the benefit of us both.

Grow Up

Growth is the logical next move in this formula for revolutionizing your marriage. Specifically, we're talking about allowing the natural anxieties and conflicts in your marriage to compel you toward maturity. Few things in life ask us to grow up as much as our marriage, and few things can. This is because nothing else asks you to be more vulnerable than revealing and representing your true self to another. Particularly the "other" whose opinion and thoughts about you matter more than anyone else's. Well, as we'll talk about at length in Part Two following this chapter, there's no escaping this whole conflict process in marriage, so it certainly makes the most sense to allow it to teach you all it can about yourself. And that's the first step in Growing Up.

Spot Your Pattern. As you learn to pause, and take yourself to the balcony, you will begin to see things differently. You will learn the difference between a purely isolated incident and an ongoing pattern. I say *pattern* because this is usually the most helpful way to think about marital "problems." Very rarely do couples come into my office complaining about a one-time event that they consider problematic. Usually, they come complaining about recurring issues that they just can't seem to resolve. They will sit down, take a deep breath, and tell me, "We have a problem." More often than not, the person saying this is the one who initiated the session and she'll usually cite something about communication or conflict or incompatibility. But let me ask you the same question I put to my clients: When you go up to your spouse and say, "We've got a problem," what do you *really* mean? Be honest. What you really mean is *"I've* got a problem . . . and that problem is *you."*

All of us do this, and here's why. We human beings love to jump to narrow definitions of the problems we encounter. We like to break a thing down to its essence, isolate the cause of the problem, and pinpoint the exact diagnosis. Combine that tendency with the one we discussed in chapter 1—too much focus on the other—and you'll see why so many couples find their way into therapy. We isolate whatever problem we may be having and we pin the blame on our spouse because it seems logical, clean, and neat. But I'm here to tell you something both humbling and hopeful. You don't have a problem—you have a pattern.

I can hear you now. "Sure—I can see that there is a pattern. My spouse keeps doing the same [stupid, hurtful, spiteful] things over and over again." This is not the kind of pattern realization I'm talking about. The issues that you face in your marriage are more about patterns that *you* and *your spouse* have co-created than they are about serious character flaws or deep-seated emotions in one person.

Jenny made it very clear to me that "our" problem (running late for church each week) really was *my* problem. If I would just pull my own weight, then everything would be just fine. I didn't argue too much, but instead agreed and promised to do better the next week. Only try as I might, each week it got progressively harder to do any better. What neither of us realized was that the pattern we thought we saw (me imitating a sloth each week) was only half the problem.

You see, not only do problems have patterns, but these patterns always have *partners*. This is because patterns are always perpetuated by interactions. Patterns are the interactional dances that we all take part in all the time. And these dances all have a few things in common: They are powerful, they are familiar, and they take two people in order to continue.

Like it or not, each of us helped create the exact marriage we have. All the problems we complain about, all the expectations that haven't been met—each one of us has been an active participant every step of the way. This means that whatever you are most unhappy about in your relationship, you had a direct hand in creating. Boiling resentment and insults? Yep. Boring sex life? Uh-huh. Even ridiculous inequality around the house? You guessed it. Either by aggressively reacting in kind to the undesirable behavior of your spouse, or by passively allowing it all to happen, you've been a part of it each step of the way.

Whenever I tell this to people, they all look at me the same way, with a raised eyebrow and a tilted head. Their body language tells me, "Hold on a minute there. Are you trying to tell me that it's my fault that my wife is terribly insecure?" "Are you telling me that I'm to blame when my husband flies off in a rage every time we talk about money?" Well, no, your spouse's behavior is never your responsibility; you are not that powerful. But *your reaction* to your spouse's behavior is always your responsibility. And it's your reactivity that helps perpetuate the problem you most complain about.

Sometimes this participation is active, like criticizing your spouse right after he criticizes you. Sometimes your participation is passive, like simply acquiescing, "yes-dear"-ing your wife whenever she wants to, again, remodel the kitchen (or the bathroom or the basement). Both ways are emotional reactions that do nothing but keep the pattern going. Again, the real problem is not the problem at hand. The real problem is not that your husband criticized you in the first place, nor that your wife never seems happy with your home. No, the real problem is thinking that by reactively criticizing back you'll somehow remove the sting of the original insult and stop it from ever happening again. The real problem is that we either cannot or will not see ourselves as the co-creators of our own situations. But the truth is (and this is a truth that will definitely set you free) that you are an individual capable of making decisions, even in the most heated or annoyingly mundane of circumstances.

And Now, Back to the Story . . .

In our Sunday morning pattern, my behavior—or lack of it—was only half the equation. Jenny had been there each Sunday, too. So what was she doing that had any sort of effect on the outcome of the day? In an effort to wake me up, get me going, and join her in the routine, Jenny tried several different tactics in a very predictable and specific order. These were her reactions to my problematic behavior. We both now think of these as well-rehearsed dance steps that we both knew by heart. First, there was the "Oops, I didn't know you were still sleeping" maneuver. She would usually begin by making an excessive amount of noise in the bathroom, and then she would turn on the closet light so that it would shine directly in my face. I followed her lead by turning over in bed.

She would then move on to her next step. The loud sigh that communicated, "I can't believe that I have to do all of this while I know perfectly well that you can hear me; you're just too lazy to get out of bed and help." Jenny was a master at the sigh—she would flawlessly execute it at just the right moment when she knew I could hear her—brilliant. That's the point when I would begin my patented promise-making-but-still-stalling two-step. It consisted of one step forward—actually getting out of bed and moving toward the shower—and two steps back, finding the sports page and heading back to bed.

Finally, Jenny would transition to her grand finale: overt nagging, dripping with sarcasm. "How about just a *little* help with the kids this morning? You didn't seem to have any trouble being awake when they were made." This usually got my begrudging butt off the bed and into gear, but with a costly price. Every

Sunday, we ended up pulling into church late, fuming at each other. What's worse is that the more often we did this dance, the better we got at it. Because these dances, these patterns—they feed on themselves.

What is fascinating about marriage patterns is that not only do they run counter to how we want to act, but sometimes they even run counter to how we *otherwise do* act. Contrary to what you may think, based on the interaction above, I was definitely not your typical lazy husband. In fact, on every other day of the week, I was the first one out of bed. I would wake up around 5 a.m. in order to do some studying before class. I worked two extra part-time jobs and also managed to do a fairly equal share of the night feedings and diaper changes.

It's also true that Jenny was not the stereotypical nagging wife. She was not the kind to hassle me or keep score on all the household duties. And on most days, she beat me to the sports section. But for whatever reason, the Sunday morning dance was always the same: Lazy Hal and Nagging Jenny nimbly following the same steps, which always left us exhausted and resentful. Neither of us was fully aware of this process at the time (couples rarely are), but as a family-therapist-in-training, I knew something was going on.

See, at this time in my graduate studies, I was learning a lot about how relationships worked, and I was constantly sharing this information with my wife. It was even at this time that I was beginning to articulate the ScreamFree philosophy—the power of focusing on ourselves, calming ourselves down, and growing ourselves up for the benefit of everyone around us.

So *I* should have known better, right? I should have recognized what was going on during these Sunday morning dance steps, stopped complaining about Jenny's nagging, and made a positive change, right? Right. But I didn't.

Jenny, however, did.

Ironically, it turns out that while I was beginning to talk about this new philosophy, Jenny was actually starting to really hear it. Thanks to all those late-night discussions we'd been having about family functioning, Jenny realized a fundamental truth. She had had an active hand in creating this mess, and that must mean that she had the potential to do something about it. If all these theories I blabbed on and on about were true, then all she had to do in order to change our typical Sunday morning dance was this: Simply. Stop. Dancing. And then take a different dance step. If she had reactively participated in creating a dance that made her miserable, then what could happen if she started a new, more thoughtful dance? What if she initiated a new pattern, one more reflective of how she really felt, and what she really wanted?

Grow Up, Continued . . .

Step on the Scales. Now, before she could decide on a new action, a new dance step, Jenny had to discover a couple of things about herself. In pausing herself, Jenny was able to interrupt her own automatic reactivity. That afforded her the opportunity to go to the balcony and gain some objectivity. From there, she was able to see the problem not as some reflection of Hal's flawed personality, but rather as a predictable pattern with two participants. And then she was able to see this pattern as a voluntary interaction, one that she, as one of those participants, helped to create and perpetuate. All of this new vision about us and about herself then begged a basic question: Why? Why was she so caught up in this pattern? Why would she continue her part, even though it was actually backfiring and making things even worse?

We all ask why. Thankfully. Asking why is the seedbed of all human thought and discovery; when done in a structured, objective way, it drives scientific inquiry and all human progress. But that's the key. Just asking why in a whimsical, undirected way will not lead anyone forward. We must proceed in thoughtful, disciplined ways in order to make any genuine discovery and enjoy any legitimate fruit from the exercise.

That's why I call this step of the formula learning to "step on the scales." This is not about some carnivalesque weight-guessing game; this is about trying to examine ourselves in a critical, discerning, accurate way. In order for our marital patterns to teach us anything about ourselves, in order for us to make different dance moves reflective of our true selves, we must take as clear-sighted a look at ourselves as possible.

This is not always pleasant. Stepping on the scales and gaining a more accurate picture of our weight isn't pleasant. Neither is entering all your financial transactions into Quicken and learning more precisely about your spending habits. These are often painful exercises, not only making us aware of some more objective truth about ourselves, but also making us aware of how far that truth is from where we thought it was. "I thought I felt lighter, but I actually gained weight last week." Or, "I thought we were spending less on eating out, but it looks like we actually spent even more than last month." My most recent experience with this was having my golf swing examined on camera, then aligned side by side with footage of a professional golfer I thought I was modeling myself after fairly well. The difference was quite humbling.

These are painful exercises, teaching us painful truths, but they are truths, nonetheless. And just as there is no way to move forward on a map without knowing where you currently are, there is no way to change a pattern into a growth and connection opportunity without knowing where you currently stand.

With all that in mind, I believe there are two specific questions to ask ourselves in order to learn the most about our roles in the patterns that we call problems. These just happen to be the questions Jenny asked about herself during our Sunday morning pattern.

First, what about this particular pattern means so much? It's not so much why Jenny was so bothered; rather, why was she so bothered by this particular pattern? What about the Sunday morning dance was so irritating to her? Surely there were other things in our marriage that were larger, more anxiety-producing issues (there were). Why attach so much meaning to this one?

This is a helpful question for all of us. It is helpful because we can all recognize that some things bother us a lot more than others. And some things that bother us a lot don't seem to bother our spouses at all. And vice versa. Whenever this happens, it becomes so easy to, again, focus on our spouse. "How can I get her to care about our finances as she should?" Which, of course, means "as *I* do." But that other focus is the type of questioning we do *before* we begin to apply the formula. However, when we Calm Down and Grow Up, when we see ourselves as active participants in the patterns we complain about, then we can ask the more fruitful question: What about this pattern/issue bothers *me* so much? Why does this mean so much to me, so much that I'm allowing it to drive me crazy?

Now this question does not always produce simple answers. It could have something to do with unresolved childhood issues. Jenny could have been, for instance, projecting some "irresponsible father" template onto my actions. The answer could have something to do with unspoken, and perhaps unrealized, resentments surrounding the issue, resentments that feed an anxious need for security, stability, safety, and the like. Jenny could have been, for instance, deeply fearing any type of abandonment or isolation, and interpreting my lazy Sundays as indicative of the very thing she feared most coming to pass. In truth, the answer could have to do with a lot of things.

One way to help yourself answer the question is to revisit the lies we've been sold about marriage. What lie am I accepting as true here? Is it a lie about compatibility? A lie about perfect oneness? About meeting one another's needs? When investigating the meaning we ascribe to a particular pattern, it is very often connected to one of these lies. "I am so angry about this particular pattern because *it's not supposed to be this way!*" "We're supposed to be one, we're supposed to be together on this, we're supposed to care about this equally!"

That was certainly part of Jenny's frustration. After all, this Sunday morning issue was a pattern involving our kids, our marriage, and our God! It can't get any more important than that, right? This is a serious problem! We cannot be individuals on this one—we just can't. Can we? Thankfully, Jenny went through all of this investigation. And she was willing to learn about all the ways she was allowing her own immaturity and society's lies to guide her behavior.

And that led her to the most important, and the most informative, question of all. This is the question that I strive to let lead me in all my endeavors. This is the question that guides all my work with my clients and all my business dealings. Most important, this is the question that I hope directs me in all my relationships, especially my marriage.

What do I want *most*? What, in this situation, do I want *most* to see happen? What is my ultimate goal? What is the end I have in mind, the end that is most reflective of my highest hopes and deepest desires? This is such a vital question because it is the best way I know to discern our next moves. See, the key to life (and I am in no way the first to say this) is to clearly define success and failure. Clearly knowing what it would mean to succeed or fail is the only way to measure how you're doing, and whether you need to make a change. Well, here is the clearest definition of failure I've ever come across.

Failure: neglecting what we want *most* for what we want *right now*.

It doesn't take long to see the accuracy, and helpfulness, of this definition. One of the things I want most, for instance, is a healthy, fit, lean body. What I want right now, sitting at my desk writing these words late at night, are two warm, fresh-out-of-the-toaster Brown Sugar/Cinnamon Pop-Tarts. You know the ones I'm talking about. They're so good they could actually tempt a man to give up sex just to have one (but don't tell Jenny I said that). Now, the point is this: If I say yes to what I want right now, the crispy gooey Pop-Tart goodness, I'm actually saying no to something else. That healthy, fit, lean body—the machine God gave me to take care of so that I might use it to pursue my highest aspirations in life.

You can actually see parallels in all of life. For instance, saying yes to the procrastinating distraction of the moment actually says no to the project deadline that would afford you some genuine free time later.

Or saying yes to the anxious need to make your children obey, by whatever means necessary, actually says no to what you want most with your kids—a mutually respectful relationship that leads your kids to voluntarily seek out your influence.

And back in our story, saying yes to needing her husband's "help" and togetherness helped Jenny say no to what she wanted most—a husband who actually *wanted* to act responsibly, no longer relying on a nagging wife to finally get him going.

Asking herself, What do I want most? allowed Jenny to move past any neediness so that she could pursue what she really wanted. Jenny wanted to go to church. She wanted the kids to go to church. She also wanted me to go to church, but not as a result of her begging, cajoling, or nagging. She wanted me to *want to* go to church, and to *want to* share the responsibility of getting the kids ready. And she realized this one fundamental truth: *We cannot force people to want to do anything.* We can only inform and invite them, and then respond accordingly. We can only Calm Down, Grow Up, and Get Closer. And that's exactly what Jenny did.

Get Closer

The last part of the formula is the one that, on the surface, involves the most change. That's because this is the most visible action move. This is the action move that other people see, so it seems as if it's the primary component of the whole change process. But, truth be told, getting closer is simply the logical outcome of all the work that comes before it. Getting closer is about coming out of your pause, stepping off the scales, and taking the risky first dance step toward a new pattern with your partner. It is about taking all that you've learned about your pattern and yourself and then acting on that knowledge in a way that is supremely representative of who you are and what you really want. It is the first outward manifestation of all the inner work of the formula. It is the culmination of all that's gone on before, and therefore in no way belittles all that hard work. Getting closer does carry more significance, however, because that is the endgame of this whole effort. Getting closer is why we get married. Getting closer is the hope that keeps us married. Getting closer is the move that most clearly represents our truest, most vulnerable desires for connection.

Show Your Cards. And the first step in getting closer is, naturally, quite revealing. It is quite risky. It is the move we so often avoid in all our relationships, especially our marriages, because it necessitates so much openness and vulnerability. And yet, do it we must if we are going to have a chance at getting what we want most. What are we talking about? We're talking about doing or saying that one thing you've been so reluctant to do or say for fear of rejection, abuse, looking stupid, feeling weak, or simply not getting the response you'd hoped for. We're talking about laying down your hand and showing your cards.

Now, for those of you totally unfamiliar with poker, this

metaphor may not mean anything. My guess is that most of us, however, can understand the meaning here quite clearly. Showing your cards is about mustering the courage to recognize that it's your turn to reveal what you've got. In the game of poker, this is always the tensest moment, because it's the boldest effort to win—and thus carries with it the opportunity to lose. Showing your cards in marriage is daring to risk revealing who you are, what you're thinking and feeling, and what you want most. This is the clearest, starkest move of Authentic Self-Representation.

You've gone through the formula to discover these things about yourself. Now's the time to choose what to reveal, and how to reveal these things to the one who matters most. What you need to understand is that this is the move that most spouses simply avoid at all costs. I daresay that the number one way we all scream in our marriages is by passively avoiding this incredibly risky self-revelation, and then aggressively demanding that our spouse change in a way that alleviates our anxiety. Most often, we want our spouse to do the risky revelation first, whether it's being the first to say "I love you," the first to apologize after a fight, or the first to initiate sex. But, of course, experience and logic tell us that such a strategy can only lead to a stalemate, with each partner waiting for the other to make the first, vulnerable move. My guess is that's where you find yourself quite often, stuck in a gridlock of emotions with your spouse, neither one willing to reveal your true feelings or hopes.

For instance, you want to tell your wife how much you really appreciate all she does to make your life enjoyable, but you're afraid that doing so may allow her to then beat you over the head with all you're doing to make hers miserable.

Or you want to let your husband know how hard it is to re-spect him when he yells at your son, but you're afraid that he'll just stop doing any parenting at all.

You want to go ahead and set up an appointment with a

marriage counselor, but you're afraid your wife will react so defensively that it'll end up being a waste of time.

You want to finally build up the courage to approach him with the role-play sex fantasy you've thought about for years, but you're afraid that he'll think it's stupid or too much work, or it just makes him too uncomfortable.

It is precisely in the midst of these gridlocks where the Scream-Free Marriage approach, and the ASR formula, can be so helpful. By calming down enough to truly gain some perspective, by growing up enough to willingly look at and get to know yourself, you begin to see the risk of showing your cards a little differently. First of all, this is not about opening yourself up to possible abuse; it's not about "casting your pearls before swine." If you suspect that telling your spouse your true feelings and intentions, and then acting accordingly, is going to lead to physical or emotional battery, then I strongly caution you against it. At least against doing it alone. Consult with a professional and let that person guide or preside over your self-representation.

Secondly, this is not about revealing yourself in order to get your partner to do the same. In fact, it's not about trying to elicit a particular response from your spouse *at all*. If you get nothing else about this whole formula, I implore you to get this. This is not about your spouse. It is not about getting your spouse's attention, stoking your spouse's passion, forcing your spouse into submission, or awakening your spouse's guilt. It's not even about inspiring your spouse's higher self. This is about one thing, and one thing only—making yourself known.

Representing your whole self to your spouse is not something you do in order to elicit any sort of response from your spouse. If it were, then it wouldn't really be authentic. It'd be manipulative and controlling, and it would give you no chance of creating the voluntary connection you crave. No, authentically representing yourself means carefully considering what you want to say or do,

and then doing it because *at the very least, you want your spouse to know you*. You want a voluntary connection with your spouse, and you want him/her to pursue one with you as well. You realize that you cannot force such a connection, because then it would either backfire or lead to a needy attachment based on anxiety and weakness. It wouldn't be a willing connection based on desire and strength. So you realize that the only logical step is to take the risk and make yourself known.

"This is who I am on this issue, and this is what I want most. I'm revealing this to you not because I need you to change. Whether you do anything differently is up to you. But I realize that you cannot make an informed choice without having all the information, so I'm telling you as clearly as I can what my hopes are, and what my intentions are. I'm not telling you this to change you. I'm telling you this because I love you, and I want you to know me."

Now, this was not the exact quote Jenny shared with me years ago, but it was definitely the message. Going back to the story, there was nothing significant about the particular Sunday morning she decided to act. But when she chose to reveal her cards, it changed Sunday mornings, and several of our dances, forever.

Jenny woke up early, as she usually did, but this time, she made no effort to stir me. She did not go out of her way to tiptoe around and let me sleep, but neither did she make any unnecessarily loud noises in an effort to passive-aggressively let me know how useless I was. By the time I did get up, she had some light music on the stereo and she was feeding the kids. There was something different about her mood—I could swear she was smiling and even humming to herself a little as she kissed me good morning. I got up, then sat down to read the paper, as usual, with the intent of getting up to head to the shower, eventually. But as I got to the sports section, I noticed that Jenny had made no overtures toward getting me to hurry up or help out with the kids. In fact, she hadn't paid much attention to me at all. And suddenly I didn't know what to do with myself.

I couldn't focus on the paper, so I decided to take my shower a little early. And that's when Jenny did finally address me directly. It was nothing like our usual Sunday morning dialogue, however. In truth, it was like nothing I had ever experienced from her before (but have plenty of times since). In one sentence she was able to clearly hold on to her truest desires, take responsibility for her choices, and authentically pursue what she wanted most from me and her marriage. She had calmed herself down enough to pause, discover, and confront her part of the pattern. She was growing up enough to ask herself what she wanted most in this situation. And she was getting ready to get closer by showing her cards in a new way.

Now, those of you who have read my first book, *ScreamFree Parenting*, may feel a sense of déjà vu when you read this part of the story, but I assure you this really did happen. In a scene remarkably similar to the single mom and her daughter in that first book, Jenny respectfully knocked on the bathroom door. She then slowly poked her head through the bathroom door, and invitingly announced (without a trace of sarcasm or animosity), "Hey, honey. The kids and I are leaving for church in ten minutes, and we'd love for you to join us." Jenny then calmly closed the door and left me alone to ponder my response. (A note of background here—we only had one car.)

Champion Your Spouse. Now, I know you're cheering Jenny on at this point, and I don't blame you. Her move toward me was very calm, very mature, and very representative of her true self. Again, she knew what she wanted, and she knew what she couldn't force. Her only choice was to authentically discover what mattered to her most and then act on it. Before I tell you the rest of the story, we need to highlight this next step in the ASR Formula.

While getting closer is all about focusing on yourself and representing that self to your spouse, it is also about welcoming, and encouraging, your spouse to do the same.

Now I know that sounds a little contrary to what I was saying earlier about not doing this in order to provoke a particular response from your spouse. That's not what this is. Championing your spouse is working hard to communicate—not so much with words or actions but by your very calm presence—that you welcome, and even invite, any response at all. Even if that response is reactive screaming (non-abusive, of course). Even if that response is silence. Even if that response is confusion, frustration, or choosing to voice a concern right back at you. By championing your spouse, you are again communicating what you want most— that voluntary connection that makes both partners feel prized, valued, and stronger as individuals. In reality, you cannot have that connection without your spouse choosing to reveal himself, in some way, back to you. Again, this is why I like the "show your cards" metaphor we used earlier. In poker, laying down your hand is a signal for your opponent to do the same. Yet, we don't want to think of our partner as an opponent to either defeat or succumb to, and that's where the poker metaphor breaks down.

What you do want your spouse to do is show you what he's got. You don't want him to "play it close to the vest," hiding himself and his true feelings and desires from you. You want him to reveal and represent himself because just as you want to make yourself known, you want to know him. That's why you got married! To share yourself with someone who wants to share himself with you. It's ironic that we can't wait to get to know each other better, until we get a few years under our belt. Then our fears, and memories of disappointment, make us a little gun-shy. We either shy away from conflict or reactively reveal ourselves in aggressive, attacking ways that force our partner to shy away from us.

But not when we follow the formula. When we go through

these steps, as hard as they are, we develop an appreciation for how equally hard it may be for our spouse to do the same type of internal discovery and external representation. Therefore, by our clear revelation and genuine invitation, we work to champion our spouse to do the same. And that's exactly what Jenny did with me that Sunday morning.

I initially thought she was just upping the ante of her nagging, throwing out some mature-sounding ultimatum designed to get me out the door. No way would my wife actually pull this stunt, I thought. If she were to actually leave, then I would have to walk to church. Jenny would *never, ever* let that happen . . . would she?

Those were my first thoughts. But then something changed. As I started the shower, I recalled the look on her face and the tone of her voice, and I realized something that shocked me. *She meant what she said*. Something about her matter-of-fact announcement and sincere invitation sounded just that, matter-of-fact and sincere. Instead of the usual anger and immature resentment that I normally showered with, I now felt something else toward my wife: respect. It was perhaps begrudging respect, but it was respect nonetheless.

Something in me was motivated to hurry up a bit. I found myself hustling to get dressed because I realized Jenny was not making some idle threat: She had every intention of leaving the house with or without me. It wasn't a threat at all; it was *an invitation*.

I slowly finished my shower, however. Perhaps all my thinking made me lose track of time. Perhaps patterns are just so powerful that even with such new radical dance steps, I was still too accustomed to my old moves. Regardless, I came to my senses and quickly became aware of the time. I was afraid that the ten minutes had come and gone. Sure enough, I opened our bedroom door, and found confirmation of my suspicions. There was my bride at the front door, casually escorting our two little ones out to the car.

Repeat

Jenny and I were University of Texas students years ago, and thus we're diehard Longhorns. That means we hate Oklahoma Sooners and love to make fun of Texas A&M Aggies. In fact, there's an old Aggie joke that asks, "How do you keep an Aggie in the shower all day? Give him shampoo that says lather, rinse, repeat."

That joke's not very funny, but it illustrates a potential problem with our formula: The very last step of the ASR Formula, Repeat, has the potential to come across as either confusing or exhausting. Confusing, because you might think that there's no end to the process, that there's never any resolution. Exhausting, well, for the very same reasons. You might think, "Repeat? How long can I keep this up? This is a lot of very difficult work. It's hard work, emotional work, risky work. It's wearing me out. And besides, when is it my spouse's turn? Why am I the one who has to repeat?"

In response to those questions, let me first say that they are all understandable, and all legitimate. This type of relationship work can be exhausting. And it can seem never-ending. And your spouse *should* be doing this himself as well. All that is true. But you already know what I'm going to say next, don't you? Of course this is hard—it's supposed to be hard. This is about growing in strength and maturity and capability—how could that be easy? It's not just that it isn't easy—it can't be, because that would violate one of the bedrock rules of the universe: Nothing grows without strain, struggle, and conflict. Nothing. Not a tree, not a muscle, not a nation, nothing. And certainly not a marriage. Or a person. The last step of the formula is Repeat because there *is* no end to the personal, emotional work your marriage has in store for you. Just as muscles atrophy without strain, so people and relationships weaken without difficulty, struggle, and continual conflict.

Now that's the theoretical answer. Here's the practical one. The last step is Repeat because whenever you choose to represent yourself to your spouse, and then champion your spouse to do the same, you've just invited more potential conflict. So Repeat is the step we take after we've received our spouse's response. We've taken the risk of revealing and representing ourselves, and we've welcomed our spouse's response to that new information. Now what? Our next move will look drastically different, depending on the situation, our initial revelation, and our spouse's response. And in order for our next move to be representative of who we are and what we want, we have to Repeat. We have to again Calm Down, Grow Up, and Get Closer.

For instance, let's say that after twenty years, you revealed to your wife that you've always wanted to spend Christmas just with your immediate family. You knew this was risky because you know that your wife loves to spend the holidays with as much of her extended family as possible. But as you've grown, you've wanted to more accurately represent your stronger self to your wife. You no longer want to simply "yes-dear" your way through life; you want to authentically make your true self known. So you do. And then, by your very calm, welcoming presence, you invite your spouse to do the same. And she does.

Let's say your wife reacts defensively. She feels attacked by the thought that you want to change how the family celebrates the holidays, and doesn't want to hear any more about it. Now what?

Repeat.

Calm Down by pausing yourself and going to the balcony. Are you hurt by her reaction? Do you need to soothe your pain for a while before returning to the conflict? While upstairs, evaluate how calmly you represented yourself, questioning whether you allowed some pent-up resentment to color your revelation.

Now, Grow Up by spotting your pattern. How has your decades-long habit of acquiescing to your wife's holiday plans actually contributed to her resistance to anything different? How can you own your part and yet still express a desire for something different? Step on the scales by asking yourself what this means to you. Are you unfairly taking your own feelings of emasculation out on your wife? And what do you want most here? Christmas at home, or a more balanced relationship, where both partners feel stronger about expressing their desires, even if they differ?

Get Closer by showing your cards. Apologize for participating in this pattern all these years and then springing something so different on her. Explain your growth process to her and let her know that you don't intentionally want to make her feel guilty or uncomfortable. Let her know that you just want to reveal more of your real self to her, especially now that you're facing an emptier nest soon. Champion your spouse by welcoming any reaction that comes your way, even asking her whether your newfound strength is making her uncomfortable.

Repeat. As she then reveals to you her own concerns about the emptier nest, you calmly listen. As she represents her strong desire to keep holiday traditions alive with the few remaining years you have left with all the kids, you realize that you just got what you wanted most. There you are, two strong people revealing some risky, painful emotions, letting yourselves get to know each other more fully. Who knows, with such vulnerability and strength combined, you may be able to negotiate a way to keep the old traditions and create some new ones.

Well, that's just one way the Repeat process can look. As I said, this is a responsive process. We do not need a particular response from our spouse, but we do need to respond to however he/she does respond. Sometimes, as in the case above, that involves reentering the dialogue with new conversation. Other times it means responding with clear action, action that naturally flows from your original self-representation. Throughout the rest of this book, we will look at multiple examples of multiple types of responses. For now, let's return and conclude our Sunday morning story.

And Now, for the Rest of the Story . . .

When we left the story, Jenny was choosing to respond to my lack of a response. She had informed me of her intentions and invited me to join the rest of the family. As the ten minutes came, she went. Upon seeing that I was not ready, she calmed herself down enough to resist the urge to remind/nag/mother me. She then grew herself up enough to proceed with her stated intentions.

It was at that time, watching them all walk out the front door, that I threw on some pants and a shirt, grabbed a pair of shoes, and hightailed it. By the time I reached the garage, Jenny was already backing down the driveway. With my shirt unbuttoned and my shoes in hand, I ran down the street after her, waving my arms like a moron. Thankfully, I caught her attention and she stopped the car.

We lived just a couple of minutes away from the church building, but that trip felt like an eternity. Jenny and I didn't exchange any words, and the kids certainly weren't going to say anything. Funny how even the littlest of babes can sense when something is going on between their parents. We were all in uncharted territory. When we finally arrived at the church, Jenny and I exchanged enough nonverbal communications to get both kids out of their car seats and on their way to their classes. And after that handoff, we both began walking toward our class. It was then that Jenny, with one gesture and one sentence, completely altered our all-too-regular Sunday morning pattern once and for all. Reaching out to take my hand, she got closer and warmly said, *"I'm really glad you could join us."*

I was waiting for a snide comment, a rude remark, a rhetorical jab. But nothing except earnestness followed. Surely she was angry, or at least feeling superior, right? But the truth was, Jenny showed no judgment toward me and my actions that morning. In fact, she wasn't even thinking that much about me at all. *And that's what made all the difference.* Jenny was tired of trying to motivate me. She was tired of coming up with new tactics to wake me up and get me to help with the kids. What she decided to do was focus on herself and on *her* part of the pattern. Once deciding to stop her part, she could then focus on herself and her truest desires.

And with that our Sunday morning pattern was forever changed. You may find that hard to believe, thinking that surely I went back to being my lazy self the very next Sunday. Or you may think that Jenny's actions did little to change me into a responsible father— after all, she still had to do all the work, right? You especially may be thinking that taking this sort of action would have no effect on *your* spouse at all, or it might just make things worse.

That is certainly one way to look at it. And that's how Jenny chose to look at it *before* she took action that Sunday morning. She believed that she was responsible for changing my behavior. But that belief was her part of the negative pattern. She used to drive herself (and me) crazy by trying to figure out how to motivate and manipulate me into doing what she wanted me to do. Once she became self-centered in the ScreamFree way, once she focused on the only part of the dance that she could control, everything changed. Since then, Jenny has told me how difficult that was for her to do. The last thing she wanted to admit was that somehow she was playing an active role in my acting like a lazy bum.

But the beautiful thing was, when she no longer focused on my behavior, *I was forced to look at it on my own.* For the first time in a very long time, I had to take a long, hard look at *my own* part of the pattern. And wouldn't you know it, after seeing my behavior in the harsh light of reality, I changed in response. I changed because I saw myself in a new way, apart from Jenny's attempts to make me behave the way she wanted me to. Now I knew that it was *me* who needed to make me behave. It was me who was acting like a child, and, consequently, it was me inviting her to treat me like one.

I also saw Jenny in a new light. This was not a needy, whiny little girl I needed to placate. Nor was she an overbearing, nagging mother-type I could depend on to be responsible for me while I then immaturely complained about her efforts to smother me. That morning Jenny became an independent individual, a self-sufficient human being who didn't need me and didn't want to need me. Jenny was a woman, a full-grown adult who wanted me to join her life. And I'd never been more attracted to her. I wanted to grow up and assume more responsibility *precisely because* she didn't need me to.

In becoming ScreamFree that morning, Jenny took great steps toward becoming a *centered self*. She became a person clearly aware of herself and her place in the world. And upon encountering that centered self, I took steps toward becoming a stronger self as well. That's the power of one spouse deciding not to dance, but still wanting to have a partner. That's the power of one partner choosing to authentically represent herself. That's the power of Calming Down, Growing Up, and Getting Closer.

Okay, we've reached the end of Part One. Congrats. This is difficult stuff, and you could probably use a break. So take one. Mark this page and come back to it in a little while. However long you need. Then, when you're ready, join me in Part Two. There we'll take this formula and make it real in some of the most heated arenas of conflict any couple can face.

You ready? Turn the page.

parttwo

The Fires of Marital Commitment

How can you really ever know yourself
until you've been in a fight?
—BRAD PITT AS TYLER DURDEN
IN *FIGHT CLUB*

Up to this point, we've talked about focusing on yourself, confronting the lies that keep you stuck, and following the formula of Authentic Self-Representation. This was all vital for equipping you with a new mentality, a new ScreamFree mind-set, preparing you for what's next. Now's the time to look at this theory and formula in practice. Now's the time to start steeling yourself in the fires of marriage.

Are you familiar with the expression "steeling yourself"? It's not a reference to theft of any kind; it's a process of making yourself stronger, like raw iron turned into steel. It means stripping away all that's weak and unnecessary in order to reveal the truest part of you, the part that cannot be easily broken, bruised, or burned. And that last one's important, because the literal way of "steeling yourself," or forging that steel part of you, always involves fire.

Every couple, in every culture throughout history, has had to deal with the "fires of marriage." These fires are the inevitable arenas of conflict involved in joining two lives into one new family. Fires like extended families, finances, household management, sickness and aging, sex. Why are these fires inevitable? Because each of these areas involves necessary conversations and decisions. Why are these called fires? Because each calls for conversation about culture, tradition, and gender. Each of these areas invites debate about roles, rules, and expectations. Each of these areas of committed life together requires negotiation and decision making. Sound like the ingredients for heated conflict? Of course.

In reality, these are all just the challenges inherent in living together in a committed relationship. These fires have to do with how a couple chooses to organize and operate their life together, and how they continue to make these choices as their life situation evolves through the years. I call these challenges "fires" because they can be arenas of extreme friction. And where there's friction, there's always heat. I also call them "fires" because this heat, these "fires" of conflict, provide a refining process that can "steel" the best, strongest parts of ourselves. These fires force us to evaluate what we truly desire, and what we're willing to let go of for the sake of our relationships.

No couple can walk through these arenas without feeling passion, discomfort, and doubt. And no one can walk through these areas unchanged. However, these are fires we all *must* face if we want to develop the type of invested, lasting, and deep connection we all crave.

Whether a couple faces these fires is non-negotiable; we all have to make decisions about these issues again and again (and again!) throughout our years together. *How* a couple faces these fires, however, requires very definite negotiation between partners. Some couples cannot handle the intense heat of these fires, and thus sidestep these potentially contentious subjects as much as possible. Their trepidation guarantees a marriage that is either cold and disconnected or, at best, lukewarm and superficial. Some couples, on the other hand, fling themselves directly into these flames without care or thought—and find that they cannot control their emotions. They run the risk of having the fire consume both of them in rage, and the marriage as a whole. The pattern most couples engage in is an unhealthy combination of the two—explosive attempts to connect and icy attempts to douse the flames.

That's where *ScreamFree Marriage* comes in. This section will give you the insight and tools to face these fires throughout your committed life. By Calming Down, Growing Up, and Getting Closer, you can enter these conflicts with a calm confidence that will likely lead to greater intimacy, as well as individual growth and marital satisfaction. I firmly believe all of that is available to everyone, including you, if you're willing to embrace two principles that lie at the heart of the matter:

1. **In order to steel yourself in the fires of marriage, you have to learn to keep your cool.** As you undoubtedly know by now, the ScreamFree philosophy is ultimately about learning to keep your cool, staying calm and connected, no matter what. This means holding on to your truest self, steeling yourself, even as you embrace the conflict at hand. It means creating a pause for yourself, between stimulus and reaction. That is the essence of what it means to be ScreamFree—pausing just enough to make an authentic, hope-filled, intimacy-pursuing choice. Without this pause, we have little chance to attain our deepest desires and little chance to act from our highest principles. Without this pause, we are far too easily controlled by the anxiety of the moment and the fear of the unknown. The ScreamFree way makes us willing to embrace the fires of conflict, and at the same time calmly pursue what we want most for ourselves and our spouse. This way turns each fire from a destructive force into a refining one, a refining fire that can shape each spouse into a stronger and more authentic self, and thus create the possibility of true intimacy between two whole people.

2. **It's better to get rubbed the wrong way than never to get rubbed at all.** I know this sounds comical; but it is actually a very serious principle and I want you to really breathe it in. *It is better to get rubbed the wrong way than never to get rubbed at all.* It is better to be actively engaged in constructive conflict than to avoid it altogether. It is better to be involved in warm friction than staying away in cold comfort. See, there's no such thing as bad conflict. There are only bad ways of dealing with conflict. I believe conflict is an intrinsic good, because it is the natural path of growth. Think about it. Conflict with weights is what builds

muscle. Conflict between ions is what creates electricity. Conflict between elements is what creates chemistry. Without conflict we only have stagnation, atrophy, and lifelessness. (Sound like your marriage?) *With* conflict we generate growth, electricity, and chemistry. (Sound like what you want your marriage to experience?)

What to Expect in Part Two . . .

This part will spotlight four of these fires in a way that invites and inspires you to see the common issues in your marriage, and the common issues in all marriages, in a totally new light. This part will excite and encourage you to see your day-to-day life as rife with marital challenges endemic to all relationships, and how these challenges provide the very opportunities to renew and reinvigorate your marriage and yourself. The four fires I've chosen to lead you through involve arenas of conflict that are especially commonplace. They are also powerful in shaping the relational patterns in every marriage. In particular, in the next four chapters I will guide you through the fires of time accountability, extended families, household management, and, of course, sexuality.

Here's how each chapter will work. First, we'll examine the inherent conflicts that make each fire just that, a fire of conflict. You'll read stories of real-life couples engaging in struggles very similar to your own, and you'll see patterns that will help you make sense of it all. What we'll do next is identify the extreme, yet all-too-common, reactions to those struggles. By staking out these extremes, we can set the stage for new, more balanced, and exceedingly more effective ScreamFree responses. That way you'll learn principles that deal specifically with each fire and yet can be applied to them all.

Then, at the end of each chapter, you'll encounter "The Lab." Here you will find real-life case studies, coming from real couples that I've worked with in marriage relationship coaching. I can promise you that while I've changed the names and specific circumstances of these examples, all these cases are real and powerful. And while none of these cases will mirror your life perfectly, I promise you can see yourself in here somewhere.

What I cannot promise is that after reading about each of these fires, and engaging with each of these questions, you'll immediately have all the answers. No, I'm going to show you more respect than that; your challenges in each of these arenas are real, they did not arise easily or quickly, nor will they go away that way. What I *can* promise you is that all you need, in order to drastically grow yourself into the spouse your marriage needs, is located within the fires of your marriage. As marriage expert Dr. David Schnarch so perfectly puts it: "It's not about working on your marriage, it's about letting your marriage work on you." Your marriage is doing a number on you—for your own, and your spouse's, great benefit. By learning to examine your own conflicts, and learning to apply the formula to yourself as you go and grow through them, you will see profound change. You will get closer to the marriage you crave.

What I know is that you want a calmer, deeper, lifelong connection. That's why you picked up this book. What I also know is that you're a person of incredible integrity, willing to have your deepest convictions questioned and your highest hopes revealed. That's why you're *still* reading this book. Now, I challenge you: Walk into these fires with that same willingness, face these fires with that same integrity, and you will learn the incredible power that comes from steeling yourself through conflict. As you'll see, it's the best way to pursue and forge the connection you seek.

Chapter 4

Time Belongs to No Man, Especially a Married One

[The Fire of Time Accountability]

*I'm twenty-six, and you know what that means . . .
all my friends are getting married.
I keep getting that same annoying invitation,
"Hey, come to my wedding!" . . . which
really means, "Hey, we're not gonna hang out
anymore—buy me a gift."*

—MO MANDEL

*Time is the school in which we learn,
time is the fire in which we burn.*

—DELMORE SCHWARTZ

At the airport the other day, I saw two different guys, at two different times, wearing the exact same T-shirt. It was a black shirt with a white silhouette of a bride and groom. It looked just like the top of a wedding cake except for one detail: trailing out from the groom's foot was a ball-and-chain. And, as if the picture weren't telling enough, there was a large caption underneath the whole silhouette, written in bold white letters: GAME OVER.

Now, this occurrence is troubling on many fronts. First of all, from a fashion standpoint, these were two different grown men wearing this thing. Men past the age of twenty-five just shouldn't wear shirts with cutesy graphics. Period. Second, what makes a guy wear such a message out in a public place like an airport? Are these guys "bound" and determined to literally show the world how unhappy they are in their marriages? Most likely, they're single, and obviously want to stay that way (and, according to my wife, they're on the right track).

The fact that someone created the T-shirt at all says a lot. It says that there is definitely a perception in our culture that marriage does in fact mean GAME OVER. No more fun and games. Your decisions, particularly about how you spend your time, are no longer yours. They belong to your spouse, and you had better get used to being a prisoner in your own home.

Now, the stereotype would say that this is a uniquely male point of view. After all, the ball-and-chain is connected to the groom, and I doubt we'll ever see a baby-doll version of the shirt made for women. But the truth is that, once we get married, we all experience a profound shift in the way we think about and experience time. Our decisions about how we spend our time are forever changed, and they should be. As married people, we share something that previously was all our own.

We get married because we want to join our lives together forever, which necessarily means we join our uses of time. This quickly leads to differing expectations about what that looks like. One partner inevitably expects more time together—and the other more time apart. And those expectations can change from week to week. What happens is that a pattern of time choices develops over, you guessed it, time. One partner works hard to increase the *accountability* of each partner's time choices, and the other works hard to increase the *autonomy* of those choices. One partner works to increase time together, and the other works hard to increase built-in excuses for time apart. Before you know it, you are in the midst of a fire that threatens to consume you. In this chapter, you will meet two couples who are caught in this fire for different reasons. What you'll learn from both is that staying ScreamFree in this fire is not easy. But it is doable. And it is powerfully effective in facilitating the growth of both partners. All it takes is a careful appreciation of two seemingly opposite principles.

You Are Accountable to Your Spouse for *All* Your Time Choices

The first principle to remember is that, after marriage, you are responsible to your spouse for all your time choices. No, this does not necessarily mean giving a minute-by-minute account of each day, but it does mean that all your choices affect another person in a new way. As Annie Dillard so eloquently wrote, "How we spend our days is really how we spend our lives." That's right— what you do with the twenty-four hours given to you shapes every aspect of your life, including your marriage. It is a reflection of your priorities, your principles, and your preferences—and there's only so much of it to go around. As you probably already know from experience, that can make for some tremendously heated conflicts. And that's a good thing.

Meet Tracy and Mark. They met in their senior year in college and have been married for eleven years. Mark owns his own business and works very hard to provide a good life for Tracy and their two kids. He's a great dad, who coaches Little League and helps around the house. Tracy is the primary caregiver for their children, works part-time from the house, and is very involved at church. They've got a relatively happy marriage, but there is one issue that concerns her. Or really irritates her. Or can drive her insane. Listen to her admission:

I love Mark like crazy, I really do. But he hasn't been on time to *anything* in the eleven years that we've been married. He'll tell me I can expect him for dinner at 6:00 and then he won't pull into the driveway until 6:45. And it's getting worse each year. I know that when you own your own business sometimes things come up, but c'mon—every night? And why can't he at least pick up the phone and call so that I can be prepared? It even happens at events, like our kids' events at school. I arrive an hour early to get good seats for both of us, giving up time that I could be working on my website. Then he swoops in at the very last minute and acts like he just found a great seat by magic. Not even a thank-you! I have to say that I get pretty steamed. I usually either seethe or explode every now and again. It helps, but only for a day or two. I just don't know what to do.

After talking to Tracy for a while, it becomes clear that her time issue is more about *respect* than time. Mark is not malicious in his miscalculations, but, in Tracy's mind, he is sending a pretty clear message: *My time is more valuable than yours.* There is a lack of accountability for his tardiness and his lack of consideration, and Tracy feels powerless in the situation. But that is far from the truth. See, as long as Tracy is focused on Mark's lack of accountability for his actions, she'll simply perpetuate her resentment and, more than likely, Mark's tardiness. But if Tracy could focus on *her own* accountability, then she's not powerless at all.

So what is Tracy responsible for? *Her* choices. In this case, her choices have led to the very thing that she's complaining about. Instead of going ahead with her plans despite Mark and thus highlighting his accountability, Tracy just keeps pushing back dinner and the kids' bedtime when Mark is late. And she keeps showing up early for those seats in the auditorium to make up for Mark's tardiness. In this ongoing scenario, why in the world would Mark *want* to change? The only motivating consequence she could previously think of was throwing a fit. But that always backfired and made her more resentful, not less. And it seemed to make him more reluctant to change.

So instead of focusing so much on figuring out why Mark does what he does, why not examine her own behavior and her own motives? Why had she continued accommodating Mark's tardiness and apparent lack of respect for so long? Did Tracy need Mark's presence in order to feel secure? Validated? Worthy? Was she afraid to be alone, both literally and metaphorically? Was she afraid that Mark didn't really want to be with her? How much (or how little) did she value her own time? Was she afraid that if she truly represented herself to Mark, confronting him about her anger and pain, that he'd disrespect her even more, even dismissing her altogether?

By asking herself these questions, Tracy could recognize and deliver to herself a difficult truth: "By giving in to my fears, I've helped to create this mess." Difficult, but powerful. Owning her own role could empower her to take the next step, talking to Mark about her role in the situation and how she plans on changing. Notice I said *her* role. After all, she is not responsible for his part in this pattern, just her own.

She is responsible *to* Mark, though. She's got to stay calm and connected in this process. It won't do her or their marriage any good if she flips out and issues ultimatums. She has to Calm Down, Grow Up, and take the bold step to talk to him about what's really behind her resentment. She has to represent herself to him in a very adult way, spelling out that she feels devalued when he arrives late on a regular basis. Then she has to be willing to listen to what his perceptions are. Finally, she has to become willing to act differently, *with or without Mark's cooperation.*

And Tracy indeed did all of the above. As it turns out, Mark had no idea that she felt disrespected. From his perspective, he was just trying to squeeze in a few more minutes at work so that he could really relax at home and be with Tracy and the kids. Once Tracy approached him in this new way, without all the accusations and nagging, he was able to see that the extra minutes weren't the problem at all, it was the not-knowing and the lack of respect that drove her crazy. So he gave her a time when she could expect him that was actually later than he needed to finish up at work. He built in a little cushion so that he would always arrive home by then and, on many nights, early. As for the school productions, Tracy still goes early. As it turns out, the good seats were more important to her than they were to Mark anyway, so she made peace with that choice and happily saved him a seat. And guess what? He usually remembers to say thanks.

You and You Alone Are the One Who Makes *All* Your Choices

How we choose to spend our time is a reflection of our priorities. And by choosing to be married, we are stating that we are willing to place our relationship as among the very highest of those priorities. Thus we are highly accountable *to* our spouse for our choices.

But in no way does this mean that we make our choices as a unit. Nobody died at your wedding, and there is no "we" without two "I"s making individual choices to agree. You are a grown-up, and in the immortal words of Dr. Seuss, "You have brains in your head. You have feet in your shoes. You can steer yourself in any direction you choose." No one, including your spouse, can make you do anything; what you do with your time is solely up to you. Now, that's not to say that your choices aren't informed by others—we'll talk about that later. But the point I'm making is that you, as a functioning adult, have to:

1. Own the choices you make about your time. Owning your choices entails more than you might imagine. If you take ownership of the choices you make, then you also are taking ownership of any consequences that come from that choice. Gentlemen, this means that there is no "ball-and-chain" or "boss" or "old lady" who's making out your schedule. Not unless you wanted to marry your mother.

2. Examine your motives for your desires. If you are going to be an adult and own the time choices that you make, then you need to take a close look at why you want to do the things you want to do. Does your time allocation really represent the things you value the most? What *are* the things you value most? Are they reflected in your calendar? Asking and answering these questions honestly means that you cannot with full integrity tell someone, "Oh, I wish I could have been there!" The truth is that you could have, but you chose not to. It doesn't matter why you weren't (work, family, previous commitment, finances, your spouse didn't want you to go)—you simply made a choice of priority. And that's fine. I learned this the hard way when I missed my daughter's piano recital because I was traveling on a speaking gig. When I talked to her about it later, I told her, "Honey, I so wish I could have been there!" She then instantly replied, "Then why weren't you? You always tell me that I'm the one responsible for my choices, that no one can make me do anything. If you really wanted to be here the most, then you would have been. Right, Daddy?" She was just twelve. I was left speechless. And ridiculously impressed.

3. Represent your choices to yourself and your spouse honestly and with integrity. This means saying, "No, honey, I'm sorry. I really don't want to go to the boat show with you." Instead of going along to keep the peace and showing him with every roll of your eyes that you'd rather be anywhere else. Or maybe you say yes to the boat show, but you do so because sharing something that he loves is more important to you than your level of entertainment on that particular afternoon. Then you own that choice and you go there with a smile on your face. Either way is ScreamFree because you've focused on yourself and you've taken responsibility for what is yours.

Let's look at another couple in the heat of this fire and see how this principle helped them. Mike and Allison had been married for less than a year. Before the wedding, Mike used to play basketball every Friday from four to seven in the afternoon with his buddies—a chance to unwind after a long week. Ever since the honeymoon, though, Mike hadn't made it back to one game. After all, he's married now, right?

When I met Mike, he was visibly upset about this situation, but he had a difficult time articulating why. He told me, "It's not that I don't like spending time with Allison. It's just that I don't feel like I get any say in the matter. Allison is super-organized, so she takes care of our calendar. She loves to spend time doing all sorts of things together and she doesn't really seem to need to hang out with her old friends. I guess I didn't see this coming—being together all the time. I suppose I'll get used to it."

Yikes.

"Mike—how did you and Allison discuss how Friday nights were going to look for you two?" I already knew the answer to this question, but he clearly didn't. He looked at me with a quizzical expression and sat back in his chair. It took him some time to remember.

"Well, the first time the guys asked me to join them after we were married, I asked Allison if it were okay. It turned out that she had already scheduled a dinner with her parents, so I told my friends that I couldn't." He said this with a casual shrug of his shoulders, as if I were obtuse to even ask the question.

"I see. So you asked for her permission." Mike stared at me for a moment and then broke into a sheepish grin. Then I followed, "Did you also ask for your binkie?"

Mike thought that by asking her permission, he was being considerate and thoughtful. He thought he was being a nice guy. The only problem is that marriage doesn't call for nice guys and girls. It calls for men and women. By asking Allison for permission, he was setting her up as the gatekeeper of his calendar and as the parent figure in the relationship. And that's precisely what is behind the ball-and-chain, GAME OVER T-shirt. "If I have to be accountable for my time," this extreme position screams, "then I may as well hand over all the responsibility to my spouse. At least that way I get to blame her for my growing resentments, without having to do anything about it."

And that's how a lot of couples choose to handle this fire, by abdicating their responsibility for their own choices. Then they can hold their spouse, their marriage, or just the institution of marriage itself responsible for their lack of freedom and subsequent unhappiness. But integrity calls us to something higher than that. Integrity calls us to be ScreamFree, to be free from extreme reactions, for the benefit of ourselves and our spouses. It calls us to Calm Down, Grow Up, and Get Closer.

I asked Mike if he could think of another way that he could have handled that situation. He quickly responded, "Well, sure. I could have just said, 'Hey, I'm going to play ball on Friday. I'm not sure when I'll be home, so don't wait up.' That would have gone over real well." And he was right in his sarcasm. You can imagine what kind of message that would have sent to Allison: *I may be married, but how I choose to spend my time is only up to me, and I am not accountable for it. So what if you want more time together than I do? Deal with it.*

The problem Mike was facing is a very common one. He could only think of extreme ways to make his decision about having any time for himself. He felt guilty for wanting time away from his new bride, and he didn't know how to handle his wife's and his seemingly different preferences. He could either abdicate responsibility to her, or he could just take what he wanted with no accountability.

But there is always a third way. And it's the way of truth.

And the truth is that Mike was responsible *for* his choices. He wanted to be with his friends again—not necessarily to get away from Allison, but just to keep that part of himself alive and well—the competitive, fun-loving guy she had fallen in love with. He had to own that choice and its consequence. He had blamed Allison for taking away his friends when it was really his doing in the first place! Now, he had to represent his desire for time away with honesty and maturity.

Mike also had to take into account who and what he was responsible *to*. He wanted this marriage to work. He loved Allison and he valued her preferences. He had to take into account her desire for couple time, but he wasn't doing their relationship any favors by allowing her strong preferences to dominate his own. He also was responsible to her in the way that he went about handling himself as he spoke up about his true feelings. That wasn't going to be easy. It never is.

The following week, I saw Mike again, and he told me that things had gotten much better. Turns out he had again heard from his buddies about playing ball. This time he handled it a bit differently. He approached Allison and said, "Hey, honey, I wanted to let you know that I've received an invitation to play basketball with the guys this Friday from four to seven. I'd love to go, so I wanted to check if you had something scheduled that night that might interfere." He was on his way to adulthood, and asking his wife to join him.

Common Pitfalls

In order to steel yourself in this fire, you have to own both of these truths at the same time. You are in charge of your choices—no one else. You also owe an account of your time to your spouse, because your choices profoundly affect your spouse. This is the fire of time accountability in a nutshell. The biggest mistake you can make in this fire is choosing to believe one truth to the exclusion of the other.

With that in mind, here are some common pitfalls and some strategies for success to consider as you learn to turn this common conflict into a deeper, lifelong connection.

Moralizing Your Preference. In the brilliant book *Boundaries in Marriage,* Drs. Henry Cloud and John Townsend discuss the all-too-common mistake couples make of one claiming his/her preferences as somehow superior to that of his/her spouse. They cite an example where the husband wants to relax on the weekend by playing with the kids and watching sports, while the wife wants to work on household projects. The wife would moralize her position thinking that "work" was good and TV bad. But is it? Just because she finds it satisfying and relaxing to work outside in the garden doesn't mean that her preference is *better* than his. Remember, preferences are just that—preferences. They usually aren't character badges or flaws, although many times we'd like to make them so.

Scorekeeping. Cloud and Townsend also point out that the way many couples attempt to balance their time often looks more like an exercise in accounting than a loving and considerate exchange. If you find yourself keeping mental track of what *he* gets to do versus what *you* get to do, get it out in the open. Usually we keep these feelings under wraps instead of making them known. Go ahead, literally keep score for a while; you just might realize that things aren't as one-sided as you think. But ultimately, remember, balance does not have to mean equality. As long as you are both satisfied, things don't have to tally up just so.

Failing to Adjust for Growth. As you steel yourself through this fire, remember: Steel is strong but still flexible. As time goes on, your stage of life, particular circumstances, and opportunities will often be in a state of flux. Time priorities need to be constantly reviewed and reevaluated as each partner grows and changes. Keep things fluid and keep talking in order to stay cool and get stronger in this fire.

Strategies for Success

While working to avoid those pitfalls, here are some common-sense strategies to rememer and employ as you strive for growth in the midst of this fire.

Build in a Time Margin. Margin is that extra bit of time that you give yourself when you are making plans. Too many of us live life without any room for error, and it often creates more stress than necessary. Estimate how long it will take you to do something or get somewhere and add an extra 15 percent. That way, you'll usually end up underpromising and overdelivering, instead of the dreadful opposite.

Plan Ahead. Date nights don't just happen. Neither do retreats. Take an active role in planning these and don't leave it up to your spouse to nurture your marriage. On the flip side, if you're the project manager type of partner who likes to plan and then feels resentful because your spouse doesn't, think about loosening your grip on the day planner just a little. Ask your spouse to plan something and then let her do it.

Ask Yourself Some Tough Questions. The only way to make changes in any pattern is to willingly focus on yourself. Here are some guiding questions to help you begin to do just that.

- What do you do when confronted with scheduling conflicts between you and your spouse?
- As a couple, what do you end up doing when there's a conflict between spending time together and spending time apart?
- Is there always one way you typically make this decision? (Does one person, for instance, always seem to sacrifice his/her position in order to avoid a conflict?)
- Do you automatically follow the typical pattern of capitulating to the together time, because you've bought into the lie that separate time is bad for a marriage?
- Do you always let the same person get his/her way? Why?
- Do you yield to whoever's the most forceful at the moment?
- Is there a pattern concerning time that is particularly troublesome for you?
- What are you doing not only to contribute to the tension surrounding time accountability but also to making it worse?

the**lab**

My wife, Jenny, has been a high school English teacher for more than ten years. She is an educator at heart. But, as she'll readily admit, she hates tests. She hates giving tests and she really hates grading them. Tests imply there is only one right way to solve a problem, or one right way to find a solution. But life just doesn't work that way. The way we really learn is not through right-or-wrong tests, but through trial-and-error experimentation. And what better place to experiment than in a laboratory?

So, in the pages that follow, and at the end of each of these four "Fires" chapters, I will lead you into a section we simply call "the lab." Here I will provide a real-life scenario and ask you to place yourself in the role of one particular spouse in the situation. You'll then get to experiment using the Authentic Self-Representation formula.

Step-by-step through the formula, we'll actually have space on the page for you to jot down your initial thoughts on how you would like to see yourself responding to the situation. Now, when you read the scenario, look carefully for those lies that lead to faulty assumptions, helping to create the patterns that have left them stuck. And then get creative! Use these labs as a chance to be ScreamFree without the threat of "messing up" or "getting it wrong." After all, marriage isn't a series of tests you either pass or fail; it is a process that you grow through. And you grow through it by going through it with intentionality and with integrity.

At the end of your write-in section, I'll give you the

actual details about how this real-life couple applied the ASR formula and learned to respond in a ScreamFree way. Please do not consider this the one and only way to handle the situation, and please do not be overly critical of yourself in comparing your thoughts to their actions. For many people, this way of approaching common conflicts is so new that they find it difficult even to get started. That's why I've created these labs, and that's why I've laid them out this way. My sincerest hope is that by examining another couple objectively, and placing yourself in their shoes, you can begin to recognize patterns and creatively come up with new alternatives. This can only build your ScreamFree muscles, and make it all the more likely that you can and will begin to Calm Down, Grow Up, and Get Closer in your own real-life scenarios.

Ready? Let's get started.

The Setup: Becky met Trey while she was in nursing school. He lived in the apartment above her and they would see each other in the complex's gym or laundry room. At first, Trey was intimidated by Becky. She was pretty, athletic, outgoing, and daring. He made small talk for months until he finally got up the nerve to ask her out. She said yes and they clicked immediately. They dated for two wonderful years and enjoyed a life filled with friends, travel, and adventure. After they married, Trey quickly began to advance through the ranks of his engineering firm. They soon had the first of three children and decided that Becky should stay home. Over the course of their eighteen-year marriage, Trey was transferred quite a few times and moved the family with him each time. Becky did not go back to work until three years ago, when their youngest began school. She then reentered the workforce full time.

At that time, she also began playing tennis again—something she hadn't done since college. She quickly remembered why she loved the sport so long ago, and was soon playing in a competitive league. She lost a few pounds, made new friends, and seemed happier than ever. And Trey was thrilled. At first.

But gradually, he became less enthralled with Becky's new hobby. While he wanted to support her newfound passion for tennis, he couldn't help feeling a little squeezed out by it. What began with her playing one night a week had morphed into her playing two, sometimes three nights a week. Then she added daylong matches and tournaments on the weekends. Recently, she had joined a *second* league to play during those "off weeks" when she didn't have a match. Gone were the date nights between she and Trey and the lazy evenings in the backyard the whole family would all spend together.

Now, Trey was growing more frustrated over Becky's preoccupation with tennis. He resented her playing so much; this was evident by his constant requests to find out about her schedule. But Becky didn't know how angry Trey was until one night when he snapped at her as she was headed out the door. "Are you serious? What is this, the third time this week? By all means, go hit that little yellow ball. It obviously means more to you than spending time with your family. Hope you have a *great* time."

Trey didn't normally yell or get sarcastic with Becky, so she was really taken aback and hurt by his tone and his accusation. Her actions at this juncture were critical. She had a chance to either damage or repair the relationship. What do you think she should do? Try to place yourself in Becky's tennis Nikes, and take a stab at applying the formula to her situation.

CALM DOWN

Pause Yourself:

How might Becky create some space here, giving her time to calmly reflect and consider her response?

Go to the Balcony:

How might Becky give herself some objectivity here? Talk to a friend, perhaps? Pray? What would you do?

GROW UP

Spot Your Pattern:

How might Becky be contributing to Trey's resentment explosion?

Step on the Scale:

What about tennis means so much to Becky? What do you think she wants most here?

GET CLOSER

Show Your Cards:

How might Becky respond to Trey's outburst? What might she need to reveal about herself?

Champion Your Spouse:

How can Becky encourage Trey's authentic self representation?

REPEAT

Regardless of Trey's response, Becky has to be prepared to remain calm and make any appropriate adjustments. What do you think happened next?

Now that you've tried your hand at the formula, take a look at how it actually happened.

CALM DOWN

Pause Yourself: Becky was stunned by Trey's comment. She wanted to smack a zinger right back at him. She wanted to yell out, "What about all those conferences you went to while I was home nursing our babies? What about all those golf trips you just had to take while I stayed home with three toddlers? Why can't it be my turn now? Why can't I have a little fun for myself?" Instead, she took a few moments to just sit in the car and let Trey's comments sink in. Nothing good could have come from yelling right back at him, even though it may have made her feel better in the short term.

Go to the Balcony: "Surely he's overreacting," Becky told herself. But, in an effort to be objective, she decided to "go upstairs" and take a hard look at her tennis schedule. She looked at her calendar, and she looked at the math. Just how many hours a week had she been pouring into this sport? Usually, she attended one two-hour practice session at night and one three-hour match on the weekend. So, five hours in all. "That's not terribly unreasonable," she thought to herself. But, she began to look closer. Occasionally, her two leagues overlapped for a few weeks. During those times, she would spend *ten* hours a week on the court. Wow. That's more than she thought. And come to think of it, that's just court time. She was actually gone from home much longer than that, since it took her thirty minutes to get to and from her facility each time. What's more, almost every weekend, she stayed after her own match to cheer on the team. Suddenly, Becky realized that she often spent up to sixteen hours a week on tennis.

GROW UP

Spot Your Pattern: Sixteen hours a week was certainly more than Becky was expecting to find. Yet at some level, she wasn't surprised. When she's honest, she can usually tell when she's playing too much. There's a guilt that creeps into her gut when she crosses that line between enjoying her hobby and becoming consumed by it. When she feels that guilt, she starts to underestimate how long a match might take, and sometimes she would even drag the kids to matches with her in an effort to create "family time." She tended to spend an inordinate amount of time and energy arranging her schedule to squeeze tennis in and it sometimes became more of a burden than a joy. But up to this point, she reacted very strongly whenever Trey pointed that out.

Whenever Trey pressed her about tennis and kept tabs on her schedule, she found herself "protecting" her tennis time even more. And when she played even more, he would get even more frustrated, wanting to know more specifics as to how long she'd be gone. It's as if the more he chased her, the less she wanted to be with him. In fact, it was exactly like that.

Step on the Scale: Becky now saw that (a) she was playing a lot more tennis than she thought and (b) she tended to play even more whenever Trey gave her grief about it. Obviously, something besides tennis was going on here. It was time for Becky to face the scale and ask herself the tough questions.

What does tennis mean to me? Why is it so important to me? She had never really tried to articulate it before, but Becky felt . . . different . . . on a tennis court. On the court, she wasn't anyone's mother or sister or wife or nurse. She was just Becky. She felt free of worry and care. She felt light, graceful, strong, and powerful all at once. She felt the way she used to in college. Whenever those fleeting moments of guilt would surface, like when she chose to play that extra set or pickup match, she felt justified in staying on the court. After all, she spent *years* following Trey around the country and caring for everyone except herself. It was finally her turn to be pampered. Her turn to be a little selfish. At least that's what the prevailing sentiment seemed to be from the other ladies on the team.

Now that she allowed herself to think about it, she felt resentful with Trey for all those years where he took time to "develop himself" through work and play, while she was home changing diapers and wiping noses. She also felt so torn. It's not as if she were forced to do all those things for the kids. She felt blessed to have had those times, but they were awfully lonely and difficult. Was she being fair to blame them and Trey for her lack of "me time" back then? Hadn't she been the one who suggested that she stay home until the kids were in school? Hadn't she been the one neglecting to take care of herself all those years? Maybe she wasn't only angry with Trey; maybe she was angry with herself for letting all that time go by without making even a little effort to stay connected to her "old self." Maybe that's why tennis seemed to have such a hold on her.

So what does she want most? Did Becky really want to leave behind all her cares and play tennis seven days a week? Of course not. The thought itself was laughable. She loved her children, her husband, and her job. What she wanted most was to be happy and to reclaim a little of that lost youth without losing her family or herself in the process. She wanted to feel alive again—on and off the court. She wanted that fun and spontaneous relationship that she and Trey once had. She realized that tennis had become an escape for her, but she didn't want to run anymore. She wanted to be balanced.

GET CLOSER

Show Your Cards: Becky went back in the house and walked over to Trey. He barely looked up and said, "I thought you had practice." She sat down next to him and said, "I've thought a lot about what you said to me. I didn't realize how much tennis I've really been playing. And I didn't realize how much it bothered you. The truth is, I don't really like playing as much as I have been. I think I've been using tennis as some sort of escape—a way to make up for lost time. It makes me feel young and I haven't felt that way in a really long time. I think that, in some weird way, I'm angry about waiting so long to do something just for me. I don't know if I'm angry at you or at me, but I think that is what's going on with me. I don't want to give up tennis altogether, but I do recognize that I've gone overboard."

Champion Your Spouse: She then said to him, "I want to hear from you. Tell me what you think about all this." Trey was surprised to hear Becky's comments. He'd spent the last half hour or so stewing in his anger and he was ready to continue his diatribe. But her demeanor caught him off guard. Even though he was still angry, he wasn't so sure he wanted to let her have it. He told her that he needed a little time to think about what she just said.

Trey didn't mention their conversation for two days. Things were a little strange between them, but Becky seemed to exude a sense of relief. She just wasn't as frantic as usual. Finally, Trey said, "Bec, I've been thinking about what you said. And I can understand where you are coming from. It's not the tennis that upsets me. It's the fact that you spend more energy arranging your schedule for tennis than you do paying any attention to me. Now that the kids are all in school, we've got this whole other chapter in our lives starting. I started seeing us all going in different directions and it scared me. The kids are busy with their activities, I've been dealing with crazy hours at work, and then you just dove headfirst into tennis. I guess I kind of panicked. I really do want you to have something fun that is just yours. I think it's great . . . and you look amazing in those little skirts. But I also want more time with you. I want 'us' to be the thing that we revolve everything else around—not tennis."

REPEAT

Once Becky saw that Trey's frustration about her tennis was never about holding her back, she stopped feeling the need to escape as much. She decided to play at a facility closer to home. She also limited the number of hours she played each week and even voluntarily sat out the occasional season. She now feels remarkably free and actually started having more fun . . . on and *off* the court. Now that she knows how both she and Trey really feel, she wants to spend more time with him. This is a strange feeling for her because, usually, he is the one pushing for more time together and she is the one edging away. But after walking through that whole awkward and tense moment between them, she actually feels quite a bit closer to him. And she recognizes that the tennis court isn't the only place where she can reclaim her "old self." So, for the first time in years, she took the initiative and planned a weekend away for the two of them. She wasn't sure how he'd react, but one thing is for certain. The ball was in his court.

Chapter 5

In Order to Move in Together, You Have to Move Out on Your Own

[The Fire of Extended Families]

The umbilical cord of a family is infinitely elastic.

—RABBI EDWIN FRIEDMAN

I told my mother-in-law that my house was her house, and she said, "Get the hell off my property."

—JOAN RIVERS

For clarity's sake, let's establish what this chapter is *not* about. It is not about the logistics of moving in together. It is not about the advantages, or disadvantages, of living together before marriage. No, this chapter is about something far more important. This chapter is about what it means to be an adult, particularly as you join together in marriage with another adult.

And, finding out what it means to be an adult is no easy task. It's not even easy to define the word *adult*. Think about it. What term do we use to describe the act of infidelity in our marriages? *Adult*ery. As if cheating on our spouse were the pinnacle of adult behavior. And what about the word *adulterate*? You would think, based on word construction, that it means something like "to make something more mature, more-adultlike." But no, *adulterate* means to make something impure, like adding cheap, inferior grapes to mass-produced wine.*

These aren't the only ways we add confusion to the notion of adulthood. Allow me to illustrate. Back in August 2000, I had just finished my family therapy internship in Texas, and Jenny was offered a great teaching job at a premier private school in the metro Atlanta area, Greater Atlanta Christian School. I had been offered a part-time position there as well. Now, when I say "just finished" my internship, I really mean it. I graduated in Texas on a Friday night, and we were scheduled to begin teaching in Georgia the following Monday. You can imagine how hectic that last weekend was, trying to get packed and relocating halfway across the country with two small children in tow.

Thankfully, we were not alone. My dad and brother were there to help load and drive the truck, and my mom was there to help get everything packed and labeled. Also, our new boss, Bill Burton, GACS's high school principal at the time, had agreed to bring a volunteer crew to help us unload once we arrived. And, sure enough, when we finally drove up to our new house on Sunday evening, there he was waiting in the driveway along with a handful of eager teachers to help. You can picture the scene: everyone sweating on a humid August evening, working swiftly to unload our huge moving truck and get us settled in before the real work kicked in the next day.

Mr. Burton, a big strong guy, was fantastic. Not only had he brought a small crew of people to help, but he was right out there with them leading the charge. At one point we noticed him

---

*Now, for you language geeks, I know that the etymology of *adult* and that of *adultery* and *adulterate,* are different. But the fact remains that they share the same English root phonetically, and that is good enough to confuse the vast majority of us.

carrying a heavy load out of the truck, a massive box labeled KIDS' VIDEOS. It was full of our toddlers' VHS movies (pre-DVD days, of course), like the entire Disney catalogue, along with the entire Barney and Teletubbies collections. After setting the box down, and commenting on how many movies our family had, Mr. Burton went back into the truck to get another one.

Now, remember that my mom had done all the labeling of the boxes, and she did so—like the rest of us—in a big hurry. I therefore do not fault her at all for what was about to unfold. See, Jenny and I also owned a number of VHS videos of our own, like all the *Star Wars* and *Indiana Jones* movies, along with some other favorites—*Gandhi, Schindler's List, Saving Private Ryan*. Well, apparently, in an effort to differentiate these videos from our kids', my mom had put them in a separate box, with a separate label.

Well, you can imagine the horror on our faces when we both turned toward the van to see our new principal, from our new Christian school employer, bounding down the ramp of the truck with a big box labeled ADULT VIDEOS. We stood motionless, holding our breath and praying that he hadn't seen the labels that adorned all four sides of this box. He didn't—or at least he was too much of a gentleman to say anything. (Thankfully, he didn't pick up the ADULT TOYS box—just kidding.)

As this story shows, our culture generates a lot of confusion about what it means to be an adult. This chapter is going to attempt to bring some clarity to that confusion. In particular, we are going to look at what it means to become your own person in relation to your parents and the rest of your extended family. This step is absolutely critical before being able to fully join your spouse to form a new married couple.

Now, it's important to insert a cultural note here. At the beginning of Part Two, when referring to the fires of marriage, I made a bold statement. I said that every couple, in every culture throughout history, has had to deal with these fires. I stand by that statement; the fires *are* all the same, but *how* those couples have dealt with these fires has differed drastically, given the disparate historical, socioeconomic, and cultural settings through the ages. These differences still continue today, particularly concerning this Fire of Extended Families. The notion that I'm prescribing here, of leaving your childhood family relationships in order to fully connect with your spouse, can certainly be viewed as my own culturally biased prescription. I am a white, Protestant, Texan by birth and upbringing, after all, and even though I don't really have an accent, I know I have certain biases.

But many other cultures have chosen to deal with the fire of extended family in other ways, from some having the wife join the husband's family upon marriage to others prescribing just the opposite. It is a decidedly American ideal for both men and women to literally live on their own, independently as individuals, before marriage. But allow me to clarify again: I am not, in this chapter, talking about the physical logistics of where or in what manner people live. I am talking about the crucial *emotional* journey of becoming an adult in your marriage. Without that trek, you will continue to find yourself in the midst of exhausting relationship dynamics between you, your spouse, and your extended families. Let's examine a few common ways this fire manifests itself in marriages.

Say your mother seems to have latched onto the idea that she can come over anytime she likes, à la Raymond's mother on *Everybody Loves Raymond*. You don't like her intrusion, but you do like how she watches the kids for you, and you're afraid that if you address the problem you'll lose the relationship (not to mention the free babysitting). Your husband is begging you to do something about it, and you feel desperately trapped in the middle between them. What do you do?

Or let's say you've worked in the family business for years, and this legacy and effort has afforded you a very comfortable lifestyle. But that lifestyle comes with a price tag. Your parents expect a great deal of loyalty from you, especially in the areas of time and access. Neither you nor your spouse particularly likes the situation, and her parents are putting pressure on her to visit *them* more often, but both of you are afraid of biting the hand that feeds you. You've got a complicated mix of conflicted feelings, from gratitude to resentment, from loyalty to anger. Where do you go from here?

Finally, here's one more. You had a rotten childhood, full of dysfunction, and you only survived by leaving early and staying away. You're still in contact with your parents occasionally, even exchanging holiday gifts and cordial pleasantries. But all it takes is one objectionable phone call and you're right back to feeling abused or overwhelmed, and therefore cutting yourself off once again. To complicate things, however, you've now got kids. Your extended family would like to be in their lives, and even your spouse has encouraged you to reestablish a relationship. What now?

What do each of these scenarios have in common? They all can create a tremendous amount of stress on even the healthiest of marriages. But, thankfully, that's not all. They can also create a tremendous amount of growth in even the most miserable of marriages. It all depends on how each individual is willing to approach the situation.

And, according to the ScreamFree view of things, that approach involves two related principles. In order to grow through this fire, you must: 1) leave your own mother and father and cleave to your spouse; and 2) work to develop a direct relationship with your in-laws. In this chapter we're going to talk about both of these difficult tasks. But take heart: What you'll find is that one feeds off the other.

To Cleave, You Have to Leave
(A Garden-Variety Marriage)

You may not be able to see it, but I promise you, there is a direct connection between (a) leaving behind and growing beyond your dependency on your parents, and (b) connecting to your spouse in a deeper way. One directly precedes the other. Now, I'm not the first to say this, mind you—not by a long shot. This idea of leaving Mom and Dad in order to become an adult in your marriage goes back centuries. Millennia, in fact. Almost three thousand years ago, some Hebrew writers reported to us a story about our beginnings. This narrative about Adam and Eve—literally, The Man and The Woman—can teach us something that is universally true about our own humanity.

As the story goes, The Man was created out of dust, long before The Woman came along. God saw that The Man was alone, however, so He put him to sleep, took out a rib, and voilà, created The Woman. After waking and seeing his new companion, The Man marveled at God's creation, crying out, "At last! A creature with the same bones and flesh as me!" After chronicling this joy, the narrator then adds a fascinating parenthetical statement. "For *this* reason, every man must leave his mother and father and be joined to his wife as one flesh."

For *what* reason? According to this story, because man and woman were created to join as one, that relationship should take precedence over the parental relationship when the time comes. That's the instruction here. Even thousands of years ago, people recognized the wisdom that leaving behind, and growing beyond, our childhood connections to Mom and Dad is integral to having a successful union as husband and wife.

This doesn't just mean leaving in the literal sense. Leaving your mother and father means leaving behind and growing beyond both the *excuses* and the *resources* of childhood. What do I mean by *excuses*? Becoming an adult means working very hard to overcome the inevitable pains and shortcomings you experienced in childhood. This includes what your parents did or didn't do *to* you, and what your parents did or didn't do *for* you. It also includes all the painful insults on the playground, the broken hearts and scars of adolescence, and yes, for some of you, even the horrors of abuse. All of these experiences have shaped you, and all of these experiences help *explain* who you are. But none of these experiences *excuse* you. If you don't move past these excuses for your immaturity, then you cannot grow into the kind of adult you really want to become—the kind of adult your marriage is *demanding* that you become.

I know that sounds harsh and very direct. You may have experienced an especially traumatic childhood, and you may still be struggling mightily to make sense of it all. I know. I work with clients every week who fight this battle on the way to mature adulthood. It's not easy, but it is doable. And necessary, if you really want to grow your life and your relationships. Especially if you want to connect with your spouse and forge a unique, lasting intimacy.

Leaning on Ourselves

You might be thinking, "Okay, Hal, I get that we should leave behind the excuses, but are you sure we have to walk away from the resources?" I know it sounds strange to advocate leaving behind the resources from childhood and extended family, but allow me to explain what I mean by the term *resources*. See, we all learn coping mechanisms growing up, things we turn to in order to survive all the pains and shortcomings I mentioned above. These resources include seemingly positive efforts, like commiserating with friends, or looking for Mom or Dad or Sister or Grandma to make everything all right. These resources also include the many childish attempts we use to make ourselves feel better, such as running away, fighting back with insults, or turning to alcohol and drugs. If we don't leave behind these kinds of emotional resources, which occasionally served us well in our youth, we'll have a very difficult time creating healthy ones as adults. The same coping skills that worked for you as a child can easily become destructive as an adult. Especially in your marriage. Skills like pouting. Or defensiveness. Or running to family. Or dumping your current job and looking for another one.

I'm reminded of a fascinating conversation I had with a ski instructor a few years ago. Since it was our kids' first time on skis, and since Jenny and I had not been on skis ourselves in many years, we decided to hire a couple of instructors for our first day on the slopes. As it turned out, we hired an actual married couple. While the husband took our kids off to learn the basics, the wife stayed with us. She was a phenomenal instructor and a graceful skier, even though she was seven months' pregnant at the time! We found out that they also had a three-year-old daughter, and, out of curiosity, I asked a question about their little girl on the lift ride up the mountain.

"So, I take it, having two ski instructors for parents, she's already up on skis?"

"Oh, definitely, she's learning quickly," our instructor said.

"Wow. When did you start teaching her?"

"Oh, gosh! We didn't teach her! Any good ski instructor knows that you don't ever try to teach your own kids how to ski."

"Really? How come?" I inquired.

"Well, skiing is hard. Really hard. There is just a natural difficulty to it. And when children encounter this natural difficulty, if their parents are anywhere in sight, they will naturally go to lean on them." At this point she paused and offered some profound wisdom: *"And they will never learn to lean on themselves."* I knew she was an expert on skiing, but I didn't expect her to be an expert on relationships as well.

Some of the biggest mistakes we can make in our marriage stem from never learning to lean on ourselves. Instead, we lean on our parents too much, either by actually calling them after a fight with our spouse, or by using them as a comparison standard to justify our spouse's shortcomings. In the process, we don't learn how to lean on ourselves and our own marriages. And clinging to either the excuses or the resources of childhood and extended family doesn't just prevent us from fully becoming adults; it prevents us from enjoying the kind of deeper connection we crave with our spouse.

Moving Out and Moving On

Like it or not, we learn about relationships from our parents, and we bring whatever we've learned right down the aisle with us when we get married. These relational imprints may seem obvious to us, but we get into trouble when we underestimate how influential these imprints can be. Whether we came from a wonderful loving family that we want to emulate, or a wretched broken family that we wish we could forget, we must deal with this specific fire over and over again or it will consume our relationships. That's because trying to re-create or run away from your past inhibits you from participating in something truly unique with your spouse.

There's a great scene from the 1999 movie *The Story of Us* that perfectly illustrates this principle. Bruce Willis and Michelle Pfeiffer play Ben and Katie Jordan, a couple married for fifteen mostly good years. But they are in the midst of a serious crisis and decide to discuss their marital issues with a therapist. The good doctor tries to explain to the couple how care must be taken when communicating, for oftentimes, each spouse unknowingly brings his or her own family-of-origin into the argument. Ben and Katie brush off the therapist's words until the very next scene. The strained couple is in bed together on the cusp of a very sweet and romantic moment. Suddenly, one seemingly innocent comment by Ben is taken the wrong way by Katie. The camera slowly pans out as she starts to articulate why she is offended and you see that she is not alone on her side of the bed. Just as the therapist said, her parents are lying right there beside her, commenting on everything taking place. Then Ben defends his remarks and the same thing is true for him: His parents are sitting by his side. The marriage bed is holding six people, not two. Both spouses hear everything their spouse says through the filters of their own extended family.

For better or for worse, we all enter our marriages with a unique perspective cultivated through our own families-of-origin. Our extended families shape our beliefs in subjects ranging from gender roles and work ethic to money management and child rearing. Most couples find themselves fighting the same battles over and over again about these important issues without ever realizing how influential their own backgrounds and experiences have been in shaping their points of view. This fire of extended family is a complex and intricate force. It entails incorporating new family members, recognizing and unpacking tons of baggage (most of it tucked away and hidden), creating a brand-new family unit, and then navigating the ripple effects of the choices we make as a couple, both within our new family units and in the ones we grew up in.

Obviously, all of this is incredibly complex, and it involves, in many ways, a lifelong process of moving out of childhood and moving on into adulthood. While there is no one clear way this is done, there are some large emotional steps that are necessary to the process. Like Kübler-Ross's famous stages of grief, these are not meant to be neat, linear processes that one can simply schedule at will. These are complex emotional experiences, after all. But becoming aware of these steps can help us learn to recognize, and even actively participate, in our own growth needs. Here they are:

1. **Disillusionment.** At some point, in order to be able to relate to your parents on an adult level, you have to realize a harsh truth: Your parents weren't perfect. Far from it. Now, for some of you, this was made readily apparent long ago. And you've got some emotional scars to prove it. For others, this is still hard to accept; your instinct to defend them, regardless of their behavior, is still very strong. What you have to learn, however, is that seeing your parents' flaws allows you to see them as people, not pedestals. It is not fair, and certainly not honoring, to elevate one's parents above and beyond reproach. What is honoring is to see our folks as fallible creatures, just like everyone else.

2. **Awareness.** We all must take time to reflect on where we can begin to evaluate all our parents did, all they didn't do, and most importantly, what they cannot do for us now. This isn't a chance to blame them for our own failures, but it is a chance to learn how truly influential our parents have been on our own development. That is truly a remarkable step toward taking ownership over the rest of your life..

3. **Self-confrontation.** Most people can accomplish the first two steps toward adulthood, but they don't press any further. But this next step is perhaps the most challenging and the most important. You have to acknowledge any resentment you have toward your parents and figure out in what ways you are still too needy of them. Staying connected to them by bitterness isn't the kind of connection that you want. In fact, in many ways, it is holding you back.

4. Self-representation. I'm not an advocate of digging through your past only to create another rut. In fact, I think you should only dig until you find something useful, which normally doesn't take very long. Acting like an adult with your parents and addressing the present patterns that you don't like (which usually stem from your past issues with them) is crucial. That can be one scary step for many people, but taking it will do wonders for your self-respect and the respect your spouse—and your extended family—has for you.

5. Forgiveness. Forgiveness is an active process, in which you let your parents off the hook for their failings and recognize that they did the best they could. In forgiving, you seek to be fully reconciled with them and you pursue a new, vibrant adult-to-adult relationship with them. When reconciliation is not possible (either through death or an unwillingness on their part to engage with you), you can still forgive by letting go of your resentment.

Connect the Dots (Making the Outlaws In-laws)

If you'll recall, there are two key elements to consider when dealing with the fire of extended family. The first is to put aside childish behaviors and engage in an adult relationship with your own extended family. The second is to grow up even more and engage in a direct adult relationship with your in-laws. As I mentioned before, these two elements are intricately linked.

Not only does holding on to your childhood make it difficult to create a new family with your spouse, but it also makes it difficult for your spouse to relate to your own parents in an adult manner apart from you. Now, earlier I asserted that these two processes were crucially linked. Well, here's how it works. Each step toward adulthood makes the next step a bit easier, not only for you, but for your spouse as well. As you begin to leave your childhood relationships with Mom and Dad (and your entire extended family), you necessarily begin to establish yourself as your own individual. This makes Mom and Dad less needed, which frees them to be seen as individuals in their own right. This, in turn, makes it easier for your spouse to relate to them directly, rather than only through you. And in doing so, your spouse grows in his own individual maturity, which then smooths the way for him to grow beyond his own childhood relationships with *his* family. These steps certainly aren't easy, but if you're willing to lead your spouse through the heat of this fire, you will be amazed at how much stronger you, and your adult relationships, will become.

What exactly do those steps look like? A good friend of mine entered the fire of extended families very early in his marriage. About three months after the wedding, Steven and his new bride, Leslie, went to her father's house. Upon arriving, they were immediately whisked into the family room, where they were shown all the newly received and framed professional wedding photos. My friend marveled at how beautiful his wife looked in all the pictures, especially the large portrait of her alone in her gown. She also looked lovely in the photos with her extended family. There were probably ten to fifteen framed photos in all, and they were all beautiful. Then he noticed something peculiar. They all had one thing in common.

He was nowhere to be found.

Not one of these expensive, framed photographs from the expensive, elaborate wedding gave any indication that a *marriage* had even taken place. Steven tells this story now without a trace of bruised ego, but that certainly wasn't the case at the time. He was crushed. He was even more upset when he talked to Leslie about it on the way home. He posed a simple question. "Les, did you notice anything strange about *our* wedding pictures?" She was quiet for a moment. When she spoke, it wasn't what Steven wanted to hear. He was hoping for something like, "Yes, I did notice and let me tell you something—my father has some serious explaining to do!"

Instead, he saw his new bride shrug her shoulders and say, "Notice what?"

He was disappointed in her answer, to say the least, but he mustered enough self-control to Calm Down, Grow Up, and Get Closer. He saw a few possible choices in the path before him. He could choose to be angry at his father-in-law for this slight. He could also choose to be angry at his wife for not noticing the oversight in the first place. Or he could choose not to be angry at all. Maybe, just maybe, there was something going on with these photos that had nothing to do with him.

Steven wisely took stock of why he felt put out and what it was that he wanted most. He wanted to be respected by his new in-laws and his new wife. Would whining about it and insisting that she take it up with her parents get him closer to that goal—or further away?

So, as Steven says, "I made a determination. I was married to this woman I loved. I was a part of this family, whether they wanted me or not. I couldn't make my new father-in-law accept me, but I could make it awfully hard for him not to." Instead of putting Leslie in the middle of the situation, or standing toe-to-toe with her father, he decided to forge ahead with this new attitude. He made a sincere effort to get to know this man—outside of his relationship with Leslie. He took him to sporting events and golf outings. He called on occasion simply to catch up. He even made it a point to ask his advice on a few business matters. After a few months, the old man started to soften up. And after a couple of years, he considered Steven a second son. They even got to a place where Steven told him about the picture incident and they spoke about it openly and candidly.

As of this writing, Steven and Leslie have just celebrated ten years of marriage, and each year, on their anniversary, they take a picture of the two of them and send it to her dad as an inside joke between the three of them. Sometimes, Steven just sends him one of himself. Even with a rocky start and some deep-seated issues, this is proof that it's possible to cultivate both a healthy, long, and loving marriage *and* good relationships with your extended families. But you must grasp one crucial lesson: You have to become an adult in both of those relationships. No matter how childish and immature either your spouse, his family, or your family may act, you must rise above the fray and pursue what you want most with the utmost integrity.

Some ScreamFree Tips for the Journey

Admittedly, this issue of leaving and cleaving deserves not only its own book, but its own academic department. And my fear here is that I'm giving you just enough information to be dangerous. With that in mind, I want to break my own rule a bit and give you some very direct tips on making this emotional moving out and moving on as productive a journey as possible.

Be Playful. One way to sabotage your marital relationship when it comes to the fire of extended family is to be defensive and take things too personally. This is especially true when it comes to comments made by your spouse, or your in-laws, about you and/ or your own parents. When it comes to our parents, we can say whatever we want about how frustrating or annoying they can be. But the minute someone outside the family comments about their tics and habits, our protective instincts kick in and we start circling the wagons.

Why is that? Why do we feel the need to defend our extended family at all costs? Are we really that valiant or is there some other reason? Do we think that it says something about us if our parents are criticized? If we have not truly left Mom and Dad, then of course we get riled up. We are still connected by that umbilical cord and it hurts when they are attacked because we are still attached. But if we can get to the place where we feel confident enough in ourselves and secure enough in who we are as individuals, then we can hear things about them and about us a bit more objectively. We can defend them out of love, rather than insecurity, if the situation calls for it.

Now, I'm not advocating holding a parent-bashing party with your spouse. But there will likely come a time when your wife or husband will notice some dynamic about your family that you cannot see. How will you act when he brings it to your attention? Being overly sensitive and defensive about your family-of-origin (or anything for that matter) just isn't helpful. It doesn't do anything for you—in fact, it just keeps you stuck. If you can develop a little thicker skin and more of a sense of humor, you'll be amazed at how free you can feel, even when your partner tells you things that are difficult to hear.

Change Your Vocabulary. Years ago, as our first Christmas in Atlanta approached, Jenny and I were asked a very common question by many of our new friends. They would ask, "So, are you guys going home for the holidays?" They wanted to know if we were staying in Atlanta or going to Texas in order to see extended family. An innocent question, mind you. But pay attention to the way they worded it: "Home" is wherever your parents are or wherever your extended family resides, or wherever you called home as a child.

But Jenny and I felt (and still do) that if "home" meant someplace other than our current location, then that would imply that we hadn't really ever left our childhoods behind. If "family" meant something other than our immediate configuration of Hal, Jenny, Hannah, and Brandon, then that would mean that our hearts, and our priorities, lay elsewhere. So, we answered these friends, "No, we as a family are *leaving* home to go and see extended family in Texas." If you think this is just semantics, you're missing the point. Home is not someplace we long for, many miles and memories away; home is *wherever* we reside *together*. Family is not the separate lineages we hail from; family is first and foremost the new creation we're forming together. We have to think this way in order for ourselves, and our kids, to become full individuals on our own.

Redefine Respect and Loyalty. Whenever I lead people through this material, I usually get some pushback at this point. The idea of "leaving" Mom and Dad, addressing issues with them directly, or watching our spouse address them, is just downright offensive to some. I remember one client who could not stand the idea of recognizing his parents as anything other than saints. He likened my questions about this to some sort of "character assassination." Of course, it was easy for him to recognize his wife's family's faults; they were "clearly in need of some psychiatric help." But his own family? Never. They were perfect. Never mind the fact that both his wife and I had no trouble spotting his dysfunctional family-of-origin issues, which, as you might have guessed, stemmed from his "saintly" parents.

My response to this resistance is always the same: Redefine what it means to respect and honor your parents. Is it more respectful to let your or your spouse's resentments build up toward your parents in silence while your marriage bears the scars? Or is it more respectful to treat your parents like fallible, yet responsible, adults capable of handling and growing in their own right? I think what most people mean when they say they respect their parents too much to confront them is that they *fear* their parents too much to confront them. And they fear what such a confrontation may say about themselves as "respectful" children. The problem I usually see is that people allow this situation to build up to something so large that to address it feels insurmountable. I hear you. I'm not saying this is easy. In fact, it may be among the most difficult emotional journeys you will ever take. But I cannot encourage you enough to consciously explore what it would be like to place loyalty to your principles and your marriage above loyalty to members of your extended family. Principles are more important than people. Loyalty to principles means that your behavior is governed by something far larger than other people's opinions, whims, and insecurities, including your own. Loyalty to principles makes it possible for you to discover a new level of maturity that inspires others to join you—even the parent you think could never handle confrontation.

the**lab**

You might be saying to yourself that the ideas in this extended family chapter are easier said than done. And you'd be right. But here's the truth: *Everything* is easier said than done. Doing this "adult" stuff is hard work. It's uncomfortable, it's painful, and it's messy. But it is also vital to the health and happiness of your marriage. Jenny and I know how hard this is—we've had plenty of practice with our own families. Since both of our parents divorced long ago, we've had the . . . privilege . . . of forging adult relationships with *four* sets of parents-in-law instead of two. And we've found one thing to be absolutely certain. You have to leave childhood relationships with your family in order to pursue adult relationships with them. These relationships are characterized by mutual respect, an ability to confront one another, praise one another, give space to one another, and forgive one another. Then, and only then, will you be able to achieve a level of closeness with your *spouse* that you never dreamed possible.

In this lab, we're going to take a look at Brent and Jenna, a couple struggling with these very issues. Read their story carefully and then see how you could help Brent apply the formula in the midst of this fire.

The Setup: Brent met Jenna at an office party soon after college and knew immediately that she was right for him. His mother, Betty, wasn't so sure. From the moment that he brought Jenna home, it was obvious that the two strong women did not see eye-to-eye. Even after four years of marriage, Mom still hadn't really accepted his bride, and she didn't do much to hide that fact. Jenna really made an effort to reach out to her mother-in-law, but not much progress was ever made. This frustrated Jenna, but what truly angered her was how Brent refused to accept that his mom was anything but perfect. He'd always make excuses for her complaining and overbearing presence by saying, "She just cares about us—that's all. Give her a break."

About a year ago, things got even more tense. The young couple had their first child, a beautiful baby boy named Christopher. It was the third grandchild for Jenna's parents, but the first for Brent's. And ever since Christopher was born, the relationship between Jenna and Betty deteriorated further. Each time Betty visited, she literally shoved her way past Jenna to get to the baby, making snide comments about Jenna's lack of experience as a mother. Invariably, Jenna got hurt, lashed out at Betty, and then complained to Brent. Before he knew it, he was defending his mother to his wife and vice versa yet again. Brent was at wit's end. The two women he loved most in the world just couldn't seem to get along, despite all his efforts to keep the peace. In fact, it seemed as if the harder he tried to get them to see eye-to-eye, the bigger the rift became. Many days, he just wanted to get away from it all. He found himself spending more and more time at the office, even though he adored his time with his new son.

OK, now it's your turn to take Brent through the formula to see if you can help him find a way out of this dilemma before he checks out altogether.

CALM DOWN

Pause Yourself:

How might Brent detach himself from the triangle between his mother and his wife long enough to just stop and think?

Go to the Balcony:

How might Brent gain some objectivity on the situation, and what are some possible patterns he may discover?

GROW UP

Spot Your Pattern:

With his pause and objectivity, what might Brent learn about his active, or passive, contributions to these patterns?

Step on the Scale:

Why does reducing this tension between the two women in his life mean so much to him? What does he want most here?

GET CLOSER

Show Your Cards:

How may Brent calmly confess his newfound knowledge about his role in all this, both to his wife *and* to his mother, and how might he also show what he wants most with each and all of them?

Champion Your Spouse:

How could Brent welcome both Jenna's and Betty's input, communicating clearly that he longs to know their honest concerns and truest desires?

REPEAT

So what do you think would happen next? How might Brent, after hearing from both Jenna and Betty, have to repeat the formula with both his wife and his mother?

Now that you've had a chance to pause and reflect from Brent's point of view, let's compare notes on possible applications of the ASR formula.

CALM DOWN

Pause Yourself: Instead of allowing the pressure he felt to creep up on him, Brent decided to be proactive about taking intentional retreats from his house of horrors. He developed the habit of taking his son on a quick walk in his neighborhood right after work to clear his head (and do a little male bonding). He took this chance to pause before he got caught up in the emotion of the moment. If he didn't take time for these retreats, he would have continued to feel the need to escape the situation, which never helped anything in the long run.

Go to the Balcony: From above, without either Jenna or Betty in his face, Brent could start to sort out what was really going on. He could clear his head and recognize that his stress was not caused by these women or their conflict. It was caused by the fact that he felt responsible for solving their issues. He felt caught between the two of them and stuck in his role of peacemaker. He felt as if, no matter whose side he took, he would get into trouble . . . and the thing he hated more than anything was for someone to be angry at or disappointed in him.

GROW UP

Spot Your Pattern: Brent was doing two things that kept him stuck in the very position he hates. First, Brent was refusing to "leave and cleave." Brent thought he had good intentions when he would defend his mother to Jenna. In his mind, he was honoring his mother, but when he took a long, hard look at his pattern, he saw that he was more concerned about gaining his mother's approval than he was in truly honoring her. His fear had gotten in the way of really leaving home and creating a family of his own. And his fear of Mom's disapproval created real (and deserved) disapproval from the one he had pledged the rest of his life to, his wife. He had not done a good job of shifting his primary loyalty to Jenna, and everyone was now suffering because of it.

Secondly, Brent was playing peacemaker. There was a game of human tug-of-war going on between Jenna and Betty that had more to do with Brent than it did with anything personal between the women. No wonder Brent's nerves felt frayed. By trying to make sure that everyone was happy, he ensured that no one was. It's not his job to fix Jenna and Betty's relationship. It is his job to support his wife publicly, and then privately encourage her to solve her own problem with Betty.

Step on the Scale: Brent was ready to face his part of the problem and do something about it. He started with the first tough question, "What's the meaning behind my actions? Why am I allowing myself to be the rope in this tug-of-war?" He could now see that he felt the pressure of trying to honor his mother while at the same time pleasing and supporting his wife. In this instance, those two desires felt incompatible. He feared appearing ungrateful to his mother if he supported his wife, and he feared appearing unloving to his wife if he sided with his mother.

What Brent wanted most, when he really thought about it, was for all of them—himself included—to act like adults. It was easy to see that Betty and Jenna were acting a bit childish, but now that he was looking closely at himself, he could see that he was the one acting the most immature. He had yet to move past his role as Betty's child, and then he wondered why Jenna sometimes also treated him like a little boy. He now knows that in order to have a happy marriage, he has to establish his relationship with Jenna as a priority above his mother.

GET CLOSER

Show Your Cards: Brent's first step was toward his wife. He apologized to her for choosing his own sense of false security over her. He hated for anyone to be angry with him and, ironically, that fear is what is created all this drama. He went to Jenna and said, "I have not done a good job of growing up and for that, I am sorry. My primary family is you and Christopher and I don't want to do anything more to jeopardize that. I have allowed my own fear of being the bad guy to my mother to get in the way of that. I'd love to know what you think about all of this and how my playing referee has affected you."

Champion Your Spouse: This time, when Jenna decided to open up to her husband about Betty, he welcomed it. Jenna said that when Betty basically pushed her out of the way around Christopher and Brent did nothing about it, she felt as if he had "chosen your mother over me." Brent heard his wife's pain, without defending himself or his mother, and he encouraged Jenna to say more. He worked very hard to keep his cool and to maintain a sense of humor about the whole thing. After all, Betty's annoying actions did not reflect on him. He and Jenna even had a laugh or two about Betty's tendency to literally push Jenna aside when she came to see Christopher, and they decided to use the code word "Elbows" whenever they saw her doing it, out of solidarity. After their conversation, they could be amused by the situation, rather than upset by it.

REPEAT

Brent still had more work to do. It is one thing to tell Jenna that he will value her more, but it is quite another to put his words into practice. So, he sat down with his mother and told her plainly, "Mom, I really appreciate your help and wisdom, especially when it comes to Christopher. You obviously have done this before and I happen to think you did a great job. I also recognize that the only way that Jenna and I are going to become as wise and experienced as you one day is if we're allowed to do more on our own. I know that's hard for you to watch, but I really think that's how you can help us the most."

He didn't address all her critical comments or rude remarks, but he did take the first step in seeing himself as an adult in relation to his mother. And this step opened the door for many further conversations between the two of them in the years to come.

Follow up—Brent and Jenna recently reported to me that soon after applying this formula, they both started relaxing a little around "Elbows," who, in response to their relaxed attitude, calmed down quite a bit herself. To this day, Jenna and Brent can laugh about those early days without either one of them feeling defensive or resentful.

Chapter 6

This Mess Is a Place!

[The Fire of Household Management]

Housework, if it is done right, can kill you.
— JOHN SKOW

*It is physically impossible to French-kiss a man who leaves a new
roll of toilet paper resting on top of the empty cardboard roll.
Does he not see it? DOES HE NOT SEE IT?*
— RITA WILSON AS RACHEL IN *THE STORY OF US*

Let's face it, folks. Housework stinks. I mean, it really, really
does. I know I'm a guy, and I know I'm a youngest child, so my
disdain for keeping up the household makes perfect stereotypical
sense. I'm *supposed* to hate housework, unless it has something
to do with the garage or the yard. But I don't even like that stuff,
either.

And I'm guessing that, regardless of your gender, you don't
like doing housework, either. It's annoying, exhausting, and never-
ending, and it seems so trivial in light of the bigger concerns of
life. Yet despite how trivial doing the dishes or mowing the yard
can seem, the little tasks of household management can be a
huge point of contention between spouses.

Of all the fires we're talking about, the fire of household man-agement may seem to be the least important. After all, how can something as ordinary as grocery shopping and picking up after yourself possibly compare to the intricacies of extended family dynamics or the excitement of scream-filled sex? It can't. Which is precisely why it needs your attention.

See, it is often the little things, which build up over time, that cause the most damage. Dale Carnegie tells a story in his classic book *How to Stop Worrying and Start Living* about a four-hundred-year-old tree. This tree had been struck by lightning on fourteen different occasions, and had managed to survive each blast. It seemed that nothing could topple this steadfast giant. So the townspeople were shocked and saddened when the tree, seemingly out of nowhere, grew sick and just died. What was it that finally felled the mighty tree? Beetles. An army of tiny bee-tles, each one small enough to crush between two fingers, had attacked it over a number of years from the inside out and killed the once-strong beauty.

I believe that there is no other area in your marriage more prone to this same kind of destruction than household manage-ment. Tiny slights, perceived imbalances, and gender-based dou-ble standards, all coming together over time, form an army of resentment that can bring your marriage down as much as "big crises," such as abuse or affairs.

And this is now more true than ever. Despite incredible ad-vances toward the equality of men and women around the globe, there is still proof, in study after study, that married women do far more housework than their husbands. And this is true regardless of whether the woman works outside the home. It's even true for women who work more hours or even make more money than their men. So not only is there an army of resentment growing within these women, there is a growing army of women uniting their resentments into a movement.

Thus, this fire warrants our attention. It has all the potential to rot your marriage from the inside out. And my guess is, such rotting may have already begun. So that means we had better begin as well.

Our Attempted Solutions

First, a disclaimer. I'm not going to talk to you about dividing chores equally or agreeing to a set schedule of duties. There are plenty of books out there that can help you become more efficient or more effective in your cooking or cleaning, if that's what you're really after. What I'm here to do is far less tactical, but much more insightful. I'm here to show you how the fire of household management can actually help you see yourself and your spouse in a whole new light. A new light that makes cooking, cleaning, and any other task feel less like a chore and more like a labor of love.

Besides, those agreements we forge when we first get married, those neat little arrangements about who does what and when . . . well, they just don't work. And you know it. Despite their clear rationale, and seemingly indestructible logic, our best-laid plans for keeping the mice away and balancing the chores done by husband and wife never really pan out.

Here's why. In the heat of a fire, this fire of household management, the couple has to make decisions. These decisions are important, and they can dramatically affect both spouses and those around them. The home—inside and out—has to be taken care of, for instance. Certain tasks have to be completed in order for family life to run smoothly. The bills have to be paid. The bathrooms have to be disinfected. The family calendar has to be updated and clearly communicated.

In the midst of all these important decisions comes friction— friction between the desires, aptitudes, standards, histories, and expectations of two separate individuals. One partner likes a spot-less kitchen, the other likes an error-free checkbook. One is more skilled at planning, the other more skilled at execution. One grew up in a dust-free home, the other in a dander-filled animal haven. There's nothing like marriage for these two backgrounds to clash into one another. No wonder it gets heated!* Where there's fric-tion, there's always fire.

And there are three main ways we end up trying to dampen this fire.

1. The Best-Laid Plans

One way of trying to dampen this fire is the mutually agreed-upon business agreement. One partner takes more responsibility in one particular area of the relationship, and the other partner does more in another. It all ends up balanced in a fair way, one that makes sense, given the couple's current situation.

Now, sometimes, we believe that this is a rational, workable solution. Sometimes we mete out duties by perceived aptitude. "You take the finances, because you're better with numbers. I'll take the laundry, 'cause I actually know how to keep lights and darks separate." Or, we ration out the duties according to sched-ules. "I'll cook on workdays, and you take over the weekends. On

---

*Here's one example: Whenever I return from a long business trip and try to insert myself into the routine, Jenny almost always confesses in frustration, "I know you're just trying to help, but now that we've settled into a routine, I think it was easier when you were gone!" Of course, she means it, and she doesn't. It is easier to make unilateral decisions about household management, but it's a lot harder to execute those decisions. So she does want me home as her partner. But inviting me back into full involvement is always difficult. You can just imagine how difficult it is for military families trying to reacclimate after one spouse is gone for a year or more. I've had the privilege of working with military families all over the world, and they can teach us all about the difficulties of reintegration, the necessity of self-representation, and the pos-sibilities of two individuals working together in a shared household.

days you work late, I'll get up and make breakfast for the kids. Then you can take over dinner and bedtime the next night."

These are all the little processes we try to go through to cool down the heat of this fire, and settle on some workable solutions. And we think, especially early in our unions, that there's no reason this shouldn't work. Sadly, however, these solutions rarely do work, at least not for very long. And you probably know this on a personal, experiential level. Perhaps you've said this to yourself: "Things would go so smoothly if she would just let me take care of the books on my own." Or maybe something like this: "I am so tired of holding up my end of this deal while he always seems to have an excuse for not doing his."

So despite the surface logic of these arrangements, they continually fail. Here's why:

A. You are not an organization in an office, you are a family in a home. You cannot operate based on carefully matched skill sets, according to clearly designated organization charts. Those arrangements are based on the premise of a clear set of understood, and legal, expectations. In a company, anyone can always be removed and replaced. As a family, you must live together as people brought together by intense emotions, ridiculously loyal commitments, and even shared biology. And while the removal of someone is possible, it is less like a firing and more like a surgery. We are not simple machines and gears, working together toward a goal of increased efficiency and productivity. We are men and women, living together as a way to feed one another's souls and create a warm home that is anything but mechanical and operational.

B. There is no such thing as perfect equality, or perfectly mutual cooperation. Neat operational arrangements only work if they are perceived as equal and mutual. This means that: (1) the duties and obligations had better be divided up perfectly to suit both partners' expectations, and (2) the arrangement is only as strong as the perceived mutual cooperation. If one person feels slighted in any way, the beetles of resentment start to feed. "This is a partnership! I'm doing more than my share! Why do I seem to be the only one who cares about this mess?" You might fend off these beetles with justifications and little compromises for a while. But not for long.

C. These arrangements discourage mutual input, and ultimately personal growth. When originally designated, these roles and tasks feel consistent with the perceived aptitudes, habits, and preferences of each partner. But what happens when one partner wants to get more involved in an area different from her previously designated role? Let's say the husband wants to learn more about and have more input into the couple's family schedule. As he starts to ask his superorganized wife about carpooling, she begins to feel a bit threatened: "Look, I don't question the way you do the yard. Don't you trust me?" Or, let's say the less financially savvy wife happens to open a credit card statement to find a shockingly high balance. Is she supposed to leave it alone because it's not her agreed-upon area of expertise? Even though these financial habits dramatically affect her life? What if she really wants to grow up and play a stronger role in her own financial future?

D. Such arrangements do not adapt well to changing circumstances. See if these scenarios sound familiar. A man loses his job, and he's out of work for six months. His wife is still working full time, but their agreed-upon roles and tasks don't seem to change. Sure, he's home more, but that just creates more work for her, since he now makes more of a mess!

Or let's say a woman decides to stay at home after she has a baby. The man agrees to bear the sole burden of financially supporting the family for a few years. But as his hours and her days get longer, and both their nights get shorter with a crying baby, they both develop unspoken expectations about who is now supposed to do the cooking and cleaning and yardwork. Sure, friends and family tell them to relax their standards during this tough time, but all this stuff still has to get done eventually, right?

2. The Overresponsible/Underresponsible Dynamic

The second way couples end up trying to cool the fire of household management is by unwittingly falling into a very common, but very dangerous dynamic. Here one partner begins to take on too much of the responsibility for maintaining the home, and the other partner "cooperates" by doing too little. And the more the responsible one does, the less the other has to do.

In therapeutic terms, this is called the overresponsible/ underresponsible dynamic, and it's remarkably prevalent in marriages. It's one of the five ways couples "scream" at each other.* That's because these patterns develop as a way to alleviate the anxiety of the friction we spoke of earlier. Usually, they are filled with bitter resentments and back-and-forth periods of explosive arguing and cold distance. Sometimes, however, couples just accommodate to it: "Let's just do it this way, so we don't have to keep negotiating and arguing about who does what, and who likes it this or that way." Check out this quote from a woman attending one of our ScreamFree Marriage seminars:

Hal, I've been married for twenty-four years and I keep my husband as far away from housework as humanly

---

*You can read more about the over/underresponsible dynamic in Appendix A at the end of the book.

possible. He has ruined too many loads of laundry mixing colors, broken too many dishes "helping out" after dinner, doesn't know how to turn on the vacuum cleaner, and his idea of cleaning something is scary. His idea of cooking is to toast a muffin or open a can of soup . . . What can I say? I think it just works better for us this way.

You can imagine that she was none too pleased when I explained to her that, as a kid, I *intentionally* broke a few dishes and burned a few meals in order to demonstrate my incompetence in the household arena. But my mom didn't buy it, unlike this woman, who, one could argue, was definitely acting like a mother to her husband. And that's why I questioned her further about whether such a conflict-avoidant solution really did "work better," as she professed. Turns out that while the woman had accommodated to this situation, her marriage was not well suited to grow toward the intimacy she craved. She was royally ticked at her husband for allowing this arrangement to go on, and royally ticked at herself for trying to justify it all these years as simply "what works best." Even more aggravating, she was beginning to recognize what had been missing from their relationship all these years: connection. Mothers and their sons simply cannot experience the connection offered in true marriage.

That's why the over/under dynamic doesn't really work for anybody. Anytime our patterns are driven by the anxiety of facing a potential conflict, we're not rationally choosing—we're reactively "screaming." And, as we've learned throughout this book, whenever we scream, we create the very outcomes we were hoping to avoid. Making up for one partner's incompetence or immaturity may help you avoid arguments in the short term, but it only serves to create even worse dynamics in the process, dynamics that can ruin any chance of true connection.

As we stated earlier, the more the "responsible one" picks up the slack, the less likely the "slacker" will ever step up his game. Thus, the cycle continues. But then it gets worse. The overresponsible one doesn't just assume responsibility for the task at hand, be it balancing the checkbook, doing the laundry, or cleaning the dishes. As the cycle continues, the overresponsible one assumes responsibility for *getting* the underresponsible guy's butt in gear. You can definitely see where this is headed. It's headed to a constant battle on Sunday mornings before church, with a nagging wife trying to rouse a slothful husband to at least "help" her get their two kids ready.

3. The Gender Wars

The third way couples attempt to quell the fire of household management is to simply default back into traditional stereotypical roles. Perhaps more than any other fire, the fire of household management sets the stage for a firefight between the sexes. Thus, I believe it invites an examination of these stereotypes.

Husbands in our culture are commonly portrayed as overweight, blundering imbeciles who passively plod around the house like overgrown children. This image is so pervasive that you're probably thinking right now, "How is that a *portrayal?* Sounds pretty accurate to me!" And yet, despite scores of responsible men who defy this stigma, the portrayed stereotype prevails. Think Papa Bear from the *Berenstain Bears,* Homer from *The Simpsons,* or any character played by Jim Belushi. Think about every beer commercial, and every commercially successful family comedy. According to these images, men do not, on their own, clean up the house. They do not clean up after themselves. Very often, they don't even clean themselves!

Their female counterparts, on the other hand, have their own stereotype to combat. Wives are far too often seen as sexless, martyred nags who necessarily carry the heavy load at home. They are the responsible ones, responsible for running the whole household. They always clean up after themselves, and they routinely clean up after their kids. And, yes, resentfully, they even clean up after their husbands.

These stereotypes are powerful, pervasive, and persuasive. They can tempt you to quench this fire of conflict with a ready-made solution, before even properly diagnosing the problem. Check out this excerpt from a relationship website, which will remain nameless, advertising *the* "cure for home-related arguments" between spouses. As you'll see, it taps into the dynamics mentioned above. It reads:

> Ladies, this is the perfect solution to get your man to help out around the house. It is simple. Your man picks a card and then does what is on the card (very easy and lots of fun!). It could be a chore, a chance to play golf, get out of the doghouse for FREE, or a night with the boys. Here are some actual cards from the deck:
>
> "You've been great this week. So you get to plan a date night. Don't forget to hire a babysitter!"
>
> "Snookums, when you bring a drink into the den tonight . . . Don't forget to bring it into the kitchen when you are finished . . . and use a coaster!"
>
> "Clean the bathroom . . . NOW!"

Sounds like loads of fun to me. For the record, ladies, I don't know a man in his right mind who would respond well to this tactic. Not if you want him to actually remain a man. But before we just dismiss it outright, let's take a moment to examine this a bit further and see what kinds of faulty assumptions this marketer is asking you to accept. Here's what the ad leads us to believe:

1. Women are the only ones who care about household matters.

2. Men don't jointly participate in chores, they "help" the woman keep *her* house.

3. Women must trick men into doing housework with gamesmanship and manipulation.

4. Men must get permission to do something fun and must be told what to do otherwise.

5. Women (literally) hold all the cards at home.

Now, hopefully, this does not sound exactly like your marriage. But if you're at all like the vast majority of couples I work with, then you're probably not that far off. As much as I hate to admit it, these gender stereotypes exist for a reason. All stereotypes do. There are usually elements of truth to them at some level; otherwise, they wouldn't persist. But while seeing men and women in this light is easy, it isn't very helpful. And I can guarantee you one thing: If you allow the idea of this stereotype to color the way you see your spouse, you are actually creating a self-fulfilling prophecy. But if you're able to Calm Down enough to confront these stereotypes, and Grow Up enough to see the real dynamics behind them, then I wholeheartedly believe that you can actually Get Closer through this whole mess.

Come along and eavesdrop with me on a conversation I heard just this week.

No One Is Ever Always Anything

The other day, I was sitting in my favorite coffee shop near a couple I assumed were married. The woman, dressed to the nines, placed her briefcase down and pulled out a stack of papers neatly folded. Meanwhile, the man, in a sweatshirt and sneakers, slumped down into his chair across from her. After ordering their coffee, they began to chat. Turns out they were a married couple and they were in the process of building a house together. They were at the coffee shop waiting for the general contractor to join them.

Once the contractor arrived, the wife laid out the house plans, and went through her checklist of items. The contractor, in turn, had his own set of questions, which the wife answered as best she could. I didn't pay much attention to what they were saying, but after a while I couldn't help but notice one interesting fact. The husband had yet to open his mouth. He was still sitting in the same slouched position with the same blank look on his face. Not once in this meeting did the man offer an opinion. Not once did he even speak! Right in front of him, huge decisions were being made about his home, and he couldn't have looked less interested if he'd tried.

Now, here's where the over/underresponsible dynamic mixes with the gender stereotypes we've been talking about. According to the stereotypes, the husband is the underresponsible one. In our case at the coffee shop, our "laid-back" husband doesn't participate much in the house-building plans because his "type A" wife has it all under control. Of course, he probably feels a great deal of unspoken resentment about everything he does to make their home life possible, which goes unrecognized.

From the wife's point of view, however, she probably feels that if she didn't shoulder the burden, nothing would ever get done! Likewise, she probably feels a great deal of resentment about having to make all the decisions all the time, because, according to their script, he simply shrugs his shoulders and says, "Whatever you like." Like Eddie Murphy's subservient African bride in *Coming to America.*

All these sentiments echo across homes everywhere, with couples believing this is just the way things are between men and women. Our sitcoms say so, our comedians say so, and even some of the most popular marriage experts in the world say so.

But this is where the ScreamFree Marriage formula comes in, and why it can help so dramatically. By first resolving to Calm Down, we can see that these stereotypes, while having the appearance of reality, are just a reaction. They are an emotional reaction to the continual friction of this fire of household management (and many other fires, too). And as an emotional reaction, these stereotypes are actually doomed to backfire, creating the very outcomes we were hoping to avoid.

For instance, ever wonder why your "lazy husband" doesn't do enough around the house? Well, you just said it—he can't, *he's too lazy.* He's a husband, after all. You married a man—what do you expect? Or, for you men, ever wonder why your "nagging wife" is always complaining and trying to get you to do more cleaning? Well, you just said it—*she's a nagging wife;* she's just doing what she's supposed to do.

See, left unquestioned, these gender stereotypes grow into full-blown stories about our lives that have already been scripted out. There is no changing anything because these are grounded in history, in biology, in our own family legacies, and our own marriage experiences thus far.

Without confronting these stereotypes, we just perpetuate them. And they simply become the blueprints of our marriages. But as we Calm Down, pausing ourselves enough to go to the balcony, we can see that the first step is to confront these stereotypes with one undeniable truth: No one is ever always anything. Let me say that again. *No one is ever . . . always . . . anything.* No one is ever always lazy, no one is ever always hardworking. No one is ever always late, no one is ever always punctual. No one is ever always responsible, no one is ever always a lazy, slothful, ungrateful slob.

Is it true that your husband *always* breaks the dishes or burns dinner? Really true? Always? Is it true that your wife *never*

appreciates all the things you do accomplish around the house? Really true? Never? Yes, there are tendencies that point us toward blanket statements about men and women in general. Yes, there are scores of personal examples you can come up with to make your point about your spouse in particular. But whenever we use absolute language (*always, never, completely, at all*), it is a telltale sign that we would rather complain about the lie than change according to the truth.

But if you believe you're ready to grow up in this fire, then you're ready to take the next step in confronting these gender stereotypes. You're ready to recognize that without shared household ownership, there will never be shared household management.

Whose Home Is It Anyway?

Let's go back to the couple next to me in the coffee shop. Obviously, I don't know them. But given what I've seen thus far, and given my arrogance about these things,* I believe I can accurately read the situation. And it's actually very instructive for us all.

The real reason this man isn't very involved in building this house is the same reason he probably won't be very involved in its management. And the reason this woman is so dominant in the building of the house is the same reason she will feel most responsible for its upkeep.

What is this reason? What is this magical key that unlocks the mystery of the fire of household management?

It's *her* house.

No, I'm not talking legally; I'm talking emotionally and relationally. It's her house, it's her home, and they have implicitly agreed on this, even if they both would explicitly deny it. Like the rest of us, this couple has been taught from their very earliest

---

*Jenny insisted I add this line.

days as a couple that most aspects of the relationship are hers to own. Think about it. What was this guy, and every other guy, told about their wedding day?

"It's *her* day."

Jerry Seinfeld makes a great joke about this, explaining that this is why grooms and groomsmen are dressed so much alike. If one doesn't work out for any reason, then the next one can just slide into place. "After all, the groom is just furniture in this extravaganza."

So our coffee-shop guy, like so many husbands, started off his union with his wife by limiting his input into or preferences for anything that involved both of them. Since then, they've both been told that letting a wife have whatever she wants is the only way to a peaceful living arrangement. This is not because she's type A; this is just because she's a woman. She needs to nest . . . or, she needs to feel secure in her surroundings, or whatever. And if a husband wants just the slightest bit of peace and harmony, then he just needs to "yes-dear" his wife all the way through the home-building process. After all, "If Momma ain't happy, then no one's happy."

So it's *her* kitchen, to arrange as she sees fit (because, of course, it's assumed that she'll do all the cooking). And it's *her* living room to arrange as she sees fit (because, of course, she'll be the one staying at home and being responsible for any entertaining). And, of course, it's *her* bedroom to decorate as she sees fit, including all fifty-six throw pillows on top of the bed (because, of course, if she has to sleep with this slob, she at least needs to feel as comfortable as possible).

All of which makes it *her* job to make sure it all gets managed. This is why, whenever a wife does allow her resentment to come to the surface, she ends up asking her husband to *help* her around the house. "Do you think you could *help* me with the kitchen tonight?" Or, "Could you at least *help* me a little by picking up your socks and shoes?" Or, finally, "I don't ask for much, just a little

help now and then." By asking in this way, the wife recognizes and even accepts that household management is *her* job, and anything her husband does is just a matter of assisting her. When he does housework, he's performing a noble gesture; when she does it, she is simply doing her duty.

But what about outside the house? What about the garage? Doesn't the husband traditionally consider these areas his domains? Well, in some ways, yes. But we must consider two trends that are wreaking havoc with this traditional form of balancing out the division of labor. (1) With the urbanization of the population yards and gardens are shrinking dramatically, thereby reducing the area the man traditionally owns and manages; and (2) with increased work hours and increased work travel, husbands are doing less yardwork than ever before. This trend has been promoted by the growth of relatively cheap immigrant labor. These trends have led to an increase in the perceived inequality between the sexes, and thereby an increased resentment among wives across the nation.

Now, I'm not saying that anyone really enjoys this setup. Quite the contrary: Most wives *and* husbands are fed up with this situation. But the problem is, of course, that they keep looking at the other person as the problem:

"I can't get him to do anything around here."

"She doesn't appreciate the things I do to make our home life possible."

"He just doesn't care about the house as much as I do, and I get really tired of being the only one who cares."

"She wants me to help, but whenever I do she criticizes me for not doing it her way."

When you decide to Calm Down and Grow Up, you can begin to take the focus off your spouse and begin to see the real culprit behind this situation. The real culprit here is not to be found in our gender differences, or in some faulty personality traits. I believe the real culprit behind any unequal sharing of household *management* is an unequal sharing of household *ownership*. Simply put, we will not move anywhere near an equal share of the caring and cleaning until we challenge these stereotypical assumptions about whose home it really is. As long as we all buy into the assumption that it's really the woman's place, then we cannot be surprised that managing that place will always feel like her responsibility.

And, therefore, the man will usually lag behind her in the care and cleaning of the home. Why? Because it is a simple fact of human nature that we do not maintain things we borrow or receive as much as things we buy and own. Remember how you kept the car Mom and Dad let you drive in high school? How messy and dirty was it compared to the first car you bought with your own money? Or think about this: Would you rather own a house on a street where all the other residents owned their home, or on a street full of rental houses? People just naturally care more for things and places they own. Especially for something as personal as a home.

So what am I saying? That women not only need to allow, but actually invite their husband's input in the design and development of their home life? Well, yes, I am saying exactly that. What else? That men need to speak up and take a more active role in decorating and running the house? Absolutely, yes, I am saying that as well. But I am also saying much more than that, to both wives and husbands.

But What Do I Do?

But before I do say much more, I want to give you a chance to speak. If you've stuck with me through this chapter thus far, you're probably ready for some clear direction. You may be thinking, "Yeah, Hal, that's exactly what I'm looking for. You've told me all the ways and reasons we struggle in this fire, but what do I do now? The dishes still need to be done! The yard needs mowing! Mail delivery needs to be stopped during our vacation! The guest-room needs to be decorated! These socks ain't gonna clean them-selves! And since I'm the only one who notices all these things, I'm probably gonna be the one to do 'em!"

Thank you for your patience thus far, and thank you for voic-ing your concern. I hear you. And yes, you're right. All that nasty housework needs to get done if you're actually going to enjoy your physical environment. So it begs a question: If the nice and neat operational arrangements don't work, and our over/underrespon-sible patterns don't work, and our gender-based stereotypes don't work, what does? What could possibly undo all the harmful lies, reverse all the negative patterns, and put in place a new pattern of shared responsibility in the running of your home?

Calming Down, Growing Up, and Getting Closer.

Both wives and husbands can change the entire dance around this fire by simply following the formula in the midst of this heat. That's the only way to break the generational and stereotypical cycles wreaking havoc in your marriage. That's the only way to begin with a new frame of vision, capable of seeing lies and patterns for what they are, and then confronting your own participation in the very patterns you complain about. It's also the only way you can really hear the clear direction I'm about to give you.

A Clear Directive to Wives

Wives, you absolutely need to stop acting like martyr homemak-ers, passive-aggressively *asking your husband for help*. This puts him in a no-win situation. See, if he says, "No, I don't want to," for whatever reason, then he's obviously a jerk. You're not asking him for much, after all, and he's just an ungrateful pig, right? If he says Yes to your request for help, however, and he goes ahead and does the cooking for a change, then he's still in a no-win situation. Why? Because you're still resentful that you had to ask in the first place! You wish he would volunteer to do the cooking because he notices, on his own, that meals don't just appear out of thin air. If he just does it when you ask him to, then it simply reinforces the very problem that's making you resentful in the first place.

Well, ladies, if you want your husband to care about the upkeep of the house, as much as you do, then you need to start telling him openly what your expectations are. This is not a request from a boss to an assistant, and this is not a chore list from a mommy to a child. This is a self-representation of what you want and what you expect. And it comes only after you've gone through a careful process of Calming Down and Growing Up. You've paused yourself enough to confront the lies of perfect equality and gender stereotypes. You've grown up enough to recognize that you've participated in those lies without even knowing it, and therefore you've actually created the gender-based ownership structure you're now complaining about. Now is the time to Get Closer by showing your cards and letting your husband know what housekeeping you want to do yourself, what you would like to see him do, and how his action or inaction affects you on a personal level.

So what might this look like? Let me tell you a quick story. At one point in our marriage, Jenny began to routinely get on me about not making the bed. Sure, sometimes I would make it, but not very often. There actually was a reason for this bad habit of mine, but I wasn't aware of it at the time. I was just, in my conscious mind, and in my words to Jenny, "forgetting" to do it. Well, this obviously didn't suit Jenny very well, and she would continue to nag me about it. Until one day she did something re-markably different. That morning, after sharing our coffee down-stairs, Jenny ventured back up to our bedroom to get something and saw that I had "forgotten" to make the bed again. I wasn't aware of her discovery until a little while later, when she came back downstairs. At that time, she came up to me and proclaimed in a very even tone:

> Just so you know, Honey, I need to tell you something. When you forget to make the bed in the morning, especially when you are the last one to get up, it makes it much harder for me to want to climb back into that bed with you later that night.

Suddenly, I was a lot more interested, for my own personal reasons, in making the bed. She did not ask me to make the bed. She did not tell me to make the bed . . . or else. She simply, and calmly, represented herself, her preference, and her feelings toward me as a wife. And then she walked away. She did not wait around for my response, because my response was not what she was interested in. She was interested in representing herself in an authentic way, making herself known as a wife to her husband.

A Clear Directive to Husbands

Now, to you husbands, here's what I'm saying: if you want your wife to stop nagging and honey-do-ing you to death, if you want your wife to genuinely appreciate all that you do to make your home life possible, and if you want your wife to feel less like a housemother and more like a wife, then you need to do one thing: You need to stop acting like a guest in your wife's home. You need to stop trying to make her happy by acquiescing to her every preference. You need to stop compromising yourself by letting her put fifty-six throw pillows on the bed, all the while resentfully hoping that someday you'll finally get that "man-cave" that she can't touch.

You also cannot keep offering to "help out" with the dishes, expecting to get a round of applause for your noble act. What you need to do is start Calming Down enough to see that you have fallen hook, line, and sinker for the gender-based lies that tell you to mute your preferences for your own home. You need to Grow Up enough to accept that you have allowed your own participation in this lie to build a growing resentment toward your wife, and toward yourself, without even knowing it. You haven't addressed this resentment openly, so you've acted it out by getting lazier, using work and the money you make as an excuse and an entitlement to this laziness, and then neglected to thank your wife on a regular basis for all she does.

Now, what could this growing maturity in your own home look like? Let's return to my making-the-bed story. See, after Jenny's Authentic Self-Representation, I was struck with a newfound respect for her. It was a begrudging respect at first, but a respect nonetheless. And I was also struck by a newfound desire to make the bed. See, I really like it when she wants to come to bed with me.

But old, stereotypical patterns can be hard to overcome overnight. The next morning I made sure I made the bed. I even placed all fifty-six throw pillows back on the bed, just the way they're supposed to be arranged. I was so pleased with myself. But apparently not enough, because I found myself needing Jenny to notice. I went downstairs and invited her back up to the bedroom. Upon our arrival, I proudly asked her to validate my efforts. "Look, Honey, I made the bed, just the way you like it."

Her response was not exactly what I was hoping for.

"Wow, good for you," she said. "Would you like a medal?"

Ouch. Now, her response was rude. But it was also right. By needing her to notice, I was just reinforcing the very over/under-responsible dynamic she was working to change. She represented herself to me as an adult wife. I reacted like a needy child.

But after calming myself down, I began to recognize something. From the balcony, I was able to see that I was actually making *her* bed, not ours. I didn't want the fifty-six pillows on there, and I certainly didn't want to have to put 'em all back there every morning. Then I grew up enough to recognize that my hidden resentment behind this situation was the real reason I kept "forgetting" to make the bed. It was my passive-aggressive way of telling her that I felt like a guest in her bedroom. So, now what? Now it was my turn to represent myself.

Hey, Honey, I need to tell you something. First I need to apologize for not making the bed all this time. Regardless of any reason, that's just immature behavior and I realize that. I also realize something else: There was a reason I wasn't making our bed. It's because it doesn't feel like ours; it feels like yours. I know you've asked me my opinion on the sheets and comforter and everything, and I've told you that I don't care, as long as you're happy. Well, there is something I do care about. I really don't like having all these pillows. They take forever to take off at night, and they take even longer to put back on in the morning. And when I do make the bed, I'm always wondering if I'm putting them back in the right order. What I'm trying to say is that I really don't want this many pillows on our bed, and I'd like to talk about finding a lesser number that both you and I could live with.

I was calm, but I was direct. I was connected, but I didn't need her to respond in a particular way. Sure, I wanted her to respond with a great "Thank you!" and a willingness to negotiate. But I was prepared to move on with or without it. I was actually prepared to make the bed up to the point I liked it, with only a few pillows on top. If she wanted to add the rest, so be it. Turns out we did end up negotiating a settlement, and now there are just the right number of throw pillows on the bed, fifty-five (just kidding). And I feel pretty confident about my habit of making *our* bed. And now, Jenny *always* wants to climb into bed with me.*

A Clear Directive to All Spouses

Now I have a message for both husbands and wives. And don't worry, I'll keep this brief. If there is one small step you can take to grow stronger as a person and closer in your marriage, it is this: Just say thank you. Make it a priority to recognize, highlight, and appreciate anything and everything your spouse does to make your home life possible. Doing the dishes. Going through the mail. Picking up the newspaper. Raking the leaves. Dusting the ceiling fans. Calling the phone company to complain about the bill. Working to get a graduate degree in order to increase income. Dealing with the accountant. Covering the plants when it freezes. Locking the doors and turning off the lights. Organizing the Quicken and online banking accounts. Grocery shopping. Changing the air filters. Hanging a ceiling fan. Cooking anything. Cleaning anything. And, of course, remembering to put in a new toilet paper roll when the old one runs out.

Take your focus off getting your spouse to recognize you and your efforts. Focus instead on growing yourself into a more grateful person, willingly recognizing and thanking your spouse for all the things he/she does, big and small, to keep the household running. Just as in any of the other fires, pointing fingers, keeping score, or waiting for the other person to change will only keep you stuck. The real key to success is focusing on your own part of the problem, finding out more about yourself than you prob-

---

*I insisted that we add that line.

ably wanted to know, and then having the courage to share those discoveries with your partner. In doing so, you create a space to figure out what's important to you and a space to hear what's important to your spouse. And you learn—maybe for the first time— that this mess you share together is a place you can both call home.

the**lab**

The Setup: Henry and Laura have been married for ten years and have two small children. Their jobs and the kids keep them busy, but they still make time for each other with date nights on a fairly regular basis. All in all, they are relatively happy. But there is one issue that continues to threaten the connection they both work so hard to establish. And that issue lives in the kitchen. What follows is a typical exchange.

The Scene: Laura walks by the kitchen sink full of dirty dishes and breathes a heavy sigh. Once again, Henry has promised to clean up after dinner and, once again, he is nowhere to be found. She even laid out the dish soap and dry towels for him. Where is he this time? Probably out jogging or upstairs watching *SportsCenter,* she figures. "Why is it that he gets to relax after a hard day, but I'm just starting my second shift?" Laura wonders aloud. She sits down at the table and tries to flip through a magazine before the kids need a bath, but she just can't relax with that pile of pots and pans staring at her. Each time she catches sight of them, she can't help but think of all the times in the past this exact same thing had happened. She has asked Henry dozens of times to pitch in and his answer is always the same: "I promise, I will. I just need to do something first."

Seething, she slams down her magazine, grabs the sponge, and starts attacking the sink. About halfway through the greasy lasagna dish, Henry walks in from his run. Immediately, he defends his choice to work out before cleaning up.

"Hey, babe, stop doing that. I was going to get to those right after my run." He steps toward the sink, but Laura won't budge. She continues to scour the pan and blurts out, "Forget it. It's too late now. Apparently, helping out even a little bit around here is just too much to ask of you."

They spend a few more minutes in this heated exchange until Henry just gives up and walks out of the room. Laura turns back to finish the dishes alone. Not exactly the nice, quiet evening she envisioned.

Now it's your turn to put yourself in Laura's shoes and practice the Authentic Self-Representation formula. How could Laura handle things differently so that she authentically represented herself to Henry, without creating the outcome she was hoping to avoid?

CALM DOWN

Pause Yourself:

How might Laura create a space for herself to calmly investigate the situation and her reactivity to it?

Go to the Balcony:

What questions can Laura ask herself, during her pause, that might help her see the situation more objectively?

GROW UP

Spot Your Pattern:

What is Laura doing to perpetuate this pattern?

Step on the Scale:

Why do you think the dishes mean so much to Laura? What significance, other than a clean house, might a clean/dirty sink mean to her? What do you think Laura wants *most* out of this situation?

GET CLOSER

Show Your Cards:

How might Laura calmly, but surely, represent herself, her hopes, her resentments, her fears, etc., in this situation?

Champion Your Spouse:

What could Laura do to encourage Henry to represent himself here?

REPEAT

What do you think would really happen here? How might Henry respond, or react? What could Laura do if he just threw up his hands and said, "Whatever!"? What if he responded positively? What would they do next?

Now that you've had a chance to help Laura, read how Laura indeed did stop the old pattern and start something revolutionary.

CALM DOWN

Pause Yourself: Laura sometimes couldn't even tell when she started to get upset, but her body certainly could. That deep sigh she would unconsciously utter was her body's attempt to rid itself of her built-up stress and frustration. Whenever Laura caught herself doing this, however, she would begin to take the hint, stop whatever she was doing, and breathe deeply a few times.

Go to the Balcony: Up on the balcony, Laura removed herself from the immediacy of the moment and viewed things a little more clearly. She was able to admit that Henry really did have good intentions, but he didn't seem to understand how his lack of action affected her. From here, Laura was also able to see some of those cultural lies that most all of us have allowed to infiltrate our minds and relationships. As you might have noticed, Laura assumed that Henry didn't care about the cleanliness of the house. She wanted him to "help" clean "her" house, but then would get angry at him because he wouldn't seem to feel a sense of ownership in it. Finally, she assumed that leaving him hints or resorting to loud gestures and sarcasm were needed in order to "get" him to participate.

GROW UP

Spot Your Pattern: From the balcony, Laura could also see much better what was really happening each time she and Henry ended up in this argument. Instead of blaming either herself or Henry, she could now see that they were each simply playing a role in their pattern. Henry would act very passively and tend to stall whenever it was his turn to pitch in. He also continued to ask Laura to trust him when there had been a few occasions when he didn't live up to his word. In reaction to that, Laura would brace for him to do the same thing each time. She assumed the worst and couldn't wait more than five minutes after dinner was over before she would clang around pots and pans in an effort to show him how annoyed she was. In short, she would give in to her anxiety and it created, of course, the very outcome she was hoping to avoid—Henry not taking part in keeping the house.

Step on the Scale: Laura did not recognize it at first, but there was a deeper reason why she would get so upset when Henry walked by the dirty sink on his way out of the door. By stepping on the scale, she could finally face her difficult reality. Dishes weren't the real issue. The real issue was respect, or the lack of it. In her mind, Henry's actions indicated that she was undervalued and underappreciated for all that she does in the home, on top of her 9-to-5 job.

What Laura wanted *right now* was for Henry to do the dishes. But what she wants *most* is to know that she's not alone in this thing called family. She wants an equal partnership, not a lopsided workload.

GET CLOSER

Show Your Cards: With all this self-examination behind her, Laura is now able to push past her anxiety instead of jumping up to do Henry's job for him. She can, instead, talk to Henry about what she's just figured out about herself. She can talk about her feelings of disrespect and inequality. So she went to Henry and addressed the fact that she feels invisible and more than a little envious of his time to relax. And she did this without pointing fingers or accusing him of being a jerk.

Champion Your Spouse: Laura's openness and lack of accusation resulted in Henry sharing things from his point of view. And she was genuinely interested in hearing it. He was quite surprised that she felt disrespected. He explained that he had no intention of hurting her; he just had a different time line for when he liked to tackle the kitchen. She took this new information he provided and walked through the formula again. In doing this, she could see how her lack of patience and hasty actions were actually showing disrespect to Henry! She then made more of an effort to refuse to do the dishes whenever Henry promised he'd do them. That way, she showed that she takes him at his word, treating him like an equal partner.

REPEAT

With Laura's cards on the table and any new information processed, she was ready to act differently. She decided to change her part in the pattern by taking Henry at his word. She told him that she considered him to be a man of integrity, and she really does believe him when he says he'll clean up the kitchen. In order to give him some space to do so, she decided to avoid the sink area altogether after dinner. She knew this would cause her a little stress, but she was willing to push past it if it meant getting closer to what she wanted most.

Chapter 7

A ScreamFree Marriage
Leads to Scream-*Filled* Sex

[The Fire of Sexuality]

If your sex doesn't scare the cat, you're not doing it right.
—ANONYMOUS

There is no such thing as safe sex. There never will be.
—NORMAN MAILER

Okay, gentlemen (and some ladies), I'm on to you. I know you skimmed the chapter titles, saw something called "scream-filled sex," and turned right to this page. Don't worry, I won't tell. Heck, I would do the same thing. Despite that nagging Victorian voice in the back of your head, there's nothing wrong with being really interested in sex. As a species, we are drawn to it, both physically and emotionally. We long for it passionately, both biologically and spiritually.

Now, we've always assumed this to be true for men. And the explosion of pornography as the Internet's number one industry is all we need to confirm that assumption. But contrary to popular stereotypes, this incredibly strong desire for sexual expression and connection is true for both men and women. In fact, I believe women are becoming more erotically engaged than men these days, and becoming more open about it. Simply look around us. From *Cosmo*'s monthly multiple-orgasm tips to the continual success of sexy romance novels, from prime time's steamy view of suburbia in *Desperate Housewives* to the ubiquitous Abercrombie & Fitch male model shopping bags, popular culture reflects a growing female desire for physical connection. Sex is at the core of all our beings; has been on our mind, in our heart, and surging through the loins of humankind since our inception; and is now more openly pursued than any time in recent memory.

So, yes, I believe this is one area of your relationship to which you should pay close attention. And, yes, this is one area that, in fact, should *not* be ScreamFree. It should be filled with screams, moans, whoops, hollers, and whatever else floats your boat . . . whenever your boat is actually floating. The truth is that this chapter's title came about because, again and again, I kept hearing the same joke from folks: "Hal, you know there's one part of marriage where it's okay to scream, right?" But while the title may have begun as a joke, I mean it very seriously. I believe sex is designed to be enjoyed immensely, as the ultimate search for physical, emotional, and spiritual connection between people. I believe our bodies and our spirits are designed to commingle in marital sex, leading us toward an experience of union and delight that overloads our senses and bypasses our own efforts to stay composed. Yes, I hope and pray that more and more marriages can experience truly scream-*filled* sex.

Yet, so many couples shy away from this type of freedom and frivolity—even find it impossible to imagine. This is especially true for those who feel as if they are either in a constant fiery battle or in the midst of a cold war. You may even be reluctant to read this chapter because you and your spouse have struggled so much in this arena, or because you are terrified of getting your hopes up for something so incredibly precious. You may believe that all that awaits you in the bedroom is more embarrassment, more pain, and more disappointment. I promise you that is not necessarily true. I do not take your past experience and current patterns lightly, and that's exactly why I am writing this to you now. What I want to convey to you more than anything else in this chapter is that I promise you, scream-filled sex is possible, even *probable,* for those willing to become ScreamFree.

As the chapter title suggests, the less we "scream" with our reactions in the heat of the moment, the freer we become to literally scream with our passions in the heat of that moment. The less we get reactive and defensive in the vulnerable expression of our sexuality, the more we can experience the kind of erotic and ecstatic sexual intimacy we crave.

What most people fail to realize is that sex is not only a by-product of a great marriage—it can also be the catalyst for one. Sex is a remarkable window into the growth process of both the marriage and the individual partners, for how we behave in our sexuality with our partner indicates how comfortable we are with ourselves. Looking at our sexual patterns in the bedroom (and hopefully, many other rooms) offers a view to how much we can fully own our desires for true connection with our spouses. Simply put—you cannot talk authentically about your marriage without taking a close look at what happens between the sheets.

Sex is the most powerful fire of all, capable of providing the spark, warmth, and heat of passion. It is also capable of generating the worst kinds of lightning, burns, even electrocution. That is why there is no more important area in which to keep our cool—knowing and pursuing what we want, championing that same pursuit for our spouse, and yet never compromising ourselves along the way. For those of us willing to stay ScreamFree, the most passionate scream-filled sex awaits.

To that end, I'm going to use this chapter to teach you one principle that, when adopted and followed, has the potential and probability of using this fire of sexuality to create a deeper connection to yourself and your spouse than you've ever thought possible.

Great Sex Is Supposed to Be Uncomfortable

Boy meets girl. Girl marries boy. Together, they settle down and live happily ever after. Or so our fairy tales lead us to believe. But the truth is much more sobering. A full 50 percent of all U.S. marriages end in divorce; in fact, most of those that break up don't even last five years. And what's worse? It's the very security and predictability that we all seek when we decide to "settle down" that is largely to blame. Yep, the thing we think we need the most in a marriage is the very thing that leads to so much marital dissatisfaction. Why? The very stability and safety our anxiety leads us toward is the very antithesis of the mystery and risk that our sexuality longs for.

Back in chapter 2, we talked about some of the lies out there, designed to help our marriages, that only keep us stuck in counterproductive patterns. One of the most pernicious lies is the one surrounding the issue of trust and safety. Most couples think that trust is the number one requirement to gaining and maintaining a healthy sex life. One partner waits for the other to become trustworthy before he or she reveals anything dangerous. Of course, the other partner follows suit. This game of chicken takes place far too often and I cannot speak out against it strongly enough. The truth is this (and it is never more appropriate than in the bedroom): *Self-respect and self-revelation at the risk of rejection are the main ingredients to Scream-Filled sex.*

Revealing yourself and representing your true desires at the risk of being rejected, redressed, or even ridiculed are the only ways of making yourself truly *known*. And that's the true power of sexuality. In the Adam and Eve story, the Hebrew Bible introduces a term to describe sexual connection. It states that "The Man *knew* the Woman, and she became pregnant . . ." That Hebrew term, *yada,* obviously meant more than a simple acknowledgment with or acquaintance of another. It meant to know someone deeply, intimately, from within. Three thousand years ago, people recognized that intimately knowing each other is far different than being just comfortably familiar. The knowledge we both reveal and gain about ourselves and the other during sex is more revealing than any other kind of knowledge. We learn about each other's basic comfort and confidence levels, we learn about each other's desires and dislikes, we learn about each other's secrets and scars. But the only way we learn this is through risking ridicule or outright rejection. This kind of *knowing* is achieved through authentic, ScreamFree self-representation both inside and outside the four bedroom walls. Knowing is about risky revelation; familiarity is about safety. Knowing is about discovering new parts of yourself and your spouse through unpredictability; familiarity is about the security of knowing exactly what's going to happen next. Knowing is a continual quest that can never be fully realized. It is leaving margin for growth and being curious when such growth happens; familiarity is finding yourself on the Love Toilet, or the TwoDaLoo, and then wondering why your marriage is going down the drain.

In chapter 2, I quoted world-renowned sex expert Esther Perel, explaining this phenomenon in her excellent book *Mating in Captivity.* Here is that quote again:

> There's a powerful tendency in long-term relationships to favor the predictable over the unpredictable. Yet eroticism thrives on the unpredictable . . . So where does that leave us? We don't want to throw away the security,

because our relationship depends on it . . . Yet without an element of uncertainty there is no longing, no anticipation, no frisson.

She couldn't be more right. So often we find ourselves stuck between security and sexuality and we don't know where to turn. The truth of the matter is that for many of us, that "frisson" she speaks of, a kind of earth-shattering tremble that only occurs on the edge between safety and danger, seems like a pipe dream. We are like the proverbial poor boy peering at the Christmas display through the store window—such pleasure is only for *other* people, not for us. Perhaps we believe it's only available to the beautiful . . . or the young . . . or the single . . . or the rich. Those who aren't like us boring married folks . . . so *settled* into the confines of security and stability.

So what do we do? We end up *settling*. We settle for the same old sexual patterns. We are afraid to rock the boat, or the bed, because we are afraid that if we seek too much, we'll end up getting even less. Or maybe we're afraid that if we really let ourselves go, we won't like who we become. We'll feel stupid, or we'll get embarrassed, or our spouse will simply reject us. Or perhaps, just perhaps, we're afraid of intimacy—true intimacy—knowing our spouses and being fully known by them.

So we work very hard to reduce the anxiety of our sexuality by reducing the shared activities of that sexuality to the lowest common denominator. We ask ourselves, and our spouses, "What is the least scary or bold activity that we can agree on so that neither one of us ever has to feel uncomfortable?" And we settle comfortably into that comfort zone. No oral sex, let's say. Or lights must be off. Or no expression of fantasies, unless they're PG. We'll do this position at this time of day, and only in this room of the house.

This is a slippery slope toward sexual boredom and it's only a matter of time before settling for only what's comfortable settles into having no sex at all.

Does any of this sound familiar? I'm guessing it does. I've worked with countless couples who found themselves going months, even years, without connecting sexually. I've worked with countless others who could only engage in safe, lifeless sex that left both of them wondering about the future of their life together. But it doesn't have to be this way. We aren't forever constrained by the lies we tell ourselves about sex, the lies we use to protect us from bravely pursuing and claiming what is available to us all. See, if you're willing, the kind of sex you've always wanted is readily available to you—in the very marriage you are in right this minute. But I must warn you. This kind of pleasure is quite expensive. It demands an investment of all you have and hold dear. It involves all of you boldly pursuing all of someone else, at the risk of incredible pain and discomfort. You see, *great sex is supposed to be uncomfortable.*

I know this sounds bizarre at best, so allow me to explain. Great sex, the type of sex that captivates us and takes us to an almost scary place of ecstatic pleasure and emotional connection, is not for those seeking safety and comfort. Dr. David Schnarch addresses this in what I believe to be the best book on this subject, *Passionate Marriage*. He says that this type of intimacy ". . . is not for the faint of heart." This is not just because the safety-seeking, unwilling, "faint of heart" folks are not equipped to handle this type of sexual connection; it is because such an experience of connection is not *available* to them.

Just as increased muscle growth is not available to those unwilling to strain under heavy weights, and just as the experience of new cultures and countries is not available to those afraid of travel, so, too, the experience of great, transcendent, scream-filled sex is simply not available to those unwilling to let go of their need for safety and comfort. But for those who are willing to let go, and learn to grab hold of their own deep desire for erotic expression and passionate connection, well, they can actually go back to Eden.

Garden-Variety Sex

Back in chapter 5, we looked at the Adam and Eve story in order to gain some insight into the fire of extended families. Now we're going back to that ancient story because it offers tremendous insight into the fire of sexuality. Again, I'm asking you to set aside your religious biases about the story, because regardless of what you believe, it offers a profound statement about married sexuality in its optimal state.

As the story goes, The Man and The Woman are metaphorical representations for every man and every woman. We know this because Adam and Eve are not really names in Hebrew. The words *Adam* and *Eve* are literally translated as The Man and The Woman, and the story is a description of how we were originally meant to be. This is vitally significant for us in this chapter because the author of the story includes a remarkable comment about the couple in their paradise. Right after making the point about how every man needs to leave his mother and father in order to be truly joined in one flesh to his wife, the writer mentions—as if "oh, by the way"—that both the man and the woman were "naked and unashamed."

Naked, and *unashamed*. Without clothes, and without any shame about that. According to this ancient story, this is the ideal couple in their ideal state. Naked, and unashamed. This is such a foreign concept to most of us that we simply cannot imagine the thought—unless, of course, we've been unfortunate enough to stumble upon a nudist colony's annual volleyball game . . . or even worse, been part of one. Try shaking that one out of your mind. (Trust me, it's not easy. They may have been naked and unashamed, but I sure wished they hadn't been.)

Anyway, back to naked and unashamed in marriage. When I'm teaching this material to an audience, I like to lead the whole crowd through a powerful word exercise. From one side of the crowd, I work to solicit synonyms for the word "naked." After we've collectively come up with several examples, I move on to the other side. There I ask for synonyms of the word "unashamed." Usually, when we're finished, the list looks something like this:

Naked	Unashamed
vulnerable	secure
exposed	proud
open	strong
revealing	confident
sensitive	bold
woundable	comfortable
w/o defense	w/o embarrassment

Take a long look at that list. You'll see that these two lists seem to describe experiences and states at opposite ends of the human emotional spectrum. Yet the way we function best in our marriages is when we can marry the two together. Exposed, yet confident. Vulnerable, yet secure. Open, and completely comfortable about it.

I saw this embodied in an incredibly mature woman I met recently at a ScreamFree seminar. After the discussion on scream-filled sex (always a crowd favorite), this woman came up to me and confessed that lately, since she turned fifty, she finds herself more erotic, and more confident than ever. "I just got tired of playing it safe, you know? I'm learning who I am, I'm learning what I like, and I'm just gonna go for it." You go, girl.

So, I'm curious. What do you think it would take for *you* to get there? A perfect body? A guarantee that your partner won't laugh you off, or reject your advances outright? Several margaritas? Not a chance. Although those things might sound enjoyable, none of them can really get you what you want most. 'Cause what you want most is an inner confidence that can transcend your aging body, pursue the edge of rejection that creates the possibility of frisson, and leave you drunk with passion. And believe it or not, that's what your spouse wants most as well (even if he/she doesn't know it yet).

But here's the good news. That's right, really good news. Ready? *Everything you need to become naked and unashamed with your spouse is already available to you.* And it's awaiting you. *Every. Single. Thing.* See, naked and unashamed is not some condition you have to attain outside of the sexual fire, whether through fitness or therapy, in order to enjoy scream-filled sex. No, naked and unashamed is a state of being that occurs whenever you do one simple thing: Authentic Self-Representation. By Calming Down enough to examine your fears, and Growing Up enough to own both those fears and your real desires, you can begin to get closer by revealing your true, erotic self. That's all it takes. Simply reveal yourself to your partner—*without waiting for any guarantee of her response.* Be bold enough to know and own your desire, and then be secure enough in yourself to make this desire unmistakably known, and there you have it—you are walking through the fire naked and unashamed.

Simple, right? But definitely not easy. In truth, it may be the hardest thing you ever do. Why? For most of us, sexuality is the most vulnerable, and thus, the most uncomfortable, part of being human. This is remarkably ironic, because no other part of being human is capable of providing such profound physical, emotional, and even spiritual comfort. What's more is that the nakedness required for that comfort and that ecstasy is also the nakedness responsible for the most pain or, perhaps worse, *embarrassment.* It takes tremendous courage to discover your true desires, your longest-held fantasies, and it takes even more courage to disclose those dreams to your mate. He may reject that desire of yours, or even be repulsed by it. She may be turned off by your newfound eroticism, and even react by shaming you for it.

This is the ultimate "I-step," and it isn't easy. But perhaps there is no arena in life where the old adage "Nothing ventured, nothing gained" holds truer. And that's why it's important to begin at the beginning. As we turn these ideas into practical advice, we need to look at your rites of initiation.

Hedging Our Bets, Protecting Our Ass . . . ets

A woman told me recently that the most used expression in her marriage seems to be "Do you wanna?" Whether it's discussing plans for the holidays or desires in the bedroom, the initiation always begins the same way: "Do you wanna visit my parents for Christmas this year?" or . . . "Do you wanna turn off the TV and go upstairs?" It's much safer to ask that way because the one asking the question doesn't really have to risk anything—the responsibility for moving forward is now on the other person.

Of course, the other person usually responds with "I dunno. Do you wanna . . . ?" Each partner is waiting for the other to make the bold, risky, vulnerable first move. And the wheels just keep spinning—until such a couple ends up in my therapy office complaining that their marriage doesn't seem to be going anywhere.

This couple isn't alone in this pattern. One thing I always investigate with couples who come to see me is their practices of sexual initiation. This is because learning how couples dance around this most intimate and risky of proposals is a fantastically clear window into the relationship, and the individual partners, as a whole.

And after working with scores of couples over the years, I've heard a lot of stories. You'd be amazed at all the passive-aggressive ways we try to initiate something, particularly sex, by risking almost nothing. "Do you wanna?" is just one way. Another way that seems popular is going upstairs at night, earlier than usual, hoping your partner follows suit. Still another is the strategic, lingering hug or kiss. This is where we try to take advantage of an otherwise innocuous embrace, by simply holding on longer than usual.

My favorite is what I call the "Recon Hand." This is when, after the lights are out and the covers drawn, one partner sends a hand across the chasm of the bed on a reconnaissance mission. This hand starts innocently, touching clearly safe body areas in an apparent gesture of gentle connection. Depending on the urgency of the sexual desire at the moment, and the relative tiredness of the initiator, the Recon Hand may then proceed slowly, or quickly, to more sensitive areas. Here the senses of detection must be in prime focus, able to discern the slightest warmth of receptivity or twitch of rejection. If the Recon Hand reads any receptivity, the mission continues. If, however, that twitch of rejection sends strong enough signals, then the Recon Hand is slowly, but surely, returned to either a safe spot on the target or back to home base altogether, as if no ulterior motive were ever involved. We just bring that hand right on back to our side of the bed.

While it's definitely fun to laugh at ourselves here, it's only helpful if we can confront the truths that make it so funny. See, all these weak forms of initiation are really just that, weak. And they can't even be called initiations, because the goal of such passive-aggressive moves is to somehow, with very little risk, get your partner to do the initiating. This may be because you're scared of rejection. It may be because you're sick and tired of doing all the initiating all the time. But this fact is undeniable: If you're even thinking about initiating in these weak ways, you definitely still want to experience an erotic, emotional connection.

And that means you have a strong desire to find some confidence in your sexuality. You want to find some boldness in your vulnerability. You actually want to become naked and unashamed.

Well, you can be. And you can put yourself and your spouse in a position to experience something new and powerfully erotic. But you cannot wait for your spouse to make it happen. You cannot try to manipulate the situation to guarantee your spouse's response. You simply cannot experience the spoils of naked and unashamed sex without taking the risk of revealing your nakedness . . . without any shame. And here's what that might look like for you . . . even tonight.

Paint the scene. Dinner is just finished, and you and your spouse are both beginning to clean up. Maybe one of you is starting the kids toward bath and bed, or toward chores and homework. In the midst of the routine chaos, you pause yourself. Where is this night headed? To something familiar? Something comfortable? You go to the balcony and see yourself participating in that dance. You'll finish cleaning up in the kitchen, work together to get the kids settled, and then collapse on the couch, scanning the DVR for the latest episode of . . . whatever. Maybe your spouse will join you, maybe not. And thus maybe you'll have a few moments together before crashing into bed, hoping to get some rest and renewed energy before it all begins again tomorrow. From the balcony you see all this happening and it is just so . . . predictable.

Now, maybe on some nights, that's exactly what you want. But not tonight. Tonight you want something different. You want to explore yourself, and your spouse, looking for the erotic connection that you read about in *Glamour*, or *Men's Health*. No, you don't feel great about your body, and that tempts you to just head for the familiar. But something in you is tired of settling for that, darn it. Why can't you get a taste of what we all assume (incorrectly, BTW) the young and beautiful get to experience? After all, just because you're out of shape doesn't mean your body doesn't work sexually.*

So you decide to grow up a little and spot your pattern, confronting all the lies that usually keep you headed for the familiar. You quiet the lies about your body. You quiet the lies about needing safety and comfort. You decide to step on the scale and ask yourself the most important question of all: "What do I want most?" After calm investigation, you discover that what you want most is a stronger you, capable of letting go of safety and grabbing hold of your passion. What you want most is a connection with your spouse, one based on the freedom and confidence of both partners, and one that dances with frisson.

So, armed with your newfound calm maturity, you decide to go for it. You decide to go up to your spouse and show your cards. Maybe it begins something like this:

> *Hey, Honey, thanks for taking care of _____ [getting the kids into bed, finishing cleaning up in the kitchen, working so hard to help provide for this home—you fill in the blank]. I also wanted to tell you something. I know things have been pretty hectic lately, and I know that nothing that happens tonight will suddenly make everything perfect.*

At this point, you take a step closer, perhaps even gently cupping your spouse's face in your hands. Then you continue . . .

---

*Some of you may in fact be experiencing physical dysfunctions in regard to performing sexually. Whether you're struggling with anything from vaginal pain to erectile dysfunction, I strongly suggest working with your physician and a certified sex therapist. I also wholeheartedly recommend reading Dr. David Schnarch's fantastic work on the subject, *Resurrecting Sex*.

But I wanted you to know that, for whatever reason, I've been thinking about you all day. And I don't want tonight to go on as normal without me letting you know that I want you. I really, really want you.

And then, without waiting for a reply, with your hand lightly caressing your spouse, you casually walk away to resume taking care of the dishes, the kids, whatever.

Now, before you can say, "Hal, there's no way I could do that!" or "Hal, you just don't understand, my spouse and I are just not like that," I want you to consider two things. One, how would you feel if your spouse approached you in this way? Would this type of confident expression of desire make your spouse less attractive, less appealing? Hardly. Two, how do you think you will feel after offering yourself like that? Forget wondering whether you could do it; think about how you'll feel when you do. Stronger? Taller? More confident? Check, check, and check. Naked and unashamed? You bet. And all those feelings are accessible to you long before your spouse has even had a chance to respond! That's because it's not about your spouse validating your efforts—it's about you validating yourself as a whole, mature, sexual person, capable of owning and pursuing your deepest desires.

Now, some of you have another objection on your mind. "Hal, that still wouldn't work with my spouse" or "Hal, my spouse would laugh at me, make me feel stupid." I want those of you ready to respond like that to consider two things. One, as we just discussed above and as we've discussed throughout this book, it is not your spouse's response that matters most. It is about how authentically you can represent yourself to your spouse, regardless of his/her response. Would it hurt if your spouse still rejected you? Of course. It would hurt like hell. If that were the case, would it be tempting to swear off such bold advances forevermore? Absolutely. But would that get you closer to what you want most? Of course not. What would get you closer, in the case of rejection or humiliation?

That's the second thing I want you to consider. Return to the formula. Remember, after you show your cards, your next step is to champion your spouse. By remaining calm and present when your spouse chooses to respond, you create the opportunity for an authentic self-representation from your partner. And whenever you receive whatever response she gives you, repeat the formula again. If your spouse rejects you, then calm yourself, ask yourself if there's anything you could have done differently or better, and then show your cards again.

> *Thank you for letting me know your feelings. I didn't need a particular response from you, I just wanted to let you know how I was feeling. I'm disappointed that you're not into it tonight, but I still love you. Is there something else you'd like to do together instead?*

If your spouse laughs at or ridicules you, again, accept it as feedback.

> *It's obvious that you're uncomfortable with me approaching you in this way, because I know you wouldn't just want to hurt my feelings by making fun of me. I assume you don't intentionally want to hurt my feelings. And I wasn't intentionally trying to make you uncomfortable. I just wanted to let you know how I was feeling at the time.*

Now I'm guessing that this kind of dialogue might sound like a pipe dream to you. Perhaps it sounds so foreign and idyllic that you just cannot picture it having any place in your relationship. Well, that's partially the point. Experiencing an erotic, emotional connection as you've never had before is going to require some intentional moves and responses you've never tried before. It is no use wishing to see Europe if you're too afraid to travel.

In order to experience all that's available to you as a married human being, you have to develop in your very bones a desire for connection that outweighs your fear of rejection.

And that's really been my only goal for this chapter.* I wanted to inspire within you a passion for and a vision of your deepest desires coming to the surface. You got married with a biological, emotional, and spiritual desire for intense connection. Now, the years and kids and mortgages and fights have a way of disconnecting you from that passion, but the fact that you're reading this is a testament that it's not completely dead. It is within you, waiting for you to Calm Down and Grow Up enough for you to Get Closer to your partner.

And that's where we're headed in Part Three. But first, step into one more lab.

---

*In truth, this fire of sexuality deserves its own book. There are just so many issues that space does not allow us to discuss, including the desire dynamics between couples, biological and psychological impediments to experiencing great sex, and religious concerns regarding sexual expression. We also couldn't address specific ways to nurture sexual desire, break through long-held patterns of emotional gridlock, or explore different sexual styles. For all these issues and more, I cannot recommend highly enough the works of Dr. David Schnarch and Esther Perel. Please see For Further Reading . . . and Growing at the end of this book for specific bibliographic information.

thelab

For all of us, stepping into the fire of sexuality, whether writing or talking or doing something about it, is a scary prospect.

But that's good news. It's that fire, that edge, that uncertainty, which keeps us from growing complacent. Without it, we become as adventurous as an old flannel nightgown and a cup of hot tea. Sex is supposed to be fun, risky, and dangerous. And I believe that you can have that kind of sex with your spouse, even if sometimes you can't stand to be in the same room together. What if you went to your husband or wife tonight and simply said, "Honey, I know we've been fighting a lot, and I know that our struggles are bigger than just one night. But I want you to know that tonight, I want you. All of you." Does even reading that make you uncomfortable? Good. That's because you are starting to see what I think of as one of life's great truths. *Sex is supposed to be uncomfortable.*

The Setup: Meet Kate. In her college days, she was a free spirit like no other. She was fearless and fun, outrageous and silly, loyal to a fault, and completely spontaneous. The only thing predictable about Kate was that she was *un*predictable. She was the type of girl who, during a long study session in the girls' dorm, would retire to her room complaining of a headache only to burst through the door a few minutes later yelling like a banshee, brandishing a plastic sword, and wearing *only* a red leather belt.

Kate was most alive when she was taking people by surprise. And that was one of her greatest qualities. She had a zest for life that was unparalleled and she was intimidated by nothing. She had a couple of boyfriends back then, but whenever they would want more commitment from her, Kate knew she wasn't ready. She really didn't want to be tied down. Plus, she had seen her parents go through an ugly divorce and she didn't want any part of that. After college, Kate dated a couple of men, but nothing was ever serious. Until she met Dan. Dan was a few years older than Kate, and he was very grounded. He came from a stable family, was driven at work, and had just recently helped his parents celebrate their fiftieth wedding anniversary. Kate was attracted to him immediately. He was so different from the less stable boys she had dated before. He seemed to really know who he was and what he wanted.

And apparently, he wanted Kate. He was direct in his pursuit of her, and they were engaged and married within the year. That was over four years ago. They've since moved into a new house and have concentrated on their careers. Recently, all of Kate's friends and family have been pressuring her to start a family, and she does her best to deflect their prodding casually. But each time one of them raises their eyebrows and asks if "little ones" are in their future, Kate breaks down and opens up. "Well, that would require us actually having sex . . . and I can't remember the last time we did."

See, while Kate and Dan were coming up on their five-year anniversary, they just passed the one-year anniversary of the last time they had sex. Now, it wasn't because of a lack of desire on Kate's end, as far as she knew. She reported that she actually had a healthy appetite for sex. They had just settled into an extremely "comfortable" arrangement. Like so many couples, Kate and Dan had learned together how to dance around any discomfort. They had believed the lies about compatibility and trust so completely, they actually worked hard to completely avoid any conflict, any friction at all. This meant learning to hide the "unpredictable, zest-for-life" Kate. This meant avoiding any difficult topics of conversation, avoiding any strong expressions of preference or opinion, and certainly avoiding any risky revelations about their sexuality. Obviously, this safe avoidance of conflict made for an extreme lack of connection.

In explaining the situation to me, Kate said, "I don't know what to do. We just don't click anymore. It's like we're living two totally separate lives and I'm back to having a roommate. But I can't even be myself in my own home. We never do anything spontaneous, we never talk about anything of significance. And we don't even come close to having sex. If you want to know the truth, I don't think Dan's interested in me at all. I finally just stopped trying to initiate anything intimate, and I've basically given up on the whole idea of it. In fact, I'm thinking of leaving altogether."

Okay, before I tell you about what incredibly brave choices Kate pursued, and what incredible changes she and Dan subsequently experienced, you take a turn in Kate's shoes. Walk with her through the ASR formula and see how you might learn to proceed through this incredibly anxious fire of sexuality.

CALM DOWN

Pause Yourself:

Before she runs to the divorce lawyer, how can Kate create some calm space to really investigate the problem?

Go to the Balcony:

Kate really needs to see things clearly, especially with so much noise around us all about sexuality. What are some possible ways to gain some objectivity, and even confront some of the lies tempting her to give up in the name of "sexual incompatibility"?

GROW UP

Spot Your Pattern:

How do you think Kate may be actually contributing to this pattern of sexual inactivity?

Step on the Scale:

What meaning might Kate derive from this lack of connection? How does avoiding sex help both Kate and Dan avoid conflict? What does Kate want most here, and how might that desire outweigh her desire to not rock the boat?

GET CLOSER

Show Your Cards:

What do you think Kate could/would do to say yes to the free spirit she is, and say yes to her desire for connection?

Champion Your Spouse:

How might Kate encourage and welcome Dan to be as open as possible about his fears, changing desires, and hopes for their future?

REPEAT

What do you think happens? How might Kate, after the initial confession and revelation, have to repeat through the ASR formula?

Now that you've had a chance to walk in Kate's shoes, let's look at what actually happened.

CALM DOWN

Pause Yourself: Kate's realization that she was significantly unhappy frightened her. She did not want to go through what she saw her parents endure and yet she wasn't willing to continue just being buddies with Dan. So she sought me out to help her sort through these problems. She didn't invite Dan—she didn't really want him there at first. She just wanted some help figuring out what she should do.

Go to the Balcony: Sometimes seeing a professional is the best pause of all. Before worrying about what their lack of sex meant, I suggested that Kate take an objective look at the frequency and intensity of the sex they used to have. I had her examine how the reality of their sexual encounters matched up with her early expectations. Kate remembers that whenever she and Dan did have sex, it was just a physical release. There was always a lack of real connection because there was always a lack of revelation. But it was just that. Eyes were closed, lips were sealed, and passion was limited.

GROW UP

Spot Your Pattern: These conversations were fascinating to Kate. She wished that she could have these kinds of talks with Dan, but the mere thought of it made her cringe. "He just isn't that type of guy," she reasoned. He wasn't comfortable with deep, intense conversations; to be fair, she wasn't, either. They both would default to a safe, comfortable rhythm early on.

Once, I asked Kate this question: "Do you still consider yourself a free spirit?" Kate laughed. "I am at work. But I cannot imagine showing that side of me to Dan. He would think that I'm being silly and immature." Kate figured out that her part in their "comfortable" pattern was avoiding any strong feelings, opinions, and preferences around Dan for fear of disturbing the peace. Apparently, Kate found the combination of being vulnerable and comfortable simply unbearable.

Kate then realized something significant. While she didn't care what everyone else thought of her antics, she was horrified that Dan would disapprove. So she would hide that part of herself from the one person who deserves to see it. She would tell herself that if she "could only be sure" that he wouldn't be turned off by her free-spiritedness, she would let loose more. But as she waited for signs of his openness, the chasm between them got bigger and bigger.

Step on the Scale: Now came the tough questions. What meaning did she attach to that kind of disapproval? Why was she so afraid of Dan's judgment when she so clearly wasn't afraid of anyone else's? She was afraid of repeating her parents' mistakes. She didn't want to end up alone, so she was choosing safety over passion. Certainty over spontaneity. Ironically, that very choice was leading her right toward the thing she feared the most.

So, while peace and stability were what she wanted at the moment, that wasn't what she wanted most. Kate desperately wanted to be herself around Dan. She wanted to be crazy and silly and sensual and erotic with the man she had chosen for life. And she wanted him to be the same way . . . willingly.

GET CLOSER

Show Your Cards: Kate felt that she and Dan were so far apart that talking about all these deep emotions just didn't seem possible right away. So I challenged Kate to "show herself" and her true desires to Dan in three small gestures this week—without telling him what she was up to. She grazed his back with her hand while doing dishes. She rented a movie that she wanted to see but feared that he would hate, and asked him to watch it with her. She sat a tiny bit closer than normal to him on the couch. These gestures were small but risky.

Champion Your Spouse: At the same time Kate started to notice her own hopes for her marriage, she started to develop ears to hear and eyes to see what was really going on with Dan. They had lived parallel lives for so long that she'd forgotten to stop and look at him as a separate person. She had assumed that he felt uninterested in her, but the truth was that he didn't even know the real her. How could she possibly know what his response was going to be? Instead of withholding the real Kate out of fear, she started to show her true self to her husband. And she learned to cherish any subtle movement he would make in her direction. And he actually started to do so.

REPEAT

Kate took all these bold steps and continued to work with me. Nothing changes overnight, but Dan did start to notice small changes in Kate's demeanor. She smiled a lot more and she seemed to be in a much better mood than normal. She seemed more confident and, in a way, charming. She seemed to be at peace with herself. Something was definitely going on and he became curious about it. Kate was careful not to push him, but she slowly started talking to him about more serious matters. She told him about her parents and her memories of their loud arguments. And she told him her fears of ending up like them. And, in a moment that completely took her by surprise, Dan asked if she would mind him tagging along to her next counseling appointment.

Follow up—I'd love to tell you that Dan and Kate are now frolicking through the countryside, enjoying the most electric sex possible. They're not, but they are getting to "know" one another more and more in that way, even as it still feels risky, and scary, and uncomfortable. They have each had moments of incredible courage, choosing to independently initiate sex at times, and choosing to openly refuse sex when they didn't like the ways things were going between them at the time. Both have been powerful ways of representing themselves, making their Nos more informative, and making their Yeses more definitive. Kate even told me that recently she ran through the house with just a belt on. "And how'd it go?" I asked. With a sheepish grin, she coyly explained that, at least that night, they did not act like roommates.

partthree

Getting Closer through

Intimacy and Love

My friends tell me I have an intimacy problem.
But they don't really know me.
—GARRY SHANDLING

Closer. That was the name of the movie. It came out a few years ago, to some critical acclaim. It presented the story of four people inter"connected" by something they repeatedly called "love." It was actually the story of two couples whose immaturity led them from one distraction to another, eventually committing secret affairs with each other. We should have known this from the tagline of the film: "When you believe in love at first sight, you're always looking."

Wow.

But the story line spoke to a number of people because it detailed a quest as natural and deep as any we experience as human beings.

Closer. We all want to get closer.

Isn't that the hope behind getting married in the first place? The hope behind trying to improve your marriage? The hope behind reading this book? Getting closer. We all want to experience the magic of getting closer.

Surely by this point in the book we can establish what this does *not* mean. (1) This does not mean becoming one and only one, becoming so close that there is no separation, no individuality, no differentiation between you and your spouse. This type of attachment is a scream-fueled effort to ease the anxiety of the basic separation of husband and wife. Not only is this attachment not the type of connection you really seek, it always leads to the inevitable screaming that ultimately drives people apart. (2) Getting closer does not mean reaching agreement on all the domestic issues, "getting on the same page" with regard to time, in-laws, housework, and the like. As we've examined in Part Two, agreement on these issues is not the end goal, and searching for such agreement never gives you the type of relief from anxiety you hope for. The goal is to grow *through* the disputes, in the midst of the fires, so that you can learn to fully evaluate your own position, openly listen to your spouse's, and try to act in the best interests of both. This is not agreement—this is mutual self-representation.

Not surprisingly, taking such a stance actually gets us closer to the "getting closer" we really seek. And that's what this section is all about. What does it mean to get closer, to experience true connection? Most important, what are the next steps necessary to begin the experience?

Well, let's trace what we've just learned in the previous section. True growth can only be forged through a willingness to step through the fires of marital conflict. As mentioned previously, all marriages face the same fires. These natural arenas of conflict should not be viewed as counterproductive hurdles to a great marriage. Rather, they should be seen as tools specifically designed to refine the individuals who are bold enough to step through them. The fires give each of us an opportunity to learn about ourselves, face our fears, and live fully in our own skin. Approaching the fires while remaining calm and connected actually changes you into the type of person capable of mature intimacy and love.

Once a couple sees that these fires can refine them into stronger, more capable, and more caring individuals, they can let go of the need to either fight against or ignore these growth opportunities. This paves the way for true intimacy to occur. It also paves the way to truly share and experience love for each other.

That's what this final section is about: intimacy and love. I know you've heard a lot about those concepts, and you've probably read a lot about them as well. I'm not going to be so bold as to say that what you're about to read is completely, radically new. Many folks have said these things before. What may be new for you is seeing the connection between your own individual maturity and the mutual intimacy and love you seek with your spouse.

From the very beginning of this book we've been talking

about the value of becoming a true individual in your marriage, a true "centered self." This has involved focusing on yourself, calming yourself down, and confronting the lies about compatibility we've all been sold. It's also involved confronting your own role in the problems you complain about, and developing a willingness to calmly enter the fires of marital conflict. Now we go a step further, nurturing our individual selves to openly pursue mutual intimacy and love.

But first, a warning. As we already mentioned, Dr. David Schnarch so aptly titles one of his chapters in his book *Passionate Marriage*, "Intimacy Is Not for the Faint of Heart." As you will see, pursuing true intimacy and love, true "closeness," means courageously revealing more and more of yourself, and championing your spouse to do the same. This will lead to several revelations and realizations. These revelations and realizations will not always be pretty, or positive. They could actually be potentially damaging to your relationship as it currently stands.

That's okay.

It's actually more than okay—it's good. If you wanted your relationship to stand pat, experiencing no challenges to the status quo, then you wouldn't be reading a marriage book, much less this one. The truth is that you *want* to share more with your spouse. And you *want* your spouse to share more with you. You don't want these revelations to be falsehoods, you want the truth. And unlike Jack Nicholson, I believe that, yes, you *can* handle the truth.

That's what I've committed to telling you in these pages, and I believe that's what, after reading them, you'll be ready to do— and experience—in your marriage.

As you'll read, it all starts with one letter.

Chapter 8

Intimacy Always Begins with an "I"

I want you. I haven't thought of anything beyond "I want you."
—WILL FERRELL AS HAROLD CRICK IN
STRANGER THAN FICTION

I'm gonna just put this out there. If you don't like it,
just send it right back, but here goes:
I wanna be on you.
—WILL FERRELL AS RON BURGUNDY IN *ANCHORMAN*

As we'll discuss in the next chapter, on love, there are some terms that are bandied about so frivolously that we don't know from one person to the next what the word actually means to them. Such is the case with *intimacy*. To a number of people, intimacy is just a euphemism for sex. Sex reveals so much of our bodies and our desires, the thinking goes, that it must represent the deepest form of intimacy with another. But the truth comes out in our experience. Every one of us with any sexual experience has had moments of connecting with our genitals and yet detaching behind closed eyes. Sometimes couples even connect sexually to *avoid* having to connect emotionally, confusing the two and confounding their relationship in the process. These couples are always wondering what's missing. "We have such great sex.

(Meaning they both experience orgasm.) Why don't I feel close to him?" Perhaps you recognize this experience as your own.

But at its core and in its totality, intimacy is so much more than physical connection. As you and I discussed in the last chapter, it can most definitely include the connection of bodies, but only when that connection of bodies is itself an expression of so much more.

In truth, intimacy is *mutual self-representation*. Authentic Self-Representation in marriage is what we've been talking about and promoting throughout this entire book. It is a term I use to try to encapsulate the attitude and activity needed to create and maintain intimacy in a relationship. At its most basic, self-representation is when an individual voluntarily shares her true self with another, warts and dreams and all. It is the movement of one person willingly making a step toward another, choosing to reveal her hopes, her desires, her preferences, her fears, everything.

Intimacy occurs whenever this self-representation becomes mutual.

Preacher and author Bill Hybels puts it this way: "For a marriage relationship to flourish, there must be intimacy. It takes an enormous amount of courage to say to your spouse, 'This is me, I'm not always proud of it—in fact, I'm sometimes a little embarrassed by it—but this is who I am.'"

Just because intimacy is *mutual*, however, does not make it *simultaneous*. It is not an experience of "1-2-3 . . . Go!" and both partners share of themselves at the same time. Even though most of us did make public vows at one point, no efforts toward true intimacy began with an agreed-upon contract, with both partners simultaneously revealing their "privates" to each other like kids behind the garage. Instead, true intimacy begins with one partner courageously recognizing that *Intimacy Always Begins with an "I."* It always begins with one partner courageously, unilaterally, taking that step toward the other.

Taking an "I"-Step

Back in chapter 7, we looked at the various passive ways we try to initiate sex. From the hand sent on a reconnaissance mission under the covers to the weak "Do you wanna?" invitation, we are all well practiced in the art of asking for a lot while risking as little as possible. It's just much safer to initiate in those ways because the one asking the question doesn't really have to risk anything—the responsibility for moving forward is now on the other person.

We all fall into the risk-avoidance trap. It's just plain scary putting yourself out there, stating your true wishes, even to the love of your life—*especially* to the love of your life—because no one can hurt you like your spouse. That's the paradox of intimacy. The one we want to feel safest with and closest to is the very person who, because of that closeness and vulnerability, can cut us the deepest. That's why it's easier to do as little as it takes to get the other person to make the first move.

Think about all the ways we try to play the game of risk, getting our "opponent" to make the first overt move. "Do you wanna?" is one way; the royal "we" is another. "Do we want to try to stick to a budget this year?" Or, "Do we have a plan for fixing the roof?" Or, "When are we going to find time for a date night?" All of these carry the same implied meaning: "Can *you* stick to a budget?" "Do *you* have a plan for the roof?" "When are *you* going to arrange a date night?" These are all efforts to get the other person in a vulnerable position without having to take the risk of doing so first.

But that's not what produces the type of interesting, intoxicating connection, the "intimacy" we all crave. When we're honest, we don't want our significant other to become vulnerable only when pressured to do so. We want truly voluntary, *mutual* intimacy, freely chosen intimacy. And that type of intimacy always begins with one partner deciding to take a risk. That type of intimacy begins with one partner boldly taking an "I"-step.

This could be a statement revealing a wish for a kiss, or a hand extended, asking for forgiveness and reconciliation. This I-step could be the slow, sultry removal of clothing, or the slow but steady disclosure that you feel pain. "Ouch" can be among the most intimate of I-steps, whether it stems from a careless comment or a physical misstep during sex, because the admission of pain is the acknowledgment of one's own vulnerability. All of the above are invitations to greater intimacy because all of the above are courageous steps from one spouse toward the other, inviting further closeness and vulnerability in return. Intimacy can begin no other way.

Beginning to pursue true intimacy is always a centered-self affair, with one spouse acting bravely to initiate with integrity. This may look like a sexual advance. It may take the form of announcing a period of separation. This may be an announcement of a desire to change jobs, or it may be an expressed desire for a more regular dinnertime with the whole family. It will always begin with one partner stating, "I want" or "I like" or "I think." Intimacy always begins with an "I."

Un "dressing" with Your Spouse

One example of this may seem familiar to you. It involves a husband and wife, a seemingly cherished recipe, and one dead grandmother. Carol, the wife, was up early one morning the week of Thanksgiving, starting the daylong process of making "Grandma's dressing." Seems that her late grandmother had the mother of all dressing recipes, and Carol was the one granddaughter who ended up with the legacy of cooking it every year. Just one problem with the whole scenario: Jim, Carol's husband, hated the dressing. I mean, he hated it. The smell, the look, the taste, everything. But in twenty years of marriage he had never even thought to tell anyone—this was dear Grandma's recipe, after all. Out of loyalty, he had kept his distaste secret for all these years.

After going through a sometimes-rough season of marital growth that year, however, both Jim and Carol had grown in their ability to represent themselves in their marriage. They had each, in their own way, grown committed to telling the truth to each other. "At the very least, I want him to know me," Carol would say. Along these lines, she had actually told Jim that she wished he would stand up for himself more around his mother. Well, now it was Jim's turn to self-represent. And it just so happened to be Thanksgiving.

He came downstairs that morning to find Carol hard at work preparing Grandma's dressing. She didn't seem happy about the task; in fact, Carol was downright pouty about it. But she did manage to turn toward Jim and exclaim, "Look, Honey, I'm making everyone's favorite dressing!" Sensing the opportunity and summoning the courage, Jim decided to reveal his true feelings and represent himself.

"You know what, Honey? I'm gonna tell you something right now that may hurt your feelings. But I just have to say it. I . . . I . . . I really don't like your grandmother's dressing."

Enter the awkward pause.

"What?!?" Carol replied in shock. "I thought you loved this dressing!"

"I'm sorry if it hurts your feelings, Honey, I really am. But I have to be honest with you. I just really don't like it. *I never have.*"

Enter a second awkward pause. Followed by tears. In the face of this emotional anxiety, Jim was terribly tempted to retract his admission, but if he were to maintain his integrity, he knew he couldn't. He wanted, and needed, to stand his ground. And then something altogether unexpected happened.

Through her tears, Carol started to chuckle. "Oh my God,"

she exclaimed. "I can't believe this," she continued, beginning to laugh. "I feel so bad saying this, but you know what?"

"What?" her confused husband asked.

"I actually hate this dressing, too. I've always hated it. I hated it when I was a kid, I hated being the one expected to take it over from Grandma, and I hate cooking all day to prepare it!"

Carol said all this while wiping the cornbread mix onto her apron. Then they both burst into laughter and embraced in their newfound commonality. Now, this episode may not strike you as particularly intimate, but this type of new revelation, self-representation, and genuine connection is exactly the stuff of long, lasting, intimate marriages.

Especially when it leads to more self-representation. And that's what happened with Jim and Carol later that night. Settling into bed after a long day of family and festivities, the couple nuzzled up close to one another. And then Jim, feeling stronger and closer after the dressing episode that morning, began to kiss his wife's ear. Carol flinched a little, but not so much to deflect Jim's nibbling. He knew she loved this earplay, and figured it would be the very thing to put her in the mood. And then Carol spoke up.

"Jim, honey?" she uttered softly.

"Huh?" he mumbled, while continuing his noshing.

"Jim," Carol stated more firmly. Her resolve was growing. "I want you to stop."

"What? Why?" Jim asked.

"Because I need to tell you something."

Jim was more than a little curious now. This had an ominous tone.

"I need to tell you . . ." Carol continued. "I need to tell you that the thing you do with my ear . . . the nibbling thing you were just doing . . . well . . ."

"Well, what?" Jim's anxiety nervously asked.

"Well, I *really* don't like it." Carol was now the one doing the courageous revelation. "I can't stand it, actually."

Jim was astonished, and embarrassed, and hurt. "What? I thought you loved it. You never said anything about it before. And you always seem to respond—"

"I didn't want to hurt your feelings," she interrupted.

"Well, is this a new thing?"

At this, Carol paused. "Well, no," she sheepishly admitted. "I've actually always hated it."

"Carol, I've been doing this to your ear ever since we've been together. I've been doing this for twenty years! And you've hated it the entire time?"

"Well, I haven't always hated it. For years I just didn't really like it."

"And now?" Jim asked.

"Now I pretty much hate it. I'm so sorry. I don't mean to hurt your feelings—"

Jim stopped her. "I feel so stupid now. I feel like such a moron, thinking I was actually turning you on . . ."

"You do turn me on, Jim. You always have. But it's kinda been *despite* the ear thing, not *because* of it," Carol explained. And then, after a somewhat uncomfortable pause, she decided that she couldn't just let things end there. She decided that just as big an I-step as her initial revelation was, she would take an even riskier one. Instead of pulling back and letting Jim feel stupid the rest of the night (and maybe longer), and instead of sitting back and hoping Jim would stop his ear gobbling and start doing something she really did like, Carol decided she would take the matter into her own hands.

"Jim, honey . . ." she started, in a lower, hushed tone. She gingerly touched his face and turned it toward her own. "Would you like to know what I *do* like, and something I've always wanted to try with you?"

At this, Jim's demeanor started to change. His ears perked up, as did another part of his anatomy. I'll let you imagine the rest.

No Guarantees, Other Than There Are No Guarantees

Sure, that's a fun story, and it certainly ends well. That is, it ends with a mutual sharing experience. But perhaps the hardest part of all this is that intimacy involves the sometimes terrifying risk of sharing one's self without having any assurance that (a) whatever is revealed will be received well; and (b) such a gesture of self-representation will be reciprocated in kind. No, it just doesn't work that way. Self-representation is risky, it is scary, and it comes with no guarantees of anything other than that.

But just because it has no guarantees does not mean it carries no hope. On the contrary, individual self-representation carries with it the hope that is deeper than most all other hopes—it carries with it the hope of getting closer, and getting truly loved.

And that's our deepest longing: getting close enough to be fully known, and still getting loved. I love the line in Rabbi Irwin Kula's wonderful book *Yearnings*. In discussing our powerful yearning for intimacy, he points out that "when we hide parts of who we are from our lover, we just ensure that it is not the full me that is being loved." What a simple yet powerful understanding of the basic issue. We reveal ourselves to our lover, our spouse, because we want to get closer. What that means is that we want to be fully known by another—and still loved. This means revealing our likes and our dislikes. Our hopes and our fears. Our positive feelings of admiration and attraction, and our negative feelings of frustration and disappointment.

We want to reveal all these things, and have our spouse reveal those things to us. But the scariest part of revealing ourselves to each other is that doing so may just set us up to be rejected. Our spouse may refuse to accept what we have to say, or refuse to reciprocate. At worst, our spouse may use our intimate revelations to specifically hurt us more. We so want to experience mutual self-representation, but we don't want to risk revealing our most intimate thoughts and feelings; we don't want to risk being rejected for who we really are.

But as the good rabbi points out, *not* revealing those parts of ourselves just guarantees that we won't be *fully* loved—which, over time, is just as bad as being openly rejected. Kula goes on to say that he and his wife occasionally go through an intentional practice of revealing and recognizing their differences and disappointments. It is a perfect example of Authentic Self-Representation. He says:

> . . . it's a way to get our disappointments and frustrations out in the open where we can look at them and hopefully work them through. We ask each other whether there's anything we might have felt too uncomfortable, embarrassing, obnoxious, or scary to share about the other over the last weeks or months. Of course, the first thing to come to mind is the one thing we'd rather keep hidden. But more often than not, after much discussion and sometimes tension, we're on solid ground again, the relationship more rich and nurturing than it had been before. Intimacy means acknowledging to each other, "Okay, I'm greedy, horny, arrogant, lazy, flirtatious, jealous, angry, nerdy, insecure." And then feeling loved. Of course, it's helpful to try to keep a balance . . . We practice sharing what is good and beautiful and pleasant about each other, and sometimes that is just as challenging; it can feel corny and vulnerable,

and we may have a sinking feeling that words just don't suffice.

All of us yearn for a person with whom we can be vulnerable, and yet be embraced.

My God, isn't that what we all crave? Isn't that the type of "getting closer" that speaks to our deepest longings for connection? Isn't the hope of that kind of intimacy what beckons us to get married in the first place? Yes, yes, and yes.

But you may be thinking that their story goes against what I said earlier about intimacy being mutual, but not simultaneous. Here's a mature couple sitting down together in a simultaneous exercise of mutual sharing, right? Not really. One of them had to suggest the idea in the first place. And ever since, one of them still has to go first. Then the other has to decide, on his or her own, whether to reciprocate. And then, depending on the content of what's being revealed, the other has to decide how to receive the information. And so on. At each step along the way, there has to be a conscious, individual choice to continue their self-representation, and to choose to love the other in their vulnerability. Now, we're going to discuss what it means to love each other in the next chapter, so hold on. For now, let's stick to this business of initiating self-representation.

If it weren't scary, then we wouldn't be revealing anything of any value. If we aren't giving our spouses the chance to reject us, then we're not giving them the chance to embrace the real us.

The Hero's Journey

Psychologist Dr. Maria Nemeth, in her brilliant book *The Energy of Money,* uses a model that can be particularly useful here. She posits that each of us walks around with three layers. On the outer layer we carry all our pretends, oughts, and shoulds. This is the pretend outer level that we believe presents us in the best light. Think of how you want to be on a job interview or on a first date, and you get the gist. This layer is the self we often put tons of energy into presenting to the outside world. It is each of us in our Sunday best, informed by the hopes we think we're *supposed* to carry, the opinions we think we're *supposed* to own, and the beliefs we think we're *supposed* to have.

The reason we put so much energy into supporting this outer layer is because we are deathly afraid of someone piercing through and discovering what's underneath, our next layer. This layer, as Dr. Nemeth puts it, is our fear-based layer. This is the layer of insecurity, of pettiness, of the deathly fear that we don't really know what we're doing and we don't really have it all together. Call this the "imposter" layer, because it is characterized by the self we are afraid people will discover, and thus find out that we've been faking it for most of our lives. This is Rabbi Kula's "greedy, horny, arrogant, lazy, flirtatious, jealous, angry, nerdy, insecure" part of ourselves that we so often desperately hope no one discovers. And Dr. Nemeth states that the reason we hope no one finds this layer is because we think *that's all there is*. We think this imposter layer is representative of our real selves, the real us. No wonder we choose not to reveal these parts of ourselves—we may be unveiling ourselves as the imposters we fear we really are!

But the truth is liberating here. As Dr. Nemeth puts it, there is a third, deeper layer. It is so deep that it's not even really a layer at all—it's at the core. This core is what she calls the real self, and it is characterized by the things we hold dearest—our desires. This self is the seat of our truest desires for connection, for significance, for acceptance and appreciation, for intimacy and love. This is the self that is dying to have everything out in the open, to at least one person. As the Indigo Girls put it in one of their songs, "There's a thousand things about me I want only you to know." This core is seeking to be discovered and revealed, so it can thereby grow and encapsulate the other two layers. The work of doing so is what Dr. Nemeth calls "the Hero's journey," because it takes incredible courage to willingly investigate, and reveal, your deepest desires, your strongest fears, and your weakest pretenses.

Thankfully, that's where marriage comes in. Your marriage, as it stands right this minute, gives you the perfect opportunity to discover, reveal, and grow your self into an integrated whole. In fact, this whole book has been talking about how marriage calls on you to grow into your strongest self. Well, here's where that self shines brightest. It begins with you as an individual becoming willing to own your deepest desires for connection with your spouse, your deepest hopes to become fully known—and still loved and accepted.

One Hero's Journey

The most courageous example I know of this risky self-representation occurred between a couple who came to me several years ago. In many ways their story serves as an illustration of everything we've tried to convey in this book.

Andy and Sonya consulted with me several years ago about a very clear problem: domestic abuse. When Andy got drunk, Andy got violent. This had been going on for years. Their two young kids were at risk, so Family Services was involved, as was a social worker from a battered women's shelter. All in all, this was a horrible situation, full of conflict and chaos that most people don't even want to hear about.

But when anyone did hear about it, they were all convinced of one thing: The problem was clear; Andy was the problem.

On the surface, it's easy to agree. Andy was a grown man, responsible for all his decisions and therefore culpable for all his actions. And some of his decisions and actions were despicable and inexcusable. I want to make it absolutely clear that in no way is our discussion here designed to excuse Andy's behavior. His form of emotional reactivity, the way he "screamed," was to inflict terror and violence on those he loved most. Nothing could ever justify such wrongdoing.

So, yes, when they first came to see me, they both had diagnosed Andy as the problem. Even he thought it was all his fault . . . at the time. That's because when they came to see me, they were in the part of the cycle sometimes referred to as the "honeymoon phase." Andy had just gone through a rage a few days earlier, and now he was shaming himself, blaming himself, apologizing profusely, and promising that he would never hurt his sweetheart again. He even volunteered to go to therapy.

To her credit, Sonya used this phase to seek out therapy herself. But like almost every partner in her situation, what do you think she wanted out of therapy? Of course, she wanted help in fixing Andy. She loved him, she wanted to believe him, and, above all, she felt she *needed* him. He was her provider, her partner in parenting, and, without fully realizing it, her project. From the earliest days in their relationship, she was the "correct" one. She was the one who had it all together, and since he was such a wreck, they were a perfect, compatible match. When she said "I do," it was to a promise to rescue him from his own violent childhood and fix him forever. She believed he needed her as well.

This was her part of the pattern. Her role was to do everything the right way, appear as the innocent victim, and passive-aggressively attempt to rescue and redeem Andy. Only she understood him, only she could protect her children from him, and only she, as his better half, could "re-pair" him. That was the exact position Sonya was in when they came to see me. It was all Andy's fault. She had done nothing except be a great wife. She just needed me to help her fix him for good.

But after a few sessions, Sonya began to focus on herself. She began to critically examine some of her own behaviors. She began to see her role in the pattern: Her efforts to fix Andy led her to believe that she had the power to change his behavior, which he obviously resisted. When he did so, Sonya's emotional need for him led her to forgive him too quickly, and then gloss over all the warning signs that he was going to rage again. Her lack of belief in her own individuality and self-worth led her to hide her bruises, and resist getting real help up to this point.

Now, I know what you're thinking. She should just grow some self-esteem and leave this jerk forever. I get that temptation. But things are never quite that simple. Especially not in an abusive attachment like this woman's. Sonya had built a family with this man, interweaving their lives so much that simply extricating herself and the kids would have involved an extensive financial hardship and a lengthy court battle. Plus, she still wanted to make this marriage work; she didn't want to throw ten-plus years out the window and start anew. Moreover, Andy was actually beginning to change. Since starting their work with me, he had entered a twelve-step recovery plan, returned to church, and was even doing individual therapy, centered on growing past his terrible relationship with his father.

There was a burgeoning hope in and for this couple because each had begun to focus on themselves. They were beginning to see their problems as couched in discernible patterns, and they were beginning to identify their own parts in those patterns. And, best of all, they were beginning to exercise their real power as individuals, calming down and confronting themselves to change for the betterment of all.

But patterns are powerful. Especially ones as reactive and entrenched as the one between Andy and Sonya. And one day, when neither one was feeling their best, Andy started to drink and Sonya started to gripe. Neither one remembers who started their part first, but you can imagine what happened next. Sonya started complaining that every bit of the work they'd been doing in therapy was useless, and Andy started to get angry.

He began to raise his voice, and she began to shut down. She began to cower and walk away, and he began to pursue her. This pattern led to their bedroom. Sonya was now trying to avoid the situation altogether, understandably. Andy was trying to provoke a reaction and promote himself into a position of power, as was typical. They were heading for a horribly familiar scenario, with Andy raising his hand and Sonya turning her back to protect herself.

And then it happened. Something altogether different happened—something that would change their lives from that point on.

At just the moment when violence would typically occur, Sonya did something remarkably different. With more courage than I can imagine, Sonya took an I-step worthy of the history books. Suddenly, she stood straight up and turned around. Then she took a step toward her aggressor. With his hand raised to hit her, she looked him straight in the eye and pronounced a newfound truth.

"You know what I just realized?" she asked as she took yet another step toward him. "I just realized that I don't need you anymore."

"WHAT?!?" Andy screamed in pain and disbelief. "YOU DON'T NE—"

Sonya cut him off, and took yet another step toward her husband. "But I do still want you."

Her revelation was met with silence. They both just stood there looking at each other, stunned by the sequence of events. Neither knew what to do next, because neither had experienced this type of intimacy before. Sonya then took it a step further.

"I want the real you, the you I've been seeing more and more of lately . . . I want you, but not like this," she explained, pointing at his fist.

What happened next was profound. Andy lowered his hand

and began to weep. Sonya just stood there for a few moments, continuing to make her stand. She bravely decided to resist the urge to comfort him. Then she calmly walked around him and left the room. The pattern had been interrupted at its most volatile point, as soon as one partner's authentic self-representation had entered the picture.

Now, you may be asking the obvious question: Why in the world would she still want this guy? Like we said before, she had built a family and a life with this man. But the question is not ours to ask or answer. Sonya's heart had its reasons; it was her responsibility to fully own those reasons and fully represent them. And once she claimed the self-respect to stop needing her husband, she opened herself up to still wanting him.

Obviously, I was not witness to the scene. I heard all about it from both of them the next day when they came in to see me. And it was Andy who told most of the story. I had never seen him so open, so willing, or so joyous. He reported that between his wife's revelation that she no longer needed him and her admission that she wanted him anyway, he had never experienced such a roller coaster of emotions. He was struck by intense pain at first, followed by intense sorrow and joy. He looked to me a changed man, believe it or not.

And Sonya was most definitely a changed woman. Her new-found self-respect had left her beaming with pride and honor. Her unbelievably courageous act of self-representation had stopped a terrible pattern dead in its tracks, and led them both into a new place.

A Lesson for Us All

Now, please pay attention. I am not suggesting this as a universal course of action for any woman in an abusive relationship. It would be tragically unprofessional, careless, and irresponsible for me to do so, given the incredibly difficult and dangerous dynamics involved in domestic violence cases. What I am doing here is offering Sonya's bold step as an example to us all of the remarkable power of self-representation.

Whenever I am feeling scared silent, wanting to express myself to my spouse but too afraid to take the chance, I often think about Sonya. If that woman could take such an obviously courageous step toward her partner, fully owning her desires in the presence of imminent physical danger, then what is stopping me from taking an I-step toward Jenny? It could be that I just want to tell her my concerns about our finances. It could be that I just want her to know that, after all these years, I think I might just be a Republican (maybe). It could be that I just want her, period. Regardless, it all begins with "I."

So now let's talk about you. What does your self-representation look like? Where do you start, perhaps even tonight, or this weekend? Here's what I believe: I believe you already know. There is at least one thing that you've been wanting to tell or show your partner for a long time, perhaps years. Before you get too nervous about that, bear in mind—this could be relatively minor. I once worked with a client who finally mustered the courage to suggest changing the radio station while her husband was driving. This was small, yes, but she had no idea how he'd take it. They had always operated with the pattern of letting him decide the music; she didn't know the effect of expressing her newfound preference. What she did know, however, was the tremendous sense of relief that the very idea of telling him gave her.

What do you want to share with your spouse? What are you dying to say? Is it that you think he's overweight (or, "jiggly") and you wish he would take care of himself better? Go for it. Is it that you're scared about growing apart after the kids leave for college?

Don't wait until then. Tell her this week. Is it that you really want to experience a profound sexual connection, starting tonight? Calm Down, Grow Up, and Get Closer. Then Repeat.

Now maybe, of course, what you want to reveal is a biggie—"Honey, I'm having an affair." Or, "Honey, I don't know if I love you anymore." For such biggies it may be appropriate to do so in the presence of a third party, perhaps a religious leader or a professional therapist. The point is that it all starts with you. Not because you're the one who always has to make the first move. It starts with you because you're the only one with *your* feelings. If I were talking to your spouse right now, I'd be saying the same things to him/her. The point is that each of us has a responsibility to our spouses and to our marriages and to ourselves to courageously represent ourselves. Continually.

This self-representation is the answer to every problem in marriage. It stops needless finger pointing arguments because you're first pointing fingers at yourself. It starts great discussions because great discussions are only possible when each side is being truthful—and encouraging the other to do the same. Self-representation makes for remarkable connection because it ensures that the two trying to connect are at least trying to be authentic and truthful. Finally, self-representation eradicates the villain of marital boredom, because the risk-filled journey of showing your cards never ends. As you continue to age and grow and change, so will your desires, your preferences, and your dreams. And no matter how long you live with one person, you can never fully eliminate the risk of having no guarantee how your spouse will respond as you take an I-step. Never. That's awfully good news for those of us wanting to retain the mystery, the excitement, and, yes, the intimacy of a deeper, lifelong connection.

And it's awfully good news for those of us who really want to love, and be loved in return. And that's where we're headed next.

Chapter 9

Let Love Rule

What you call "love" is just something we
came up with to sell nylons.
—JON HAMM AS DON DRAPER IN *MAD MEN*

It takes a second to have a crush on someone,
and it takes a day to like someone . . .
but it takes a lifetime to love someone.
—ANONYMOUS

·Here we are at the end of the book. It's been a wild ride at times, I know, so I need to tell you this: If you're still reading this far, you have given me a great deal of your time and energy, and I thank you. I don't take it lightly that people read my books, given the million other things you could be doing (or the million other books you could be reading).

What I also believe is that if you've come with me this far, you're willing to go a little further. You may think it's a *lot* further after you read this chapter. As you undoubtedly know by now, I believe your marriage, and marriage itself, is designed to help you grow into a fuller, richer individual. There are few experiences in life that can match what you're facing in your marriage right now—in its ability to stretch you, challenge you, and grow you into a full self. And, in a wonderful synchronicity, there is nothing your marriage needs more than for you to grow into that full self. You really can have the marriage of your dreams, and you really can be the person you've always dreamed of being, and thankfully, *the two are totally related*. What's more, your growth process and your marriage's transformation are also positively related to your spouse's corresponding development as well, even if he/she isn't reading this book, or even seemingly wanting to change.

That's all because of these basic truths:

1. When you are calm and present, you become a calming presence.

2. When you are focused on yourself, you can free yourself and your spouse from the binding lies that keep you both stuck in reactive patterns.

3. When you know your (and you're) part of the problem, you can change the whole pattern.

4. The natural friction of conflict between you and your spouse is the exact opportunity you need to warm up your relationship.

5. By Calming Down, Growing Up, and Getting Closer, you can turn any conflict into an opportunity for connection.

6. The intimacy you seek is always just an I-step away.

Love, Actually . . .

Those basic truths are obviously what I've tried to instill and illustrate throughout this book, and I hope you've come to see that those truths really can change everything. Those truths can even lead you to a new understanding of love itself.

And that's what this final chapter is all about.

Love, as many before me have attested, is probably the most over- and misused word in the English language, or any other language for that matter. It is bandied about in every society on earth, and throughout all our lives. It is the subject of most songs, the theme of most movies, and, I believe, the true longing of every human heart. Love is among the things we love most.

At least we think it is. The truth is that love is so over- and misused that we struggle to come up with any common meaning or understanding of it. You probably said these words to someone this week—"I love you." Maybe even to your spouse. But what did you mean by that? Let's be honest. Sometimes, we mean "I have strong romantic emotions toward you." Other times, it's "I really need you in my life right now." Still other times, it may be "I'm glad I can count on you to help me right now."

But is any of that real love? Is that expression of strong feelings or neediness or gratitude a full communication of love? And, if not, what would be?

I believe there is another definition out there—one that can encapsulate all that we really mean by the word and call us to all it requires of, and offers to, us. Are you open to a higher calling for your motive and attitudes and actions, a calling that is so transforming for both the giver and the receiver that it can only be called *love-ing*? All I ask is that you have an open mind. Ready?

"She Was Just . . . Seventeen"

Way back in high school, I began to really fall for someone. And I mean fall. I was so infatuated with this girl that I would intentionally avoid going to my locker, or even my class, just so I could get a glimpse of her in another part of the school. She was all I wanted to think, talk, or even dream about. I really, really liked her. And as we began to date, I even thought I *loved* her.

Then her best friend set me straight.

See, I somehow knew back then that the way to a girl's heart, certainly in high school, was through her friends. So I developed a semi-close relationship with this girl's best friend. Not surprisingly, we would often talk about our common friend. And when I revealed that I "loved" this girl (let's call her Jenny), her best friend spoke very bluntly.

"Really? You love Jenny? What makes you say that? Your strong feelings for her?"

"I know I love her because I've never felt this much toward anybody," I retorted.

"Do you really think the difference between liking her and loving her is just a matter of stronger feelings?" she quizzed. Then, she instructed.

"Hal, you *like* Jenny, that's true. And she sometimes likes you. [Ouch.] But loving someone is a totally different matter altogether."

"Okay, I'll bite," I replied. "What do you think is the difference between liking someone and loving someone?"

"Well, liking someone is inherently selfish," she began boldly.

"Wait a minute . . ."

She didn't let me finish. "Hal, liking someone is all about wanting that person for yourself, wanting that person to like you in return—and no one else."

I immediately protested as soon as she said the word *selfish*, but as I listened I began to see her point. "Liking" someone was fairly selfish in its intent, craving that person all for yourself and hoping the other person feels the same way.

"Okay, let's say I agree," I replied. "Liking someone is much more selfish than we usually think. So I guess that means loving someone is the opposite somehow? Loving someone is not selfish?"

And here's where a high school friend changed how I thought about love forevermore.

"When you love someone, Hal, what you're really saying is that you want the absolute best for that person . . ."

"Okay . . ." I agreed.

"*. . . even if that doesn't include you.*"

"What?!?" I asked incredulously.

She repeated her wisdom. "When you love someone, you wish the best for that person. You want nothing but the absolute best life for that person—even if that best life doesn't include you in it."

Now, bear in mind, this conversation happened over twenty years ago. And to quote the Beatles, "She was just . . . seventeen." But I was struck by her truth back then, and I've been wrestling with it ever since. According to this understanding of love, I cannot be preoccupied with my needs because I want the best for my wife, Jenny, *with or without me.* According to this definition of love, I cannot be filled with the resentment and bitterness of scorekeeping, because I wouldn't wish for Jenny's life to be filled with such negativity. This meaning of love calls me to a level of giving, of care for another, that totally supersedes my feelings and whims of the moment, romantic or otherwise.

And it does the same for you.

So, Do You *Love* Your Spouse?

Now that you've heard this notion of love, perhaps for the first time, what do you think? Do you agree, disagree? Why or why not? Does this definition of love sound too selfless, especially in a book that says you need to be more self-centered in order to have a great marriage? Hold that thought.

As you wrestle with these questions, get ready to be challenged some more.

According to this definition of love, there is a far greater question that awaits all of us who are married: Can each of us honestly say that we *love* our spouse? Do you love him? Do you love her? Do you wish for, hope for, pray for what is absolutely best for your spouse? I don't mean what is easiest, or most convenient, or most materially valuable. And I don't mean what makes life better for *you*. I mean what is best *for your spouse*. The best health, the best physical environment, the best job, the best family, the best challenges, the best friends, the best mentors.

And, of course, *the best spouse*.

That's right, I said it. And I'm asking you point-blank: Do you wish for, hope for, pray for your spouse to have the best spouse possible? A spouse who listens with attention, speaks the truth in love, confronts willingly, and cares without ceasing? A spouse who represents herself fully, apologizes quickly, and works to balance separation and closeness? Do you wish for your spouse to have a spouse like the kind we've been describing and prescribing throughout this whole book? One who willingly focuses on herself, calms herself down, and grows herself up through all the fires of marriage? One who risks rejection, hard feelings, and possibly even the marriage itself in order to pursue true intimacy?

Do you wish for your spouse to have the best spouse possible? *Even if it's not you?*

Before you answer the question, let's return to one basic truth.

The first word you said in marriage was "I." And as we saw in the last chapter, intimacy—true, mutual self-revelation—always begins with "I." You said *"I* do." You did not say "We do." You did not say, "As long as you do, I do." You said that "for better or worse, I do . . . regardless of whether you do."

At least, that's what other people, including your spouse, thought you said. Now, obviously, that was a hectic day. And even if you spent a great deal of time coming up with your own special vows, you weren't really thinking clearly up there on the altar. Right? I mean, who really means what they say up there? Who really intends to live up to it? And who can, right? Those are some pretty lofty ideals, far removed from the daily details, and the monthly arguments, and the years of building resentment. Can you really be held to such a standard? Asking yourself to be committed to your spouse, even at times when you're not feeling like it? Even times when it seems that you're working much harder than your spouse is? Even times when you don't much like your spouse? Are you still supposed to be, at those times, committed to "I do"?

Well, you tell me. Better yet, you tell you. Be honest with yourself, as honest as possible, because where we're proceeding in this chapter is to call your "I do" to an even higher standard than anything we've discussed so far. Do you "I do?" With everything you have? Do you pledge your commitment to your spouse, even if you sense or fear that he's not willing or able to do the same? I'm not asking if you're willing to subject yourself to continued abuse without doing anything about it. I'm not asking if you're willing to gloss over your spouse's negative contributions to your marriage. Neither of these would be representative of your true self, so doing so could never be a full "I do." No, I'm not asking if you're willing to be a doormat for the sake of staying committed. That wouldn't be ScreamFree, and such a doormat would *not* be the best possible spouse for anyone.

What I'm asking is if you're committed to being the best possible spouse for your spouse.

That's where this combination of "I love you" and "I do" logically leads us. You say you love your spouse, meaning you wish for the absolute best for that person, even if that doesn't include you. If so, that must include wishing for your spouse to have the best possible spouse. Now, you also said "I do" to your spouse, which, if you really want to talk about it logically, means that you honestly believe that you're it. You believe that you can be the best possible spouse for your mate. Let me state that again. *What this combination of "I love you" and "I do" really means is that you honestly believe that you can be, and indeed are, the best possible spouse for your mate.* By making both these statements, you believe that (a) you want the best of everything for your mate, including the best spouse; and (b) you believe you're it.

So, of course, that begs the question: Do you believe you can be the best? Do you believe that no one else would or could work harder to be that person? Do you believe that you're capable of living up to your promise of "I do"? If you don't believe you're that person, then you cannot fully keep promising, "I do." If you don't want your spouse to have the best possible spouse, then you cannot keep proclaiming, "I love you." If you want to keep saying both, with any amount of integrity, then you're ready to be really married.

Saying both the proclamation, "I love you," and the promise, "I do," means saying good-bye to three ideas:

1. The notion of false humility, as in "I'm just lucky to have her" and "He's the real saint here, putting up with me all these years." I know these statements can sound humble, and grateful, but they are not as helpful as you think. These are simply not the honest sentiments of someone who is willing to proudly proclaim, "I am committed to this person for the rest of my life, committed to working as hard as I can to be the best spouse possible."

2. The opposite notion that your spouse is the one lucky to have you. Even joking about the supposed inequality in your pairing ("He's lucky I put up with him" or "She doesn't know how good she's got it") can be really damaging. This is because such statements, even made in jest, are reflective of growing resentment. If you genuinely feel an imbalance of effort or commitment or sincerity, then Calm Down, Grow Up, and Get Closer by addressing it. Directly. Tonight.

3. The idea that your spouse should just accept you for who you are, without calling you to continued growth and maturity as a person. My friend, colleague, and fellow therapist and author, Neil McNerney, calls this the "Popeye defense." This comes from Popeye's favorite song, "I yam what I yam, and that's all that I yam." I run into this defense quite often among my clients. It sounds like this: "Look, if she loved me, she'd stop trying to change me and just accept me for who I am."

Allow me to talk about this last one for a bit, because it leads us perfectly into the climax of this chapter. I certainly understand the dynamic of one spouse trying to change the other, and the other trying to resist those efforts. In many ways, that dynamic is the exact pattern I'm calling people away from. I'm asking folks to stop focusing on their spouse and return their gaze to themselves. But that applies to both the spouse doing the attempted manipulation as well as the spouse trying to resist being changed. Stop focusing so much on what your spouse is trying to do to you, and start focusing on something much more fruitful: changing yourself.

What's fascinating about the Popeye defense is that when it's used, it comes across as some healthy self-acceptance that everyone needs to adopt. "I can accept me for me—why can't she?" On the surface, in our pop-psychology-riddled society, this may have the appearance of wisdom. But dig deeper, and this attitude is not only unwise, it's actually harmful to both you and your marriage. And it certainly cannot stand up to our understanding of "I love you" and "I do."

Just think about that for a moment. You want your spouse to just accept you for who you are? Really? Even if you're lazy? Even if you totally let your body go and become weak, fat, and unhealthy? Even if you drink too much or watch too much TV or read too many romance novels? Even if you neglect your kids, spend without discretion, complain about your spouse to your friends instead of addressing the issue directly? Your spouse is just supposed to sit back and accept all these behaviors as the honest, unchanging you he/she is stuck with forever?

If your answer is no, then Calm Down, Grow Up, and Get Closer by actually seeking out your spouse's feedback. Go to him and ask what you could be doing better. Ask her directly how she thinks you're doing, and what she wishes you would do more or and less of. Why? Because if you're going to be the best spouse possible, then you need continual feedback on how you're doing and how you can improve.

Now, if your answer is yes, that you believe your spouse should just accept you fully, warts and all, then I want you to listen carefully. Your problem is not your spouse's efforts to change you. Your problem is that you don't respect yourself—at all. You don't even like yourself. Anyone who respects herself is going to actively work to improve herself, rarely sitting back and remaining satisfied. Anyone who even likes himself is going to nurture his God-given desire to grow in wisdom, and build on his skills and abilities. Instead, you're just wallowing in atrophy, using your emotional muscles only to defend yourself against your spouse's efforts to change you. And you're wondering why even the good things in life just don't seem to be as pleasurable as they once were. That's because you've "accepted" yourself and demanded that your spouse do the same.

But I know you. I know that you don't want your spouse to just accept you. You want her to *respect* you. You want her to respect that you are not a child, incapable of doing anything for himself and in need of a mommy to tell him how to behave. You want him to see you as an adult, one who knows herself and knows what she needs to do. Well, there's only one way to gain that respect.

Let love rule. Call yourself to your own standard. The standard you've already set for yourself by saying "I love you" and "I do." You wish for and work for your spouse to have the best possible life, including the best possible spouse, and you believe you're the one for the job. That's what it means to love your spouse, and yourself.

You *Can* Handle the Truth

And the first step in calling yourself to that standard is a step that we all have to take, continually, throughout our marriage. First, we have to be honest with ourselves. Have I been living up to my promise? Have I been working as hard as I can to be the best possible spouse for my spouse? Have you?

No.

In no way have we behaved like the best possible spouses for our mates. I know it is easy and tempting to point out that your spouse hasn't been the best for you, either, but that cannot be your focus here. It is simply not as helpful as it temporarily feels to justify your own shortcomings by comparing them to your spouse's. This is about you, not your spouse. This is about your behavior, your attitude, your responses. Can you honestly say that you've been the best for your spouse?

Of course not.

Neither have I. You and I have each fallen far short of that ideal. And according to this understanding of love, that means we have not always loved our spouses. We each—you and I—have not always been committed. To borrow religious language, we have all sinned and fallen far short.

Now, please bear with me because I do not want you to put the book down now, chastising these ideas as too negative and too gloomy, or too insensitive to your pain. Again, I know that you are hurting because of all the ways your spouse has fallen short with you, but thinking about that right now is not nearly as helpful as it feels. What is helpful is focusing on yourself and what you can do to improve yourself, starting tonight.

So, if you are still with me, and if you are ready to move on toward the deeper connection you really seek, then there is a very logical next step. We have each come to see that we are not nearly as loving or as committed as our words make us out to be. We have each "sinned" in that way toward our spouses. So what do you do when you realize that you've sinned?

Apologize and ask for forgiveness, of course.

Again, bear with me. You may be so fed up with your spouse's behavior that the last thing you'd ever do is apologize to him. You may be so angry at me that you want to neglect everything you've learned in this book! I hear you, and I get it. Your pain is sometimes so great, your desires so woefully unfulfilled, that you cannot possibly think about apologizing for your behavior.

But apologize you can.

There's a great scene in the middle-aged comedy *It's Complicated* that is particularly telling. As Meryl Streep's character begins an affair with her ex-husband, played by Alec Baldwin, she begins to realize a great many things about herself and their prior marriage. In an especially touching scene, she opens up to Baldwin in a completely new way.

"You know, I actually realize that our marriage falling apart was not only your fault."

Baldwin is somewhat shocked by this realization and confession. He was the one, after all, who had an affair with a much younger woman and then married her after the subsequent divorce. Here it was, ten years later, and the woman he cheated on is admitting playing a part in it all?

From a therapist's perspective, I appreciate this scene for its tenderness and reality; it is not uncommon for divorced individuals to mature and take responsibility for their respective parts of the marriage falling apart. I also cringe at this scene, however, because it is so *un*common for folks to come to these realizations and admissions *before* the divorce takes place.

So much pain could be avoided, so much anguish prevented, so much money could be saved if partners could just let go of the preoccupation with their spouse's shortcomings and start paying vigorous attention to their own!

And that's exactly what this entire chapter is about, bringing us to our knees in naked honesty about the high standard of love and marriage. It turns out that those two things really do have to go together like "a horse and carriage." But they haven't. You and I haven't always loved our spouses, meaning we haven't always wished for them to have the very best in life. Nor have you and I always been proudly committed to our spouses, meaning we haven't always believed and behaved as if we're a critical component of what's best for them.

If we want to keep saying "I love you," and we want to keep saying "I do," with all the integrity we can muster, then there's only one move to make. You and I have to Calm Down, Grow Up, and Get Closer by boldly apologizing to our spouses and seeking their forgiveness. And if you're up to it, I can show you how.

The Four Rs of Forgiveness

In his book *Yearnings,* Rabbi Irwin Kula gives us a helpful model for the internal and external processes of seeking, receiving, and granting forgiveness. He refers to his model as the Four Rs of Forgiveness.

1. The First R Is for Recognition. So much of what I've tried to do in this book is help you learn to recognize the huge part you've played in creating the past and current relationship patterns in your marriage. For some of you, learning these truths about yourself is overwhelmingly frightening. For others of you, these truths are incredibly freeing. For those lucky folks, it is actually good news to learn about your part, because once you know how you helped create and further a problem, you've immediately learned how to change it. Since all problems occur in patterns, and all patterns have at least two partners, then just changing your part necessarily changes the pattern—and the problem. I know it's old hat by now, but you cannot overestimate the power of this simple message.

That's what this R of Recognition is all about. True forgiveness begins with recognizing our own clear, unexcused part in the situation. Now the tough thing about this is always that we want our spouses to equally recognize their parts as well. But you know by now where that focus will lead you, to that dark place of waiting for someone else to make the first move toward you. Intimacy always begins with an "I." As does Initiation. As does Integrity. It is up to you to recognize your part first, regardless of what your spouse does either before or after, because your life is in your hands. Your desire for connection is what motivates you, not your spouse's. Your calling toward maturity and integrity is what beckons you, not your spouse's seeming lack thereof.

And that desire and calling are wonderfully helped by the

definitions of love and commitment we're offering here. Do you *recognize* that, according to our definitions, you have not been the best spouse for the one you say you love? I hope so. There is a world of freedom coming for you if you do.

2. The Second R Is for Regret. Rabbi Kula's second R begins with an internal assessment of our own attitude toward our behavior. I always find it amazing that so many people subscribe to a life philosophy of "no regrets." The famous American statesman Henry Kissinger once admonished us all to "Accept everything about yourself—I mean everything. You are you and that is the beginning and the end—no apologies, no regrets." As a therapist, I see the value in accepting yourself, but I also see the incredible danger of having no discernment or judgment about your actions and attitudes. Far too often, people use "accepting" themselves as a justification for not growing, for not challenging themselves to be better.

The truth is that everyone has regrets, and everyone should.

Kula helps us by distinguishing between regret and guilt. Guilt, he says, is a debilitating preoccupation with our bad feelings about our behavior. It often leads us to beating ourselves up, which leads us to paralyzing inaction. Regret, on the other hand, "generates action; we are compelled to make things better." Kula continues, "When we regret . . . it becomes possible to genuinely resolve not to do the same thing again when confronted with a similar situation."

That sentence brings us to the third R.

3. The Third R Is for Resolve. When you have decided that you do indeed want to be really married, then you have entered rare territory . . . a willingness to do whatever it takes to represent yourself as the best possible spouse for your mate. This willingness is the beginning point, one that I'm sure you've reached if you're still reading this book. What follows is a resolve to do something different.

This resolve is an internal attitude, a determination to make things right. Or, at least, to make things better from your end. The hardest part is coming to this resolve about your own shortcomings without any guarantee that your spouse will do likewise. I cannot tell you how many clients have come to this point . . . and then backed off. Despite all the work to get here, going through most or all of the principles in this book, there just seems to be a roadblock when it comes to actually apologizing *without an agenda*.

See, most of us stumble through our actual apologies because we have not fully recognized our hidden agenda, especially in our marriages. Secretly, perhaps way deep down, we've all at times clung to the notion that if we apologize, it had better lead to a reciprocal apology from our spouse. Or at least some form of acknowledgment. Just give me something, please! Right?

But that just won't cut it. This whole ScreamFree Marriage program is about becoming a stronger individual within your marriage, and that means acting independent of your spouse. It means acting with integrity, with or without your spouse doing the same. If you believe that your spouse owes you an apology for something, then act as an "I" and state just that. "I believe you owe me an apology for the way you acted last night." Just bear in mind that this is a totally separate conversation from *your* apology. In order for your apology to truly stop a bad pattern and potentially jump-start a new one, then your apology has to be as genuine as your desire for connection. It has to come without an agenda, even without a desire to elicit a particular response. You just have to develop the recognition of your own individual, unforced, and unexcused part of the problem. You have to then feel the painful regret of that behavior, realizing how it contradicts the highest, most principled parts of yourself. And then, as if that weren't difficult enough, you have to develop the resolve it takes to apologize and attempt to make things right or better. All without any agenda for your spouse whatsoever.

But this resolve to apologize must be coupled with a resolve to behave differently. It must come with a promise and a plan. This begs the question, what are you willing and resolved to do differently? You've recognized your shortcomings. Are you ready to apologize for not being the spouse, the best possible spouse, you wish for your spouse?

4. The Fourth R Is for Repair. Do you actually consider yourself ready to apologize, without an agenda? If you have recognized your contribution to the problems, regretted that you did so, and feel resolved to make things better—even if your spouse hasn't— then you are ready to repair the relationship. At least you're ready to do your part.

Interesting word, *repair*. Especially as it pertains to restoring harmony in a marital relationship. In apologizing from a place of integrity, regardless of our spouse's response, we are making a sincere attempt to "re-pair" the two of us. Now, this could be understood mistakenly. We could understand this the way Aristophanes did, by way of Plato's *Symposium*. The Greek playwright told a mythical story of our past in an attempt to explain our insatiable desire for marriage. He posited that, originally, there were three genders: male, female, and a union of the two, a sort of superpair. This being was a full combination of the two, with two heads, four arms, and four legs. And it was so powerful, this perfect pairing-into-one, that Zeus felt threatened. He therefore split these beings into two halves. And those two halves have been dying to find each other ever since; they need each other so desperately that they simply have to reattach for life. This was how Aristophanes tried to explain marriage.

Obviously, given all that we've said so far, this is *not* what I would like to convey with the word *repair*. I am not advocating some necessary step to bring you back into attachment with your one and only "better (or worse) half." No, we're not talking about any sort of attachment at all. We're talking about connection here, which is always a voluntary union between two independent individuals. We're talking about becoming a *pair* of complete people, choosing to use their complete selves to share with, to serve, to *love* each other.

If you're going to apologize, you are not offering this apology because you find yourself incomplete without your mate. If you are offering this apology at all, you are offering it precisely because you are complete *without* your mate, and as such, you'd like to share your complete self with another. You are offering this because you are a whole person striving to consistently grow yourself into more maturity, more integrity, and more authentic self-representation in all your relationships. Especially your marriage. You are not offering this apology because you need your spouse's forgiveness. You are offering it because you made a proclamation, "I love you," and a promise, "I do." And you, as a person of growing integrity, don't take such things lightly. You actually mean to live up to this proclamation, and this promise—even if your spouse doesn't reciprocate. Or forgive you. Or even appreciate your effort.

And that makes you a rare creature in this world—a person of character. It makes you a person of integrity. And paradoxically, that makes you much more attractive to your spouse. See, as you strive to repair your relationship with this apology, by simply striving to be fully yourself, you greatly increase the chances that your spouse will want to re-pair with you.

Even if you're apologizing for disregarding your time accountability to your spouse, or putting her in the position of making your decisions for you.

Even if you're apologizing for never fully detaching from Mom and Dad.

Even if you're apologizing for doing less than your share of the household management, or for doing too much in order to feel superior, and feed your growing resentment.

Even if you're apologizing for not fully representing yourself sexually, whether by hiding yourself, withholding yourself in a power play, or dividing yourself in a horribly destructive affair.

Regardless of *what* you are specifically apologizing for, as an example of not living up to your own proclamation and promise, *doing* so makes you a better, and more appealing, spouse. And apologizing without any expectations from your spouse paradoxically makes it more likely that your spouse will want to, eventually, do the same.

And do you know what that means? It means that you have a great chance to establish a new, positive pattern. You've Calmed Down and Grown Up enough to stop the previous negative pattern, and now, by holding yourself to your own standard and apologizing for falling short of that standard, you've actually created the possibility, and even the probability, of Getting Closer.

I've seen this transformation over and over again, and I've experienced it time and again in my own marriage. That's why I'm excited for you to experience it. Where there was blaming and name-calling, there's now pausing and apologizing. Where there was scorekeeping and resentment, there's now self-focus and self-improvement.

Such transformations are possible for you, if you're willing to step up and stand by your proclamation and promise. Do you love your spouse? Proclaim it. Do you think you can be the best possible spouse, till death do you part? Promise it.

Hold yourself to this standard and I promise you this: You and your marriage will never be the same.

Conclusion

Reason for Hope

This ain't fun. But you watch me, I'll get it done.
—JACKIE ROBINSON

At this point in the book, my sincere hope for you is that you have already found some very practical first steps to begin introducing calm into your marriage. You may have already begun to practice these steps, experiencing some successes (and failures) along the way. Congratulations; I'm thrilled for you. *Starting* on this ScreamFree journey is the hardest part, and if you've done any of the above, you are on your way to increased calm, maturity, and intimacy. In this conclusion, what I hope to provide for you is an inspiring message of hope to propel you even further.

On the other hand, you may have been overwhelmed by this approach. You may not be convinced about this whole Scream-Free thing, saying to yourself that no amount of calm will change anything about your marriage. You may be still searching for one clear step you can introduce, starting tonight, that is both in line with the lessons you've learned here, and yet clear and practical enough to test whether this is right for you and your marriage. Well, that's what I also hope to provide for you in this conclusion. That is, I hope that you can use this conclusion to spearhead your own efforts to revolutionize your relationship, beginning with something relatively small.

I say *something small* because one of the biggest mistakes we make in trying to introduce change is that we reactively go for some huge shift right away. "Okay, kids, from now on there is no TV during the week!" we pronounce. Or, "I am through with always initiating sex—if it's gonna happen, she's got to bring it up."

The sad truth is that none of these extreme measures have the slightest chance of introducing real or lasting change. What works best is thinking big, but starting small. It's perfectly healthy and effective to dream about what your marriage could be like, and hopefully we've gone a long way in this book toward showcasing the possibilities. But it's the little shifts that make for lasting improvements.

And in an effort to both give you hope in, and give you an idea for, initiating such a lasting improvement in your marriage, I'm going to end this book with a story. Now, what you'll first notice is that this story is not about a marriage. It is about relationships, however, and it is definitely about the power of calm to change any relationship for good. What I want you to see is that regardless of the powerful patterns you're facing, regardless of the intense pressure you're feeling, you can introduce lasting change into your marriage. All it takes is a willingness to first and foremost stay calm.

The Strength to Stay Calm

In 1945, a man named Branch Rickey decided that he was going to integrate African Americans into Major League Baseball. As owner of the Brooklyn Dodgers, Rickey was in a unique position to make this move, and given the country's celebratory mood after World War II, this was a prime time to make it. So Rickey commissioned his scouts to scour the Negro Leagues, looking for a ballplayer he could bring on as the first African American major leaguer. His instructions to his scouts were clear: Find a young, dynamic talent who could overcome all the prejudices with his style and success of play. And to all that he added one more criterion. Rickey insisted that this ballplayer keep a cool head at all times. "Do not bring me a hothead," he warned his scouts. With those clear instructions in hand, all the scouts were off.

And they all came back with the same conclusion.

After a long, exhaustive search, all the scouts unanimously agreed that one Negro League player was the ideal athlete to bring into the Major Leagues. He was electric, crowd-pleasing, and fast. Superfast. He was dynamic at the plate, superb in the field at second base, and he could steal bases like no one else. Add to all that his youthful good looks and charm, and the kid was the ideal candidate.

Except for one thing: He was, indeed, a hothead. This player would spike guys sliding into second, he would argue vehemently with the umps. He would even get kicked out of games. Afterwards, he would get into scuffles and fights outside the ballpark.

Mr. Rickey was not pleased. That kind of reactivity on and off the field was precisely what he didn't want. But he agreed to interview the player anyway. Rickey brought him to his office in Brooklyn, and proceeded to tell him his plans. What follows is a paraphrase of that fateful meeting.

"I'm going to integrate Major League Baseball next year," he told him. "Everything my scouts tell me is that you're the ideal ballplayer to become the first Negro in the majors," Rickey continued. "They tell me you're a great hitter, a great fielder, and the fastest player on the field, no matter who you play. You also play with enthusiasm and heart and guts. All that is ideal. But they also tell me one thing. They tell me you're quite the hothead . . .

that you let anyone or anything under your skin . . . that you argue with everyone and even get kicked out of games for it."

The ballplayer didn't really respond.

Mr. Rickey then got serious.

"Look, I'm going to integrate baseball, with or without you. I would like it to be with you. But if you want to become the first Negro to play in the majors, then you have to promise me one thing. You have to promise me that for three years, when all the racist hell comes down upon your head from the fans, the media, everybody, even your own teammates, you *will not react in any way.*"

"What?!?" asked the ballplayer, in confused astonishment.

"When all the names, the boos, the insults, and even the death threats come your way, you have to promise me that you will not react, on or off the field, for three years. We've got no army. There's virtually nobody on our side. No owners, no umpires, very few newspapermen. And I'm afraid that many fans will be hostile. We'll be in a tough position. We can win only if we can convince the world that I'm doing this because you're a great ballplayer and a fine gentleman."

The player responded: "Mr. Rickey, let me get this straight. You mean you want me to be *so weak* that I don't do anything?"

"No, sir," Branch Rickey responded. "I want you to be *so strong* that you don't do anything—except to make your response on the field of play."

After a great deal of silence, there came an answer.

"Mr. Rickey, I'm your man."

And that's when Jackie Robinson agreed to become the first African American to play in any major professional sport in America. And baseball became the first major integrated institution in America.

During those first seasons, the hell Rickey foresaw for Robinson was worse than he'd imagined. There were death

threats in every city. The worst kinds of insults and racial prejudices rained down upon Robinson at every game. He even got this
treatment from his own team. A number of players were threaten-
ing to quit before they ever played with him, and some were plot-
ting to sabotage the whole thing. Some even talked about hurting
him with a ball or bat. But true to his word, Jackie Robinson
never got reactive to any of it. He just stayed cool and went about
his business. He was a model of calm composure and, not coincidentally, he was a model of consistent excellence. And, as you
can guess, this eventually won over even the most hardened of
his teammates. His calm became calm*ing,* and that allowed his
success to empower their own.

But Jackie still had to deal with everyone else. All the time.
One occasion stood out from the rest. The Dodgers were on the
road, and at one point, unbelievably, the manager of the other
team actually took the lead in hurling slurs at Robinson. The
Dodgers were up to bat, and Jackie was in the on-deck circle,
awaiting his turn at the plate. The fans were starting their usual
jeering of Robinson, and that's when the manager came out of the
dugout. He started to lead his players and tens of thousands of
fans in screaming the most horrific racial slurs. The one they all
eventually settled on was designed to rattle Robinson the most.
They all repeatedly called him "monkey." As a person of color,
they figured he had to be subhuman, you see. He was just another
animal. And they were bound and determined to make him act
like one.

See, if they could get Robinson all riled up, they figured, then
they could justify their own beliefs about his nature, regardless
of their own inhumane behavior. This manager and this team and
this town would do anything to make Jackie Robinson get reactive.

But Mr. Robinson would do nothing of the sort.

The entire time, during the entire chant, Jackie merely kept warming up, practicing his sweet swing over and over again. He didn't yell anything back, he didn't stop and look around, he didn't make a face. Perhaps most important, he didn't flee back into the safety of his own dugout. Robinson just kept focused on warming up. And continually calming himself down.

The chants continued, however, eventually growing so loud and disruptive that the ump temporarily stopped the game. The opposing manager was there on the field, leading the jeers, for crying out loud! Mr. Robinson just kept calming down and warming up. And it was at that point that another actor entered the stage. Pee Wee Reese, Robinson's white shortstop teammate, left the Dodgers' dugout and walked onto the field. He, too, just by being Robinson's teammate, was an object of scorn that day, and that entire year.

Now, Reese himself had initially objected to a Negro League teammate, of course. Until he encountered Jackie Robinson's nonreactive composure. Responding in kind to his calm focus, Reese eventually got to know and, as he later confessed, love his teammate. He and Jackie were starting to form what became a lifetime bond.

Well, that day in Philadelphia, Pee Wee Reese would exhibit the power of nonreactive calm, just like his teammate. In the midst of that entire mob's hatred, Reese came out of the dugout and joined his teammate. Like Robinson, he never addressed or even looked at the crowd. He just calmly walked toward his new friend. When Reese eventually reached Jackie, the racist hatred had reached its apex. And that's when Pee Wee made a simple, calm gesture, one that had a hand in changing our world. In an amazingly gracious act of connection, Reese casually reached around and rested his arm on Jackie's shoulder. White embraced black. And they both just stood there.

That was it. They both just stood there. Neither one ever made a move toward anyone else, neither one ever made a plea for anyone to do anything different. They just stood there, together as teammates, united in calm.

And you can guess the effect on the crowd. This angry mob actually began to settle down. It took a while, to be sure, but not nearly as long as you'd think. The entire crowd, and the entire home team (including their manager), eventually just stopped their rants. They saw that their best efforts were not working. Neither Jackie Robinson, nor his new calm partner, would get reactive. These men just wouldn't get riled; they would not react in kind.

Soon the umpire restarted the game (and Jackie Robinson got up to bat and hit a triple).

And Now, Let's Talk about You

This whole story is not really about Jackie Robinson, or Pee Wee Reese. Believe it or not, it's about you. Their journey is not your journey, but theirs can certainly guide yours. Like so many of the profiles of spouses and couples throughout this book, this story can teach you something incredibly valuable. It can teach you, above all, that there is reason for hope. Hope that things can be different, that things can be better, that *you* can be better. Like Jackie Robinson, you can stop your old way of reacting dead in its tracks. Even in the most heated of situations. And like Pee Wee Reese, your spouse *can* eventually come around to join you, even though it may mean swallowing pride, confronting fears, and reversing years of warfare.

And when that happens, your connection with each other will be so strong that you can move mountains together. Your marriage will be so solid that you, and everyone around you, will be convinced that, together, the two of you can handle anything.

All it takes is a single spouse making a single decision. All it takes is one partner choosing to set aside resentments and scorekeeping totals, while holding on to her strongest hopes for personal maturity and connection. That single spouse is you. And that maturity and connection are yours for the taking. All you have to do is pause yourself, willingly enter the fire that beckons you at the moment, and represent yourself to the fullest. Maybe this means finally talking to your spouse about finances and your fears about the future. Perhaps it means owning your household space a little more, with the requisite cleaning that comes with it. Maybe it means finally initiating with your spouse that precious sexual fantasy you've never told anyone about.

Maybe it means just following Jackie Robinson's lead and resolving just to stay calm and focused, no matter what your partner throws at you.

Regardless of the fire that calls you, and regardless of the big changes that await, I promise you that you *can do* these things. You *can* make these decisions, you *can* initiate these changes. And regardless of the initial response from your spouse, please know this: You will stand taller. You will feel stronger. You will be changed forevermore.

All you have to do is Calm Down, Grow Up, and Get Closer.

I believe you can. And I believe you will.

Appendix A

There's More Than One Way to Scream . . .

Our hearts were louder than our brains.
—RIELLE HUNTER,
former presidential candidate John Edwards's mistress,
explaining their affair

If you're reading these words, then that means one of three things. Maybe you turned here from chapter 1, looking to expand on the concepts presented there. Or maybe you turned here from the table of contents, wondering whether *screaming* has anything to do with you or your marriage. Of course, you could have just read all the way to this point, and you just want to keep on reading. Well, in any case, this appendix is for you.

But if you're coming from chapter 1, you can go ahead and skip to the numbered statements below. There you will find, clearly identified and fully described, the five ways that people get emotionally reactive, the five ways we all can "scream" in our marriages. Most of us practice some form of all five, but we all usually have one or two defaults that we return to when anxiety gets the best of us. Find your default form of screaming, and you're well on your way to defeating your greatest enemy. I absolutely wish you the best. Now go, start reading below, and be sure to return to chapter 1 afterwards.

I Scream, You Scream, We All Scream for . . .

If you're coming from the back cover, then I'd ask you to stay with me for a little while. You may be having some trouble relating to this whole "ScreamFree" thing. Maybe you don't ever hear yourself or your spouse yell at each other. Maybe you're Italian (or Latino or Irish or African American or Brazilian or Arab or just a New Yorker), and you don't see anything wrong with raising your voice. Or maybe, it's not the screaming you're concerned about in your marriage. Maybe it's the lying or the cheating or even the hitting.

What I want you to know is that I hear you, regardless. I know that we don't all "scream" in our marriages. At least not out loud. And I know that just raising your voice is not a crime in and of itself. (I happen to love being in New York, for instance, 'cause people are direct and to the point, without dancing around politely the way we Southern WASPs were trained to do.) And yes, most important, I know that you are not interested in reading some flippant, gimmicky relationship book that sells yet another expert's shtick. Instead, you're looking for some practical, down-to-earth wisdom that addresses your real-life concerns, says something you haven't already heard a thousand times before, and guides you with an action plan that really can make a difference.

Still with me? I hope so. Because I want you to hear what I have to say. I have devoted my life to making change possible, even probable, in people's lives. That includes my work as a therapist with clients, as a consultant with corporate leaders, and, of course, as an author with readers. And therefore, I'm honored whenever anyone, especially you right now, dares to read my words and devote even a few seconds to evaluating them. This is because I know you're not just investing your time; you're investing something even more precious—your hope.

And hope is what I wholeheartedly believe is available to you,

in all your relationships. All you have to do is become willing to become ScreamFree. Even in your most troublesome relationship, which may be your marriage at this point, you have great reason for hope. This is absolutely true if, and only if, however, one partner in that relationship is willing to stop reacting and start responding. That's all that's required. One partner choosing to stop reacting and start responding.

See, ScreamFree is not just about lowering our voices. It's about learning to calm down our own *emotional reactivity*. That's a big, clinical term that represents the process of allowing our worst anxieties to drive our choices, rather than our highest principles and truest desires. What ScreamFree is really about is learning to calm down our anxious, emotional reactivity.

And that can be exceedingly difficult, because this reactivity can take several different forms. It can arise in aggressive forms, like yelling, raging, or even hitting. It can also manifest itself through passive-aggressive behavior, like shutting yourself down and shutting your partner out. All are different examples of getting reactive, or "screaming." And here's the real truth of this book: "Screaming" in your marriage doesn't just make things worse, *it actually creates the very outcomes you were hoping to avoid*. Whenever we scream out of our anxiety, in whatever way we do, we actually bring about the very thing that we were so anxious about.

Picture the stereotypical jealous husband, trying to assuage his fears by keeping his wife claustrophobically close. Of course, his reactivity just pushes her away in search of some space and, ironically, makes it all the more likely that she will begin thinking about leaving. Possibly for someone more secure and less controlling.

Or, picture the stereotypical nagging wife, constantly searching for the right way to motivate, cajole, persuade, or guilt her husband into doing more around the house. Regardless of the

legitimacy of her claims, her reactive nagging just seems to erode any chance that her husband, on his own, will take more ownership of the household management. Her overresponsible nagging actually exacerbates his irresponsibility.

Now, this book specifically addresses those two areas of conflict, along with many others. It gives specifically crafted solutions for each of these areas, designed to open your eyes and lead you to new action.

But, more important, this book gives you a framework to see your whole marriage, and marriage itself, in a whole new way. And it all comes down to calming down. The examples above show why learning to calm ourselves down is so vital. No substantive change can take place without first stopping the very activity that's perpetuating the problem. And the very activity that's perpetuating the problem is emotional reactivity, what I call "screaming." That's why this book is called *ScreamFree Marriage*. And that's why this whole book is about learning to calm yourself down—so that you can stop negative, reactive patterns, and start new, more response-able ones. And that gives you plenty of reason to hope.

The Five Ways We Scream

In an effort to help you calm yourself down, this appendix will identify and articulate the various forms of getting reactive. There are five ways to "scream." That means these are the five ways we get emotionally reactive, particularly in our marriages. Each is commonly practiced, and equally powerful. As you read, it will be very easy to pinpoint exactly which pattern of screaming your spouse seems to exercise with regular mastery. That's not all bad, because you certainly want to confront those patterns as they arise, in a ScreamFree way. And this book guides you in what that looks like.

But in order to get the most out of this book, and certainly this appendix, you have to be willing to take a hard look at yourself. This is a valuable chance to "know thyself," as the Greeks instructed us. Only by focusing on ourselves can we learn to calm ourselves down. So find yourself in here somewhere; I promise it won't take you long. And then take heart, because we're all in here.

1. We Aggressively Yell in Open Conflict. The first way we scream is the most obvious, and it is by far the most common form of reactivity. In fact, it is this commonness that led me to develop the whole ScreamFree name and approach. In this form of reactivity, we openly scream at, accuse, berate, and hurl insults at each other. We criticize, belittle, sarcastically mock, and deride each other. At its worst, this form of screaming turns violent.

While this behavior is always offensive, it is almost always done as part of a defensive strategy. We feel unappreciated, disrespected, and hurt, so we lash out. We believe we're being attacked in some way, so we protect our hurt selves by doing whatever it takes to stop the attack, and the pain. This is why this type of screaming can seemingly come out of nowhere, set off by the simplest comment or request. "All I did was ask him to put the kids to bed that night, and he exploded with this long, loud rant about how much he already does around the house! He then lashed out at me about how I don't do enough! Well, that's when I lost it, right back at him."

Sound familiar? Most of us are at least acquainted with this form of "losing it," and looking at it from afar, we can see where it comes from and where it leads. But few of us realize what the *it* in *losing it* actually refers to. *It* is our adulthood. In the heat of our anxiety and hurt and anger, we sacrifice the very maturity we need to actually deal with the problems effectively. And whenever one partner loses his adulthood, it becomes that much easier for the other one to lose hers as well. I like how Dr. Harriet Lerner puts it in her fantastic book *The Dance of Connection:*

> When the emotional climate is intense, a couple may behave like two nervous systems hooked together. Neither party can identify and calmly address the important issues, listen to the other objectively, or take a position without blaming or telling the other what to do. The contagious reactivity between two people can be so high that almost any topic triggers immediate intensity. Within moments both persons are rigidly polarized in opposing camps, unable to consider any viewpoint but their own.

Again, I ask you. Sound at all familiar? I'm guessing yes. And these intense shouting and criticizing and blaming matches may be taxing you more than you can handle. I promise you, it can all be different, and so much better. But first let's move on to the second form of screaming.

2. We Distance Ourselves from One Another. This second form of reactivity, the second form of "screaming," is also quite common. It can sometimes precede, and sometimes follow, the open screaming we just talked about—we keep our distance until something sets us off, and then after the blowup we go to our separate corners. We then keep our distance for the next several days, or weeks. We may not talk, or even make eye contact, but we definitely still know where the other is in the house—*at all times.* If distancers do talk, the conversation stays at a surface or business level, for fear of a hurt-filled explosion. Some couples tend to continuously live at this distance from each other, choosing to avoid any potential conflict, and therefore choosing to avoid any serious intimacy, any deep connection at all. This is usually done in order to avoid heading back into the open fighting mentioned above.

For instance, one married woman recently told me, "My husband and I could never talk about our deepest concerns—I just don't think either of us could handle it." That couple is now getting a divorce. And that's the power of distancing. Like open yelling, distancing just feeds off itself and creates a new norm. This norm may look functional, but only in a superficial way. This norm may stay peaceful, but only in a cold war kind of way. In distance we live in constant tension, tension between pursuing the connection we crave and fearing the pain we figure we'll get instead. This is just no way to live, and yet so many of us do. And eventually, as with the couple mentioned above, this distance leads us to the third form of reactive screaming.

3. We Cut Ourselves Off from Each Other. In a cutoff situation, each spouse goes out of his/her way to get away and stay away from the other. In this intense form of distance, one partner needs a total emotional cutoff from the other in order to feel whole, and fully functional, as an individual. The hope here is that cutting the other person out of your life will make yours that much better. Obviously, this is the hope behind almost every divorce. And that's exactly what divorce is designed to achieve. The problem is that cutoffs don't work. They can neither get the other person completely out of their lives, nor deliver the full emotional freedom they promise. I recently sat next to a professional baseball Hall of Famer on a cross-country flight. Besides talking baseball, of course, we also found time to discuss these relationship concepts. He revealed that now, some twenty-five years later, his ex-wife and the mother of their children, could not speak about, hear about, or even stand the thought of him. She certainly could not be comfortable in the same room with him at their grown children's gatherings. She had remarried happily some twenty years ago, as had my travel companion, and their kids were all enjoying successful adult lives. But she still had to try to keep him cut off, even though cutoffs never work.

Here's why, first of all, full cutoffs are nearly impossible. Couples continue to find sustained interaction with each other and are always surprised to find how intertwined their lives had become. Now, this is obvious for couples with kids. But cutoffs rarely work even for couples without kids. For years after the last contact, questions about your ex still crop up (via Facebook, no doubt), you still come across pictures or mementos from your time together, and you're still confronted by the continued presence of memories. We may be able to cut off future contact, but we can never cut out that person from the fabric of our lives. And with this pain-filled form of reactivity, that's what people are hoping for. This dilemma was depicted powerfully in the Jim Carrey movie *Eternal Sunshine of the Spotless Mind*. The pain of his broken relationship is so intense that he hires a futuristic company to literally erase his memory of the girl from his brain completely. The burning question of the film is the sobering question about cutoffs: If you could just cut her off and cut her out completely . . . would you?

Secondly, cutoffs rarely sever the emotional cords with the other person, and that's what cutoffs are exactly hoping to accomplish. "I cannot handle having this person in my life" quickly leads to "I cannot handle my life anymore, because of this person's lasting influence." The ultimate reason cutoffs don't work is because they are a reaction, instead of a response. They are a knee-jerk reaction to the intense negative emotions in the relationship, and as such can never fully resolve those emotions, regardless of whether or not the partners ever have contact with each other. Trying to cut someone off is like taking chemotherapy, even after the cancer's gone. You're consuming the poison, presumably protecting yourself from any possibility of its return, while still staying very sick from the side effects.

What is needed, even in a divorce, is a careful, thoughtful, response-full decision to deal openly with the negative emotions, address the pain involved, and part in amicable ways. The real goal, if you are to truly grow stronger and feel better through even the most painful of relationship breakups, is to get comfortable with yourself *regardless of where the other person is*. That way, if you have kids, you're able to function as co-parents; you can work through issues with calmness and clarity. That way you don't have to avoid the other person at all costs; you can handle the interaction, and even grow to wish the other person well.

4. We Fall into the Over/Under Pattern. The fourth form of reactivity is incredibly common as well. So common, in fact, that it describes how most couples function. It's called the overfunctioning/underfunctioning pattern, and it can range from either very subtle to very blatant. Here's how it works. In reaction to both the normal and unique stresses of the marriage, one partner starts to overfunction, taking too much responsibility for the ongoing functioning of the relationship. This partner does more than her share of the housework or kid duties or relating to extended family, or takes on the business of initiating all conversation and all intimacy. This could also occur when one partner physically or emotionally takes care of the other.

Of course, none of this takes place without the full participation of an underfunctioning partner. This can take numerous forms as well, from outright laziness to staying away at work too much, to possibly developing physical symptoms that excuse him/her from too much responsibility in the relationship. Usually, couples fall into a sort of a groove here, one that feels natural, even if it makes them miserable. The point here is that while there are a number of factors at work, especially the birth order of each spouse (firstborns taking care of lastborns, for instance), these patterns are a reaction, an emotional reaction to the anxieties of life. These patterns are not chosen, willing responses, based on principle; they are reflexive reactions, based on anxiety and fear. What often happens most is that couples fall into these patterns when it comes to particular issues like housework or finances or parenting or sex, with one partner taking more responsibility in one area and vice versa. Sometimes, if we're aware of it, we rationalize these patterns as normal roles, largely matching each person's skill set or particular interest.*

But you can see the problem, can't you? What happens when the overfunctioning one gets sick of taking all the responsibility? I can tell you. Resentment is just the beginning. Nagging and complaining soon follow, along with passive-aggressive acting out. All the other forms of screaming, especially distance and cutoff, soon enter the picture. And what happens when the underfunctioning one starts to assume more personal responsibility? She wants to be more involved in the finances, for instance, and now her husband is anxious because he can no longer make unilateral decisions. He's also anxious because now even her simplest queries call him to account for all his previously unsupervised actions. His reactivity makes the conversations difficult, and it then becomes very easy to just go back to the way it was. Or switch roles altogether. "Fine, then, you wanna handle the finances? Be my guest!" Sound familiar? Often this leads to the fifth form of screaming.

5. We Triangulate Others into Our Conflict. With this fifth form of screaming, we're not talking abstract geometry. We're talking about relationship triangles, in which two people, in an effort

---

*Please turn to pages 145–52 of chapter 6 to learn specifically how and why these rational, skill-set-based arrangements rarely work in marriages.

to calm the anxiety between them, bring in or focus on a third party. This can be a wife calling her mother or girlfriend to complain about her husband, for instance, or a couple neglecting to talk about anything except their children. In reality, triangles are everywhere. They can be the most common relationship pattern in any relationship system. Just think about how many third parties are brought into work relationships, church groups, and extended family networks. From Mom calling you about your sister, to a church friend asking you to pray for a brother he's got a personal issue with, triangles are everywhere.

Especially in marriage. Wives, ever feel resentment toward your mother-in-law because your husband won't stand up to her? Husbands in this scenario: Ever feel caught between your mother and your wife, each seeming to pull you in the opposite direction? Or, have you ever felt ganged up on by these two women in your life? To both husbands and wives, how often do you take dates and vacations together, sans kids? And if or when you do, how often do these times together turn into business meetings about the kids? Are you actively searching for a deeper connection with each other, one that encourages both direct discussion of the issues between you and playful enjoyment of the one-on-one times you share? If not, then you're falling prey to the triangles form of screaming. The problem with triangles is that they are always a reaction to the anxiety of a one-to-one relationship. By bringing in or focusing on a third party, there comes a short-lived relief of that anxiety. But it usually just creates a bigger long-term problem, because it precludes and prevents the couple from addressing the issues between them, and thus experiencing the intimacy they really crave.

Well, there they are, in all their glory: the five ways we humans get reactive. These are the five ways we "scream" in marriage, and in all our relationships. My hope for you is that you were able to identify yourself in there somewhere, because doing so is a crucial first step in calming yourself down. Once you can identify your default ways of screaming, then you can begin to confront yourself: When do I scream like this the most? Under what circumstances, or about which topics, do I get the most reactive? And when I do, what am I hoping to gain? Does it ever actually work? Am I willing to stop, take a pause, and do something more authentic and productive?

Those are the questions that will free you from screaming; those are the questions that will free you to pursue and create and enjoy the deeper, lifelong connection you crave most.

Now, if you came here from chapter 1, go back and continue where you left off. I've been waiting there for you.

If you came from the back cover, and you've actually read this appendix all the way through to here, I thank you. That's a considerable amount of time and emotional energy you've given to me and my words, and I'm genuinely honored. And if you've gained all the hope and help you need at this point to revolutionize your relationship, I wish you Godspeed. If you want more, then go buy this book and dig in. And be sure to visit www.screamfree .com to supplement your experience with scores of free articles, newsletters, tips, and ways to connect with other folks around the world. There you can also see ways to support the mission of The ScreamFree Institute, which is dedicated to calming the world, one relationship at a time.

May peace be with you.

Appendix B

Should I Stay or Should I Go?

If I go there will be trouble
An' if I stay it will be double.
So come on and let me know
Should I stay or should I go now?
—THE CLASH

The one thing we have not addressed in this book is the question of separation and divorce. Sure, we've gone over the issues that can lead you there, but we haven't explicitly touched on the subject. This has been intentional, and here's why. Whenever *divorce* enters a marriage conversation, it completely takes over. It's like adding anchovies to a Caesar salad. I mean, we are all aware that there's anchovy paste in the Caesar dressing, just as we all know that the prospect of divorce is always present in a voluntary union like marriage. But add some actual fish parts on top, and the taste is overpowering. The Caesar salad has just become an anchovy salad.

Such is the power of introducing the d-word into a marriage conversation—it's a threat so emotionally overpowering that it automatically becomes a divorce conversation. And thus, introducing the topic into this book before now, I believe, would have turned this marriage book into a divorce book.

So, not coincidentally, that is my first piece of advice on the issue of staying or going: Do *not* bring up the word *divorce,* the idea of divorce, or especially the threat of divorce until you are absolutely ready for it to dominate the conversation, and your whole home and relationship. This is because the threat of divorce makes all other issues, at least at that point, inconsequential by comparison. It's like trying to have a fruitful conversation with your boss about working conditions right after she's just threatened to fire you.

You may not think that's a fair analogy, but bear with me. See, once your boss has introduced the option of letting you go, it's going to take a long time before anything feels normal again between the two of you or around the office. She has asserted her power over you in a way that threatens not only your relationship with her, it threatens your relationships with almost everyone else in your life. She holds many keys to your financial present and future, and therefore her threat carries enormous weight in your life. In light of this threat, you may feel compelled to then do whatever it takes to keep your job. Forget those complaints about the working conditions, regardless of their validity; they now take a major backseat to the very salvation of the relationship.

Consequently, the boss who wielded this weapon may be left, temporarily, feeling quite smug and pleased with herself. There she was, struggling to listen to an employee's complaints. She reactively whips out the f-word (no, not that one—the Donald Trump one) and now she's got you forgetting all about those complaints . . . and working harder than ever!

But we all know that this arrangement is inevitably short-lived. Such heavy-handed, reactive leadership never creates the kind of long-term success and warm teamwork so desperately craved in any corporate culture. No, this type of reactive power play actually sacrifices those things for the immediacy of short-term compliance and a brief uptick in your panicked productivity.

Well, the same is true when it comes to introducing the d-word into your marriage. Whoever brings it up first, or most seriously, has played the ultimate trump card in an otherwise equal relationship. That person has now elevated herself into the power position in the relationship, taking almost full control over what happens next.

Think about it. There you were, struggling to listen to your spouse's complaints. Feeling especially tired and resentful because, perhaps, you have yet to calmly address your complaints with him, you reactively get very defensive very quickly. It is then, in your unchecked state of emotional reactivity, that you throw out the ultimate threat to any relationship—the threat to destroy the relationship itself.

Now all those complaints are secondary—now you've got all the attention and power in the union. Your spouse not only lets go of his complaints, he's ready to do whatever it takes to just stay together. After all, you've just threatened his relationship with you, and thus almost everyone else in his life. You've just threatened his financial present and future, considering the ridiculously high cost of divorce and suddenly supporting two households. And, of course, you've just threatened a painful, tragic end to all his original hopes, dreams, and passions for creating a deep, lifelong connection with you.

Of course, here's where the job firing analogy breaks down. When a boss makes a threat to fire you, it really only threatens you. When you make a threat to divorce your spouse, you've just threatened all those changes and losses and costs for yourself as well.

And that fact is what brings us back to the original question. *Should I stay or should I go?* is such a powerful thought that even introducing it into your own mind is dangerous. It is monumentally so if you utter it out loud to your spouse without the careful consideration it requires. Sure, using this threat may gain you immediate attention and influence in the short term, but at what cost? Reactively introducing the possibility may fulfill an unmet need within you, and it may give you a pseudo-voice that feels powerful for a moment, but (a) it will not give you the mutual, willing, intentional intimacy that you really crave, and (b) you cannot point that gun at your spouse without also pointing it straight at yourself. Everything you threaten him with you threaten yourself with as well.

And that's what rarely gets considered enough. When contemplating divorce, the one doing the most contemplating rarely thinks enough about the personal costs that are likely to come his way. It's just easier and a lot more enticing to consider the potential gains. Gains like a new freedom from daily fights, perhaps. Freedom from the pain of the affair, maybe. Freedom to make more unilateral decisions about the house, the kids, and the like. Who knows? Maybe the one who brings up divorce desperately wants to pursue someone else. Maybe it's about finally getting free of abuse.

Regardless of the exact hoped-for and possibly fantasized-about potential gains, the best, most authentic way to consider divorce is to take a bold, bald look at the certain and likely costs.

The Cost/Cost Analysis

If you want to make a decision about staying in or leaving your marriage that is (a) reflective of the most objective facts of the situation, (b) consistent with your innermost integrity, and (c) a decision you can pursue to the very end with as little wavering and regret as possible, you must simply and thoroughly consider one thing above all else: the costs.

Here's what that looks like. Very often, when my clients are facing an either/or decision of some magnitude, I will lead them through a process called a cost/cost analysis. Instead of looking at the hoped-for pros against the dreaded cons, the cost/cost just sticks with the dreaded stuff of each decision. For some reason, looking at the expected costs of each decision side-by-side offers a more objective and authentic picture of what it takes to change your life. Looking at what you'd have to give up has a way of connecting more deeply with your true self than does dreaming about the potential positives. So, if you are seriously considering whether to stay or go, I strongly suggest that you follow these directions.

First, take out a legal pad and draw a line down the center. On one side at the top write "The Costs of Staying" and on the other side write "The Costs of Leaving." Now, draw a horizontal line underneath both and begin to honestly think. What do you know, or most honestly believe, it will cost you to stay in your marriage? Will it cost you relationships with friends and family members who believe you should get out? If so, write those down with specificity. Will it cost you any genuine shot at marital happiness, as far as you can see right now? Write that down. Will staying in this relationship cost you the chance to explore your own career, adventure, passions? Write that down. Will staying cost you money, perhaps in terms of lost potential salary, expenses associated with maintaining your spouse's lifestyle, and so on? How much? Try your best to figure out a guesstimate, and write it down. Do the same with any costs associated with your physical and emotional health, and that of your kids. And, of course, spend a great deal of time counting all the potential costs that staying may exact on your kids. Will they be abused? Emotionally damaged by the continued fighting and/or silent resentment? Disheartened by watching you cave in and sacrifice your self-respect? Write it all down.

Now, as if that weren't difficult enough, it's time to do the same cost assessment for the other side of the question. What are the likely or potential costs of leaving this marriage? Will it cost you money? (Yes.) Try your best to estimate the legal costs of the divorce itself and write that down. Do some Internet research and count the cost for any alimony/child support payments going forward, and write that down. Do the same for the cost of splitting your current income/assets across two households. Now move away from money. What are the costs you believe your leaving will exact emotionally? Do some research about the healing process in the best and worst of cases, and give yourself an honest estimate. Are depression and anxiety and maladjustment a possibility for you and your ex? What might this cost you in terms of functioning, earning potential, parenting efficacy, counseling and medical costs, and so forth? Look at all those emotional costs for your children. Be as honest as you can, thinking about each child individually and how your leaving the marriage might genuinely affect each of them. Write it all down. Now think about the real cost of your time with each of your children postdivorce. Will you lose them half of each week? The whole week, except for Wednesday nights and every other weekend? What about holidays and vacations? Will your leaving cost you every other Christmas morning, Thanksgiving dinner, and spring break? Write it all down. Finally, estimate what costs, if any, you can expect your leaving to exact on your own self-respect, your religious or moral beliefs, or your integrity. And, of course, be sure to list the potential costs to your other relationships, like your in-laws, your mutual friends, your neighbors, and so on. Write it all down.

Include any other costs, potential or certain, you may think of for either side of the list. And when you're finished, just put the whole thing away. That's right, just leave it be for a while (in a very safe place where *no one* will find it, obviously). You've just completed an exhaustive, and exhausting, list of all the real and potential costs that you may be facing in the very near future. This is grueling emotional work and it demands your respect as something far more complicated than any song by The Clash can fully express.

After a break, be it a day or a week or a month, once you're ready to revisit your list and thus, your decision, take it out and look it over. Don't spend too much time on it by yourself, because now, in order to get the best out of this exercise, you need to take it to a somewhat objective third party. A counselor, a family therapist, a physician, a lawyer, a mediator, a minister or other religious leader is ideal. If not a professional, then seek out a friend who you know (a) has not already been steering you one way or another on this decision, and (b) will honestly tell you the truth as much as possible.

Once you've brought it to this person, have her look over your list of costs alongside you, gauging as impartially as possible how well you've equally represented both sides. You are not asking this person to help you make the decision, at least not yet. You are asking her to give you some objective feedback about the list itself. After all, this is possibly the most gut-wrenching and life-altering decision you can make, so you owe it to yourself and those you love to give it your very best shot at objectivity and accuracy.

So you have your cost/cost list. And you've had it examined by an objective third party. Now you're ready to thoroughly examine it yourself. *Should I Stay or Should I Go?* is the question. Here's how you come up with your answer. Looking at these costs, some certain and some potential, which ones can you actually live with? That is, which set of these costs terrifies and bothers you the least? Pardon my pun, but here it is poetic that the song posing this question was written by a band called The Clash, because what these lists of costs do for you is highlight which set *clashes* most with your innermost self, your truest integrity, your deepest values.

Which of these losses can you live with? Which of these

losses would be the most painful to face and experience? Is it the ongoing potential of abuse you'd have to endure if you stayed? Is it the tragic loss of time with your kids necessitated by any custody arrangement? Is the prospect of having to forgive your spouse for the affair, in order to ever achieve any real intimacy, just far too intolerable? Or is the prospect of having to co-parent your kids with your ex, coordinating new households, schedules, new love interests, stepkids, unbearable to contemplate? Maybe it's the sheer financial fallout and collapse involved in so many divorces that has you bothered the most.

Which of all these kills you the most?

Which of these could you actually live with?

That is the decision before you. And only you can know the costs involved with each potential decision; only you can appreciate those costs and their full magnitude in your family life. That's why I always encourage people considering divorce to do this cost/cost exercise, because it leads you to look at and feel the full weight of your choices. Only by doing so can you make a truly authentic decision—a decision that comes from your very bones, and one with which you can stand tall and face whatever comes your way. You have to decide, at your most personal level, what you can and cannot live with.

And then, all you have to do is act accordingly. Do so with no trepidation, no vacillation, and no misrepresentation that this move was led by or caused by anyone else. This is a decision you are coming to based on your own integrity; you are simply choosing what you can and cannot live with, and representing that choice with clear authenticity.

For Further Reading . . . and Growing

Henry Cloud and John Townsend, *Boundaries in Marriage.* Zondervan (1999).

Edwin Friedman, *Friedman's Fables.* The Guilford Press (1990).

Elizabeth Gilbert, *Committed: A Skeptic Makes Peace with Marriage.* Viking Adult (2010).

Roberta Gilbert, *Extraordinary Relationships: A New Way of Thinking about Human Interactions.* Wiley (1992).

Rabbi Irwin Kula, *Yearnings: Embracing the Sacred Messiness of Life.* Hyperion (2006).

Harriet Lerner, *The Dance of Connection: How to Talk to Someone When You're Mad, Hurt, Scared, Frustrated, Insulted, Betrayed, or Desperate.* Harper (2002).

Maria Nemeth, *The Energy of Money: A Spiritual Guide to Financial and Personal Fulfillment.* Wellspring/Ballantine (2000).

Esther Perel, *Mating in Captivity: Reconciling the Erotic and the Domestic.* Harper (2006).

David Schnarch, *Passionate Marriage: Keeping Love and Intimacy Alive in Committed Relationships.* W. W. Norton & Company (1997).

David Schnarch, *Resurrecting Sex: Solving Sexual Problems and Revolutionizing Your Relationship.* Harper (2003).

Acknowledgments

From Hal:

This is my second go-round at writing a book, and like a few more experienced authors warned me, it was significantly more difficult this time. For whatever reasons—increased expectations, less available time, marriage being a more difficult subject— writing this book was significantly more challenging than writing my first one.

That's why I feel so blessed to have been surrounded and aided by such a talented and dedicated team. I consider all the following as coconspirators in this ScreamFree mission, people who are passionate about doing whatever it takes to help families around the world stay calm and connected.

First, a round of thanks to those on the book-business part of the team:

Let me begin by thanking my agent, Dena Fischer, her mentor Jillian Manus, and the great folks at Manus Literary Agency. You all have believed in me for many years now, and your relentless "reality therapy" with me has kept me grounded—and yet still soaring. Dena, I so appreciate your candor and wonderfully supportive direction over the years; I so love you and Brad and your family; and I look forward to working together for many years to come, in whatever capacity possible.

To Stacy Creamer, my first editor at Broadway Books: I thank you for the supportive vision to bring this book into reality. That you've moved on to another house does not diminish my gratitude for your original backing and support.

To my current editor at Crown Archetype, Jenna Ciongoli: I was hesitant about working with a new editor, but now I am thrilled about the direction our relationship is going. Your wise, and bold, managing of the manuscript helped it grow up to our expectations, and your clear guidance through the publishing process has helped me grow up a little as well. Here's to future books!

To Diane Salvatore and Laura Swerdloff: Thank you so much for your hand-holding through all the tough transitions. I was in good hands, and I am in good hands once again—and I never felt dropped cold in the process. Thank you also for your early direction of the material, helping me see more clearly the most pressing issues and deepest hopes of our audience.

To David Drake, Catherine Pollock, Rachel Rokicki, Ellen Folan, Jennifer Robbins, and the whole publicity and marketing teams at Random House: You guys are directly putting the ScreamFree message in front of millions of eyes and ears, and families are discovering new days of calm and connection because of your work. Thank you for relentlessly making all those calls to make it happen, and thanks so much for putting up with me and my immature impatience along the way.

Along these lines, I also want to send thanks to Brian Feinblum and Rick Frishman and the good folks at Planned Television Arts. You guys taught me the ropes about doing media. You got me and the ScreamFree message out there, and I know you're there to continue supporting this mission. I'll recommend you guys to anybody.

Now, I offer thanks to those on the ScreamFree part of the team:

To our early investors in and donors of the ScreamFree movement: I cannot thank you enough for your demonstrated faith in me, in the team, and in the ScreamFree message. Your financial faith, along with your continued emotional support, literally keeps the doors open, which literally keeps more and more families open to lasting calm and connection. You all are changing lives daily.

This is all especially true for a select few of you investors and/or donors who make up the board of directors at The ScreamFree Institute. To Fernando Nasmyth, Louie Werderich, Kirk Coburn, Tim Pownall, Gary Chamblee, and especially to our chair, Ken Shumard, you men and your wives and families are faithfully and joyously bringing God's peace to our organization, and thus to thousands of families around the world. I thank you for your gifts, your guidance, your guilelessness in telling it to me straight, and your wonderfully good examples of what it means to be a man and a servant-leader. Thank you.

To our early partners, Dave and Dorothy Markert, and Fritz and Tami Miller: I offer my deepest thanks for all the faith, the sacrifices, the passion, and the continued support. May God bless you and your families, and may God continue to bring us together in this mission. The same goes for Teresa and Mike Meyer, Tiffany Kinney, Austin Bonds, Terry and Lynn Chastain, and Nancy Hunterton. Thank you all.

To Don McLaughlin, my priest, pastor, and mentor: You are meaning more to me and Jenny and ScreamFree each year, especially this last one. You were a rock and a spring at the same time, when we needed you most, and I love you so much for that.

To Bill Aramony: You too have been a godsend in my life. Your lifestory of passion and redemption is a direct blessing to me and to all of us, and your continued efforts to advise and connect and support The ScreamFree Institute are immeasurable. I'm convinced that you are at least fifteen years younger than your birth certificate.

To Neil McNerney, who has served as our Director of Training and Leadership Development, along with his wife, Colleen: I thank you so much for your continued faith in ScreamFree, and for your continued excellence in certifying and connecting ScreamFree Leaders around the world. Your sacrificial efforts are expanding these professionals' influence, and thus directly reaching families that would not hear the message otherwise. And your families' presence in my own is a beautiful thing.

And to all the ScreamFree Certified Leaders who have welcomed us into your lives, your mindspace, and your expanding influence: I thank you for your passionate faith. This organization is nothing without you guys striving to reach new families and explore new avenues. Thanks especially to a few of you: Sarah Holley, Miriam Bellamy, Michelle Yarbrough, Brandi Diamond, Susan Heid, Dr. Abdel Azim Elsiddig, Olivia Kompier, Debbie Pincus-Ward, Carla Hugo, Gina Farrell, Teresa LeBlanc, Elise Berryhill, Rayanne Coy, Stan Austin, Michele Barber, and Barbara Hopkins-Cox. I know I've left out many of you who are working so diligently to bring ScreamFree to the families you serve, and I apologize. I also thank you for your work.

Finally, there are a special few who deserve a special thanks:

To Don and Brenda Carroll, otherwise known as Grandpa Don and Mimi (and Mom): You have gone far beyond the call of duty in terms of parental assistance, grandparenting excellence, and organizational service and support. We love having you guys in Atlanta, and we love having you guys on our side. You do too much for us and for ScreamFree, but you continually give Jenny and me a model to follow later on. Thank you so much.

To Jon and Tasha Kaplan: my deepest thanks for your presence in this organization, this mission, and my daily life. Tasha, you've always shown the utmost faith, patience, and willingness that this mission needs, and you do so many little things that go unnoticed. Thank you. Jon, this book is dedicated to you because as business manager, you make this work life possible. I shudder to think where we'd all be without you, especially myself. As friend and brother, you make this life so enjoyable. You are both tremendous examples of professionalism, parenting, and partnering, and I look forward to a lifetime of love and friendship.

To Hannah and Brandon: I thank you so much for continually giving me the chance to know you, to love you, and hopefully, to lead you. I marvel at how both of you, in your own way, seem to be picking up the best characteristics of your mother and me while leaving behind our obvious flaws. I also marvel at how you each are developing your own best characteristics, and I love to think about a long future of playing, talking, working, arguing with, and loving each other. Remember, guys, two things. Always.

Finally, to Jenny: You are my partner in crime on this book, my partner in parenting our two undeserved blessings named Hannah and Brandon, and my partner in life and love. You may never know how much you saved this book, and its writer, from the trash heap, but please know this: Regardless of where you work, you are a light shining into people's darkness. That's true about your writing (whether journaling on your cancer journey or confessing your parenting struggles), your editing (whether slashing up my words or your students'), and your teaching (whether instructing our kids or "gently" guiding me on how you deserve to be treated). It's also true about your very presence in people's lives, especially mine. The best part is that you aren't fully aware of how much you mean to people. I hope I can, through the rest of our life together, help you see how much you mean to me.

From Jenny:

As much as it pains me to do so, I must say that my husband speaks for me in his kind words about all those he mentioned. I echo his sentiments wholeheartedly for everyone who helped us in the various and sundry ways to get this blasted book finished. Now, to a few other souls who deserve much credit, I extend my heart.

Robin and Louie Werderich, your love, hospitality, support, and encouragement through the years has held us together on more than one occasion. Words are not enough. Your love story is inspiring and your friendship indelible. I love you both.

Bev Dowdy, Tracy Baird, and Tasha Kaplan, you are some of the women in my life who have inspired me by your strong marriages and even stronger spirits. Your positive energy and spirituality are contagious. I treasure your friendship.

Jon Kaplan, you deserve being mentioned twice. We wouldn't be here without you, and we wouldn't want to be. You are the glue in the organization and one of my closest friends . . . no matter what Harry and Sally say.

Anna Mae and RV Pierce, and Anna and Minos Faulk, your marriages spanned 112 years combined and you showed me what love looks like. I couldn't have asked for better grandparents and I aspire to show that same commitment and connection to my own grandchildren someday.

Hannah and Brandon, you've taught me about the importance of presence and the necessity of laughter. I love you guys more than you'll ever know, and I thank you for helping me become a better version of myself every day. P.S. I love your cowlicks and freckles to pieces.

And Hal. No one else that I know can light up a room like you. I'm honored to be the one you come home to time and time again, and I absolutely love the way you still look at me after all of these years. You are the most forgiving person I know and the one person in the world who really knows me best—a combination that I don't deserve but will gratefully take. Thank you.

About the Authors

Hal Runkel has been facilitating positive, lasting change in families and organizations for over fifteen years. A licensed marriage and family therapist, relationship coach, international speaker, and organizational consultant, Hal is the bestselling author of *ScreamFree Parenting* (Broadway Books). He is also founder and president of The ScreamFree Institute, a not-for-profit organization dedicated to helping families around the world stay calm and connected. Hal and the Scream-Free philosophy have been featured in over one thousand media interviews and profiles, and he speaks to companies, places of worship, schools, military bases, and conferences worldwide. He has been married to Jenny for seventeen years (most of them happy), and they live in the greater Atlanta area with their two children: Hannah and Brandon.

Jenny Runkel has been creating, editing, and publishing dynamic content for over fifteen years. She has worked as Director of Content at The Scream-Free Institute for the last four years, and as an AP English teacher in high schools for over ten. She writes often on women's relationship issues in a variety of publications, reaching a weekly audience

of fifty thousand readers. She has been married to
Hal for seventeen years, loves raising their two kids
with him in Atlanta, and thinks he is the greatest
husband and father in the world.*

---

*Yes, Hal wrote this bio.

Still Want More?

Looking for more ScreamFree Marriage resources?
Visit **screamfree.com/marriagebook** and
let Hal tell you how to find articles, podcasts,
webinars and other resources to help you on
your ScreamFree journey.

Follow us on:

Facebook: screamfree.com/facebook
Twitter: twitter.com/halrunkel
YouTube: youtube.com/screamfree
Blog: screamfreelife.blogspot.com